A Seed in Your Heart

'I said what I did because I saw a seed in your heart . . .

Now is the watering time . . .

I saw one seed in your heart, I wish it to produce many seeds.'

'Abdu'l-Bahá to Louise Mathew

A Seed in Your Heart
The Life of Louise Mathew Gregory

Janet Fleming Rose

GR
GEORGE RONALD
OXFORD

George Ronald, Publisher
Oxford
www.grbooks.com

©Janet Fleming Rose 2018
All Rights Reserved

A catalogue record for this book is available from the British Library

ISBN 978-0-85398-615-7

Cover design: René Steiner, Steinergraphics.com

CONTENTS

Preface and Acknowledgements   vii

Prologue   1
1. The First Pilgrimage   3
2. The Egg Merchant and His Brood   15
3. Louise Spreads Her Wings   24
4. With the Master in London and Paris   36
5. The Seed is Sown   50
6. The Seed Grows   62
7. 'A Fortress for Well-being'   76
8. 'Two Birds of the Nest of Thy Love'   88
9. 'Diffuse the Divine Fragrances'   98
10. The First Trip   110
11. 'Spiritual Gladness'   122
12. First Visit to the Balkans   136
13. Czechoslovakia to Bulgaria and Back Again   146
14. From Central Europe to the Holy Land   155
15. 'Your Name Will Be Gratefully Remembered . . .'   167
16. A Change of Plan   180
17. A Summer in Salzburg   192
18. Return to Belgrade   198
19. The Last Trip to Europe   206
20. A Trip Together – Haiti   213
21. 'Your Manifold and Truly Historic Services'   219
22. 'Your Hearts Are Young'   231
Appendix: Louise's Travels   240

Bibliography   243
Notes and References   249
Index   265
About the Author   278

PREFACE AND ACKNOWLEDGEMENTS

It was in autumn 2009 that my husband Andrew and I travelled to Bulgaria and stayed for three months in the capital Sofia. During the course of our time in Bulgaria I read Jan Jasion's inspiring book on the early Bahá'í pioneer to Bulgaria, Marion Jack, entitled *Never Be Afraid to Dare*. The story of her teaching and perseverance despite incredible hardships was uplifting and we visited her grave in the cemetery in Sofia.

Throughout the book the name Louise Gregory occurred now and then, offering a tantalizing glimpse of her life and her travels. My interest was piqued and on arrival back home in England I began to try finding out about her family and early life. I was aided in this by my companion from school days, Ann Williams, genealogist and researcher, who discovered such intriguing nuggets of information as Louise's grandfather's detention in the Fleet Prison, and without whose help I probably would not even have begun.

As might have been expected, I ran into difficulties in my research. After reading Louise's *In Memoriam* in *The Bahá'í World* (Volume 13, pp. 276–278) I ran up against several stumbling blocks. I spent an entire fruitless weekend at the British Esperanto archives in Barlaston, Staffordshire, searching in vain for any reference to a Bahá'í Congress in Prague in 1928 that is mentioned in her *In Memoriam*. I contacted the various women's colleges of Cambridge University to enquire whether their archives held a record of Louise attending the university (as mentioned in the *In Memoriam*), but frustratingly I drew a blank here too. At this point I began to look more critically at the *In Memoriam* article and noted that 'Abdu'l-Bahá could not have attended the marriage of Louis and Louise (as claimed in the *In Memoriam*) because on 27

September 1912 He was in Glenwood Springs, Colorado en route for California. Clearly the *In Memoriam*, written by a well-meaning friend of the family after Louise's passing, contained serious errors. Discouraged, I put my researches on hold.

A year or so later Andrew and I were attending the annual Persian Bahá'í conference held at that time in Watford, England. The late Professor Bushrui was one of the learned speakers at the conference and at a certain point in one of his lectures he suddenly declaimed that Mrs Louise Gregory was an Englishwoman and that somebody from her homeland should write her biography. I felt as if a thunderbolt had struck me – I left the lecture hall determined to resume my researches into her life.

At this point I began to study the outstanding work on Louis G. Gregory, Gayle Morrison's *To Move the World*, and it became a reference book of inestimable value in my researches from then on. I'm grateful to Thelma Batchelor for lending me her copy of this work (which was not available for purchase in the United Kingdom at that time), for her encouragement in the early days and, in fact, for her interest throughout the writing of Louise's biography.

My researches continued and I became ever more fascinated by this self-effacing, determined woman, her interracial marriage and her pioneering travels. I felt that her achievements had frequently been overlooked and that she was, to a large extent, misunderstood. One comment I received when I mentioned to a friend that I was researching Louise's life was: 'Oh yes, it was an unhappy marriage and she went off.' How incorrect this assessment turned out to be! I decided to set out to show that it was in fact a devoted, happy marriage and that she travelled in European countries because of the impossibility of accompanying her husband to the southern states of America.

Pat Gorman has taken a profound and continuing interest in my project and I thank her for this. In particular, she shared some of her researches into the family of Edna McKinney with me and their links with the Gregorys added another facet to Louise's life and personality. In 2015 Pat brought the forthcoming Wilmette Institute course on Writing Biographies to my attention. She was planning to participate and strongly encouraged me to do likewise. I took her advice and found the course and my course mentor Adam Thorne inspirational, so that I was kickstarted into serious research. The next stage was clear: I needed to visit the United States National Bahá'í Archives in Wilmette, Illinois.

Andrew and I made an all too brief visit to Wilmette where I discovered there was a vast correspondence by Louise Gregory and relating to her. These letters opened up a whole new vista on Louise's personality, her friendships, her marriage, her aspirations and her travels. I am greatly indebted to archivist Roger Dahl for his professional assistance in connection with this correspondence and with photographs.

On the same trip to the United States we were able to visit the archives of the Spiritual Assembly of Eliot, Maine where I discovered further gems relating to Louise's life: letters, photographs and documents. Eliot archivist Rosanne Adams was our patient and helpful guide through these fascinating archives.

Back in the United Kingdom I visited Bromley Local History Library where the staff were able to guide me to Michael Mathew's obituary in the local paper and to shed more light on the development of suburban Beckenham and Penge.

I am indebted to the archivists at the universities of Edinburgh and Cambridge as well as Royal Holloway College (now part of the University of London) who unravelled for me the mystery of where Louise had studied and the qualifications that she gained. Finally, through their efforts, it was proved that she passed her teacher's certificate under the auspices of Cambridge University but that she never studied there and that she was in fact a student at Royal Holloway College and St George's College, Edinburgh.

Another archivist who gave help of inestimable value was Paul Smith at the Thomas Cook archives in Peterborough. His archive of travel books and documents offered greater insight into the places that Louise visited and the complicated timetables of the era with which she became familiar.

The Research Department at the Bahá'í World Centre receives my grateful thanks for assistance in tracing letters which clarify Louise's travels in 1930 and 1931, and I owe a debt of gratitude to the National Spiritual Assembly of Bulgaria for their help in searching out any photographs of Louise.

I should like to thank Wendi and Moojan Momen for lending me books that I would otherwise have had difficulty in finding and also Sally Spear who raided her personal library on my behalf. Kathy Hogenson gave me useful advice, as did Jan Jasion, and Mara Khavari searched the

Portsmouth, New Hampshire Spiritual Assembly's archives for further items of information. Louise Mould gave me encouragement which was greatly appreciated, and so did Susan Pershing whom I met again at Wilmette. Clare Gittings offered me a listening ear through many stages of the project and made helpful comments on the book's progress.

My husband Andrew Rose has helped with the creation of this book in so many ways. When I announced that I needed to visit the archives in Wilmette and Eliot he was prepared to fly off to the United States at the drop of a hat. His technical knowledge has compensated for my lack of the same on many many occasions and in particular he helped me with the photographs and maps. He accompanied me with love and patience throughout the long gestation of this book.

Finally I would like to thank my editor, May Hofman, for her experienced and professional advice which made it a pleasure to work with her, and the team at George Ronald, especially Wendi Momen and Erica Leith, who had faith in my project when I needed it.

PROLOGUE

The traveller wiped the sweat from his face and took stock of his surroundings. The sun was beating down unmercifully and he felt weary after his long journey by sea.

A few passers-by stared fleetingly at the traveller's western dress, his suit contrasting markedly with their own North African robes, but his dark features passed unnoticed. He had felt extreme excitement when the ship docked at the Egyptian port. Beyond the modern streets of the port, the sights and sounds and smells of the foreign city were all strange to him and he surveyed the low mud-brick buildings, the palm trees and narrow, dusty alleys as if in a dream. His delight in finally arriving at his destination was tempered with anxiety as he wondered how, in the maze of narrow bustling streets, he was going to find the one small Persian shop that would act as a key to the pilgrimage that was his heart's desire.

He made his way to Ramleh, a suburb of Alexandria, and eventually found someone who understood his request for directions to the rue Cherif Pasha and finally to the shop of Mirzá Ḥasan Khurásání, a Persian merchant. With what joy he greeted the Persian gentlemen assembled there! And how kindly they received him, a pilgrim, a traveller from the West who, despite his western clothes and manners, was in fact their brother. He handed over the precious letter of introduction from Dr Getsinger that he had treasured and protected all during his long journey and the Persian translation was read. 'You want to see our Lord?' came the question from the dignified Muḥammad Yazdí. He already knew the answer and offered to act as guide to the Master's dwelling-place. The traveller felt it necessary to refuse such kindness on the grounds that he did not wish to disrupt the business being carried on at the Persian shop, but Muḥammad Yazdí insisted, saying 'This is spiritual business!'

Escorted by the gracious Persian gentleman, the traveller was taken first to his hotel to change into fresh clothes and then, with renewed vigour and dream-like suspense, to the very house where the Master was staying, a modest but comfortable house of two storeys with a pleasant little garden at its front. The guide climbed the exterior flight of steps to the upper floor, leaving the traveller, his breath coming now in excited gasps, to wait a few minutes at the foot of the stairs. Once the beaming guide returned he was invited to climb the staircase and enter a reception room on the upper floor.

The room was dark compared with the brilliant sunlight outside but he soon discerned the majestic figure of the Master and felt moved to kneel before Him reverently. Joy and peace surged over him as he felt the Master bend and touch his head with His lips, then raise him up and direct him lovingly to a seat.

The traveller expressed his happiness at finally attaining the meeting with his Lord, who answered, 'I am happy to have you here.' Through an interpreter there followed conversation concerning the recent 'fragrant meetings' of the Bahá'ís in Washington and New York, and letters and tokens of love sent by the friends were presented, receiving wise and loving responses.

Finally the traveller became aware of the other persons gathered in the room for this never-to-be-forgotten audience with the Master. As well as two Persian gentlemen, Tamaddun Mulk and Núru'd-Din Zayn, there were two English pilgrims who were also honoured to be meeting 'Abdu'l-Bahá: Mr Neville G. Meakin and Miss Louise Alice Maria Mathew. The traveller had, in one single meeting, attained the presence of the Master and met his future wife . . .

Based on *A Heavenly Vista* by Louis G. Gregory

I

THE FIRST PILGRIMAGE

In April 1911 three pilgrims set off by ship from Alexandria in Egypt to the Holy Land. Their goal was the small port of Haifa and its twin, the ancient port city of Akka.

The three pilgrims formed an unlikely group. Two of them were English. One of these was a 45-year-old spinster by the name of Louise Mathew, an educated woman from the south of England who was fluent in French and German, had worked as a teacher and been deeply involved in philanthropic projects such as a school for poor children. She was fine-boned and small in stature with dark brown hair framing her face and brown soulful eyes. From an affluent, though by no means aristocratic, family she had spent many years living and working in Europe.

Neville Gauntlett Meakin was the second English traveller, a young man in his mid-30s. He had suffered a traumatic childhood when his father had deserted his mother and run off to France with a woman, and later emigrated to America where he bigamously married again. Forced to provide a living for herself and her child, Mrs Meakin had taken the post of superintendent at an orphanage which is where young Neville spent his blighted childhood. Now, in poor health, he was on a spiritual quest that was to be the culmination of his tragically short life.

The third pilgrim was American, a tall upright youthful black man with an open courteous demeanour. Louis G. Gregory was an educated man of 36 years of age, the son of freed slaves from the deep south of America. Louis's father, Ebenezer George, died when Louis was very small and his mother later married again to George Gregory, who was a free-born black man and a property owner, and Louis took his stepfather's surname. Young Louis was early recognized as highly intelligent and his stepfather encouraged his education so that he attended not only the publicly funded local schools but a prestigious private school,

Avery Institute, followed by Fisk University in Nashville, Tennessee and later Howard University, Washington DC, where he qualified as a lawyer in 1902.[1]

It was a momentous time in the lives of these three very disparate travellers. They had met shortly before in Ramleh near Alexandria where they had all been drawn by their newly found attraction to a young and burgeoning religion, the Bahá'í Faith, or the Bahá'í Movement as it was then known, and their admiration for its leader, 'Abdu'l-Bahá, whose self-adopted title signified 'Servant of the Glory'.

'Abdu'l-Bahá was the eldest son of the Prophet-Founder of the Bahá'í Faith, known as Bahá'u'lláh or the 'Glory of God'. Bahá'u'lláh had been banished for His teachings from His native Persia and, after many years of persecution and exile in Baghdad, Istanbul (Constantinople) and Edirne (Adrianople), He had been condemned to suffer imprisonment in Akka in the Holy Land, passing away and being interred in nearby Bahjí in 1892. His son, 'Abdu'l-Bahá, was exiled with Him and shared in His Father's sufferings, vowing to serve Him throughout His life and beyond.

In His own words 'Abdu'l-Bahá described His status, saying:

> My name is 'Abdu'l-Bahá. My qualification is 'Abdu'l-Bahá. My reality is 'Abdu'l-Bahá. My praise is 'Abdu'l-Bahá. Thraldom to the Blessed Perfection is my glorious and refulgent diadem, and servitude to all the human race my perpetual religion . . . No name, no title, no mention, no commendation have I, nor will ever have, except 'Abdu'l-Bahá. This is my longing. This is my greatest yearning. This is my eternal life. This is my everlasting glory.[2]

After 40 years of incarceration 'Abdu'l-Bahá was finally freed in 1908 as a result of the Young Turks Revolution which restored the constitution to the moribund Ottoman Empire and all religious and political prisoners were set free. The new religion had begun to spread to the West thanks to a number of emissaries who travelled to America and Europe, and small groups of early Western pilgrims had begun visiting 'Abdu'l-Bahá even while He was still officially held prisoner in Akka. After His freedom was granted 'Abdu'l-Bahá left Haifa in August 1910 and began a series of extensive travels in Europe and America, visiting the Bahá'ís there and spreading His message. At the beginning of His travels, however, He was forced by ill health to spend a year resting in Egypt and it was here that Louis, Louise and Neville Meakin visited Him.

Louis had accepted the truth of the Bahá'í teachings in Washington DC in June 1909 thanks to the persistent friendship of a white couple, Pauline Hannen and her husband Joseph. He wrote to 'Abdu'l-Bahá professing his belief and early in 1910 he sought to meet 'Abdu'l-Bahá Himself. He wrote to Him again requesting the bounty of a pilgrimage. 'Abdu'l-Bahá replied that the time was not yet propitious and that Louis should wait a while: 'It is at present not in accord with wisdom. Postpone this matter to another and more opportune time.' When 'Abdu'l-Bahá was resting in Ramleh in Egypt late in 1910 Louis received the news that now was the time to visit Him and with alacrity and no doubt a great sense of excitement, he embarked on his first experience of foreign travel, setting sail from New York and eventually arriving in 'Abdu'l-Bahá's presence.[3]

Louise Mathew had first encountered the Bahá'í Movement while she was furthering her studies of music in Paris around 1909. She had written letters to 'Abdu'l-Bahá while she was still investigating the teachings and He had answered patiently with letters (known as Tablets) written to her in Persian which were then translated for her into English or French. She had accepted the validity of His message and immediately, like Louis, she had requested a pilgrimage to visit 'Abdu'l-Bahá, or the Master as He was known to the Bahá'ís. Like Louis, she was lovingly informed that this would be possible – but at a later date.

Eventually the invitation to visit 'Abdu'l-Bahá had arrived and Louise had hastened to accept it. An independent spirit, she had travelled alone to Egypt from France, dispensing with the need to travel accompanied as might have been expected of a woman of her social class. She was not afraid to travel on her own to unknown foreign lands where the customs, culture and conditions were quite alien. This love of foreign travel was to be a feature of her life in years to come.

And so it happened that the two newly-declared Bahá'ís, one from the new world and one from the old, who had both had to wait for a 'more opportune time' found that their visits to the Master eventually coincided in Egypt.

Little is known about the origins of Neville Meakin's search for spiritual truth. He had dabbled in occultism and was a member of the Stella

Matutina order, a magical order dedicated to the Golden Dawn and Rosicrucian tradition, when he met Wellesley Tudor Pole, a spiritualist and early English follower of the Bahá'í teachings.[4] In November 1910 Tudor Pole had met 'Abdu'l-Bahá in Alexandria and been impressed by Him. It may well have been through Tudor Pole that Neville Meakin met the Bahá'í Movement for the first time. Whatever was his introduction to the Movement, something must have inspired him to travel to Egypt to meet 'Abdu'l-Bahá.

Louise and Mr Meakin had already attained the presence of 'Abdu'l-Bahá when Louis arrived in Ramleh, a summer resort frequented by European officials and high-ranking Egyptians. It boasted beautiful parks, elegant houses and many hotels, both large and small. An electric tramway connected it to the prosperous city of Alexandria a few miles to the west. 'Abdu'l-Bahá stayed first in the Hotel Victoria in Ramleh until a few days later a villa was rented for Him and His family not far away from the hotel. Louis found the villa situated near the sea and surrounded by a beautiful garden.[5] He later described his first impressions of the Master:

> When . . . I saw Him for the first time he was about sixty-seven years of age, about the medium height, with a strong frame and symmetrical features. His face was deeply furrowed and his complexion about the shade of parchment. His carriage was erect and his form strikingly majestic and beautiful. His hands and nails were shapely and pure. His silver hair touched his shoulders. His beard was snow white, with eyes light blue and penetrating, his nose somewhat aquiline. His voice was powerful, but capable of infinite pathos, tenderness and sympathy. His dress was that of the Oriental gentleman of rank, simple and neat, yet very graceful. The color of his apparel was light, the outer robe being made of alpaca. On his head rested a light fez surrounded by a white turban. The meekness of the servant, the majesty of the king, were in that brow and form.[6]

In their meetings with 'Abdu'l-Bahá in Ramleh the three western pilgrims heard Him stress the need for racial unity in America, as He alluded directly to 'the conflict between the white and colored races' and asked Louis whether the black and white races in the American Bahá'í community were entirely united. When Louis responded that 'there was not entire unity, but that there were earnest souls of both races who desired closer unity' 'Abdu'l-Bahá responded that 'the best means' for true unity 'is to accept this Cause. All differences must fade among believers. In the present antagonism there is great danger to both races.'[7]

When 'Abdu'l-Bahá was asked whether the black Bahá'ís in America should organize their unity meetings separately He replied: 'The colored people must attend all the unity meetings. There must be no distinctions. All are equal.' Shortly after saying this He went out on to the veranda of the building and walked backwards and forwards in silence, then returned to the reception room again in silence. Soon He rose, saying sadly that He was very weary. He shook hands with his companions and retired, leaving Louis feeling that the very difficult situation in America had made the Master very sorrowful.[8]

'Abdu'l-Bahá made it clear that Louis was to play a key role in promoting racial unity in America. When asked what was His will concerning Louis He replied: 'Work for unity and harmony between the races.' He also referred even at these first meetings to the importance of interracial marriage in bringing the races closer together, saying: 'Intermarriage is a good way to efface racial differences. It produces strong, beautiful offspring, clever and resourceful.' He urged Louis, 'If you have any influence to get the races to intermarry, it will be very valuable.'[9]

On 16 April about a week after Louis's arrival the three pilgrims went to take their leave of 'Abdu'l-Bahá before setting sail for Haifa later that day. On approaching the house where He was staying they met 'Shoghi and Rouhi', described by Louis as 'two beautiful boys, the grandsons of 'Abdu'l-Bahá', adding that 'These children of the Holy household show great affection for pilgrims.'[10] Shoghi Effendi, the future Guardian of the Faith, was 14 years old at this time and had travelled to join his Grandfather in Egypt, and was attending the French Brothers' school in Alexandria. Louis and Louise were greatly impressed by the young boy but could hardly have suspected his future role in the development of the Bahá'í Movement.

In their meeting with 'Abdu'l-Bahá Louis expressed the hope that in another year the friends would see Him in America. To this He smiled and asked jokingly: 'Will you bring an aeroplane and steal Me away?' On a more serious note 'Abdu'l-Bahá asked the three pilgrims to pray for Him when they visited the Holy Tomb and added, 'I hope the

Divine Bounties will descend upon you during your visit.' With this blessing they departed.¹¹

The three pilgrims embarked on a ship of the Austrian Lloyd line in the busy harbour of Alexandria. A traveller wrote that Alexandria was

> like a progressive American city. Its tall buildings, its large department stores, its clean avenues, its double-decked electric cars, its delightful parks, its electrically lighted boulevards and streets, its fine promenades around the seaport, are all signs of a wonderful prosperous spirit. As I passed along the streets it seemed as though I was walking on an avenue in New York, and I wondered at the magical transformations which had taken place since this city was burned to the ground during the Arabi [sic] revolution thirty-one years ago. The inhabitants of all nations, Greeks, Italians, French, Jews, English, Arabs, Persians, live here and associate with one another in perfect harmony.¹²

Unfortunately the pilgrims' departure was delayed for 24 hours because of a storm. They eventually sailed on 17 April even though the sea was still rough and they had an uncomfortable passage to Port Said. Here they rested at the entrance to the Suez Canal for some hours before sailing further to Jaffa, the nearest port to Jerusalem, where some passengers disembarked and stores were unloaded. As they journeyed the 60 miles or so along the coast northward from Jaffa they were able to admire the mountain range which was formed by the southern slopes of Mount Carmel. Around dusk they finally reached the beautiful expanse of the Bay of Haifa and transferred to a little boat which ferried them to the port of Haifa itself. Their first night in Haifa was spent in a small German hotel.¹³

Haifa at this time was beginning to develop as a more important seaport thanks to the construction of a branch of the Hejaz railway (a line built by the Ottomans from Istanbul to Medina) to Haifa and Akka. This enabled the development of trade although the primary aim of the railway had been to relieve the suffering of Muslim pilgrims travelling from the north down to Medina and Mecca. Haifa had developed considerably when in 1868 German Templers settled there and built their colony of solid red roofed houses at the foot of Mount Carmel. These industrious immigrants built a steam-based power station and started factories in the town as well as opening shops, doctors' practices and hotels.[14]

Western tourists, including of course Bahá'í pilgrims, had started to arrive in Haifa and Thomas Cook, the pioneering travel company, recorded in its 1911 handbook that

> Haifa is a prettily situated little seaside town, with gay bazaars, on the southern end of the Bay of Acre, at the foot of Mount Carmel. The houses are built terrace-like on the hillside, and there is a very fine grove of palm-trees on the Acre (Akka) or north end of the Bay, greatly enhancing the beauty of the view from Haifa in that direction. The population is about 17,000, and increasing. Trade is flourishing, both import and export, and latterly large quantities of coal and material for the Hedjaz [sic] Railway have arrived there.
>
> A stone breakwater is in course of construction.
>
> About ten minutes west of Haifa is a pretty German Colony, with about 500 residents.[15]

Another district of Haifa, to the east of the Templer colony, came to be known as the Street of the Persians (Haparsim Street) because it was the area where many Persian Bahá'ís settled. This street included the elegant House of the Master where 'Abdu'l-Bahá and members of His family lived. A small stone building near the Master's House constituted the pilgrim house for western pilgrims at this time. To the west, looking out to sea on the slopes of Mount Carmel and next to the cave of Elijah, was the Carmelite Monastery and church built in 1836. The site had been considered sacred for many centuries because of the caves in this part of the mountain where hermits had earlier dwelt. The Monastery complex was influential in attracting Christian pilgrims to Haifa.

The three pilgrims having rested overnight, the following morning they were visited by two of 'Abdu'l-Bahá's sons-in-law and later taken to pay their respects at the Shrine of the Báb, the Forerunner of Bahá'u'lláh. At this time the Shrine of the Báb, situated halfway up the mountain on the slopes of the northern face of Mount Carmel, consisted only of a single storey building but described by Louis as 'stately in proportions' and with 'a commanding site' next to the circlet of cypress trees which had been favoured by Bahá'u'lláh as a place to rest and take tea. A visitor to Haifa the same year as Louis wrote of the view from the Shrine:

From this little rose-garden, tended lovingly by the Persians, one has a wonderful view of the flower-covered slopes of the mountain, the little red and white town of Haifa below and then the wide blue bay with its long crescent of sandy beach, on the further side of which Akka lies close to the water's edge within her fortified walls, white as the breast of a sea-gull.[16]

The three western pilgrims met several other pilgrims at the Shrine and then left their shoes at the door of the Shrine as was the custom and entered with great reverence to hear prayers chanted in Persian.

Their pilgrimage coincided with the Bahá'í Feast of Riḍván which commemorates Bahá'u'lláh's declaration of His Mission in Baghdad in 1863 and is a joyful 12-day festival. On the first day of Riḍván, after early morning prayers, the three western visitors accompanied by Mírzá Asadu'lláh and his son Enayatu'lláh set off in clear sunny weather to drive the nine miles along the beach to Akka in a horse-drawn carriage. There was no road between Haifa and Akka at that period and, in addition to driving along on the sand with the carriage wheels sometimes splashing through the fringing waves, they had to ford the Kishon river and the Na'aman stream on the journey. The beach was awash with unusual and beautiful shells and was famous for the quantity of spiky murex shells to be found there. On the way they might have seen herds of goats watched over by a local goatherd, a flock of sheep and even a caravan of camels led by bedouins coming from a great distance. Date palms added to the exotic scenery and spring flowers such as brightly coloured anemones, scarlet poppies and yellow crown daisies decked the surrounding hillsides.

At the city gates Louis and Neville Meakin went on foot together with Enayatu'lláh to explore the narrow alleys and hidden courtyards of Akka while Louise stayed with Mírzá Asadu'lláh outside the city in the carriage. It is possible that Louise, whose health was extremely delicate at this time, felt unwell and unable to face walking some distance through the ancient streets. Or it may be that it was felt that the sight of a European woman walking in the largely Arab city would cause too much comment.

Louis and Neville were able to visit the barracks where Bahá'u'lláh and His family were kept on arrival in Akka, and the Most Great Prison where Bahá'u'lláh and His close family were held prisoners and endured great suffering. They passed through the bazaars with all their exotic oriental sights and smells, and finally reached the House of 'Abbúd next to the seawall where they entered and climbed the staircase to the upstairs apartments. They respectfully removed their shoes and their faces were anointed with an eastern perfume before they were permitted to enter the room of Bahá'u'lláh and view the portraits of Bahá'u'lláh and the Báb.

After this sublime experience they made their way back to the carriage where they rejoined Louise and Mírzá Asadu'lláh and drove to Bahjí just outside the city through 'green fields and fragrant gardens', arriving at the pilgrim house next to the Shrine of Bahá'u'lláh. After a delicious lunch served in the courtyard they visited the Shrine. Louis later described the place as 'spiritual and its atmosphere . . . fragrant with many beautiful flowers'. The Persian friends chanted again and Louis recorded that 'according to His expressed wish, we remembered 'Abdu'l-Bahá in our prayers. The friends in the East and West were not forgotten. Our earnest desire was for unity through the power of the Greatest Name.'[17]

The unforgettable day continued with a visit to the Riḍván Garden, named by Bahá'u'lláh as His 'Verdant Isle' where many Bahá'ís including other pilgrims from distant countries were gathered. Persian tea was served and more verses were chanted before they were granted a visit to the simple little house where Bahá'u'lláh Himself often used to rest on His visits to the garden. Louis described the Riḍván Garden with awe: 'The entire garden, with its great mulberry trees, bushes laden with roses, rivulet and flowing fountain, has an ideal beauty.'[18]

Louise may have missed out on the visit to the House of 'Abbúd in Akka but it is certain that, as a woman, she had special access to the women's quarters in the Bahá'í homes and made lasting friendships with the women of the holy household. Years later in January 1922 Louise received a letter from Munavvar Khánum, youngest daughter of 'Abdu'l-Bahá, apparently in reply to Louise's letter expressing condolences on her Father's Ascension. In the letter, which is most affectionate towards Louise, Munavvar Khánum suggests Louise could come to Haifa to teach in a Bahá'í school on Mount Carmel – a suggestion which was never, however, taken up. Munavvar Khánum writes that the women of the Holy Family send Louise love and remembrances.[19] On her pilgrimage she would certainly have met Bahíyyih Khánum,

'Abdu'l-Bahá's devoted sister, as well as 'Abdu'l-Bahá's four daughters and Munírih Khánum, the Holy Mother, wife of 'Abdu'l-Bahá.

Louise's close friend and mentor, the Canadian Bahá'í Marion Jack, had spent six months in Haifa in 1908 in the household of 'Abdu'l-Bahá, invited there to teach His daughters English. Her prolonged visit had been a joyful time both for Marion and for the women of the household and Marion had emerged as an ebullient character, fondly given the nickname 'General Jack' by 'Abdu'l-Bahá. When it came time to leave she was in uncontrollable tears for days before her departure. How happy the women of the household must have been three years later to receive Louise who knew Marion well and could no doubt tell stories to them of her activities in Paris.

Louis records in his account of his pilgrimage that the day after the visit to the Ridván Garden he left for Egypt and visited Port Said and Cairo before returning to 'Abdu'l-Bahá's presence in Ramleh.[20] It is unclear whether Louise and Neville Meakin also returned to Ramleh. It may be that Louise travelled back to France or England from Haifa. Earlier in his account Louis had mentioned that Neville Meakin intended to spend more time in Haifa and Akka. It seems that he was familiar with the area because it was he who acted as guide when the party visited the Carmelite Monastery in Haifa. He may have decided to spend time in the area in the hope that the favourable climate would benefit his health. However, eventually Neville did return to England where he finally succumbed to the tuberculosis that was devouring him and he passed away in London on 4 October 1912.

It is impossible to overemphasize the importance of this pilgrimage to both Louis and Louise. Louis found himself transformed by the experience. Just the fact that it was the first time he had left America and visited foreign lands must have made an unforgettable impression on him. He was visiting Africa, the continent of his forebears, and the Middle East with its culture and history so different from his native land. He enjoyed sightseeing in Cairo, calling it 'a wealth of ancient and medieval art' and saying 'few cities in the world surpass the Egyptian capital'.[21] But more importantly he had trodden the very ground where Bahá'u'lláh Himself had lived, had visited His Tomb and the sacred Shrine of His Forerunner, the Báb. He had relished the company of his fellow pilgrims and been greeted and accepted by the followers of Bahá'u'lláh as an honoured equal. Most of all, he had been in the presence of 'Abdu'l-Bahá, had been invited to ask Him questions and had been guided and blessed by Him. 'Abdu'l-Bahá later commented on Louis's transformation, writing in a Tablet: 'Verily, he has much advanced in this journey. He received another life, and obtained another power. When he returned, Gregory was, quite another Gregory. He had become a new creation...'[22] And in another Tablet: 'Mr Gregory arrived with the utmost love and spirituality and returned with infinite happiness. He added to his faith and assurance and found firmness and steadfastness.'[23]

'Abdu'l-Bahá asked Louis to visit Stuttgart in Germany, and also Paris and London before returning to America. Louis would have had a personal connection with the Bahá'ís in Stuttgart because Alma Knobloch, sister of Pauline Hannen who had introduced him to the Faith, had settled in Stuttgart in 1907 and had taken 'the Glad-Tidings of the Advent of Bahá'u'lláh to the soul of the German people'.[24] The German Bahá'ís wrote a report of Louis's visit for *Star of the West*, the Bahá'í news journal: 'In May, 1911, we had the privilege of entertaining Mr Louis G. Gregory, of Washington D.C., who came to us from the presence of Abdul-Baha, throbbing with new life and light.'[25] Louis's visit to London was also recorded in *Star of the West*:

> Those few of the Bahais here who had the good fortune to meet Mr. Louis G. Gregory, during his four days in London on his way home to Washington, D. C., from visiting Abdul-Baha at Ramleh, were exceedingly interested and edified. To meet such a great soul, so filled with the true Bahai spirit in any man is an inspiration; but when this man is a negro, and wise enough to be proud of his colour, then it is a revelation impressive with great significance as one contemplates the difficult problems existing between the white and black populations. How these problems can be changed by a few such men aflame with God's Word![26]

Louise corresponded with Neville Meakin up until the time of his death and Louis and Louise kept in touch after their pilgrimage, acknowledging the bonds of true friendship created by such a deep spiritual experience. It is possible that they met again when Louis visited London or Paris.

Louise's whole future life was shaped by her pilgrimage in 1911. She had arrived in Ramleh physically weak and yearning for rejuvenation both spiritually and physically. Her meeting with 'Abdu'l-Bahá changed her entire being and gave her purpose in life. She later wrote to her friend Agnes Parsons:

> Abdul Baha saved my life therefore it belongs to Him to use for the Cause. When first I was in this country [referring to her later travels in America] He said to me 'I found you almost dying in Egypt and if you had not done as I said you would have been worse than Mr Meakin'. This was an Englishman, a friend of Tudor Pole's I met in Egypt and saw a good deal of who was very ill from consumption and who died 4 months after Abdul Baha said this to me. Therefore it was evident I should have died if I had not obeyed and eaten fish and chicken as Abdul Baha told me to do if I wished to get better.[27]

She obeyed 'Abdu'l-Bahá's advice to the letter – including the practical advice that she should nourish her body with fish and chicken, which she did even as a very old lady. The spiritual advice that she garnered on her pilgrimage was to be her guide and her inspiration.

For the rest of her life she cherished two guiding lights which motivated her constantly. One was her love and gratitude to 'Abdu'l-Bahá with Whom she felt a personal connection. This love flowered into her lifelong service to the Cause of Bahá'u'lláh despite manifold difficulties. The other was her love for Louis and their marriage which were both directly attributable to 'Abdu'l-Bahá.

2

THE EGG MERCHANT AND HIS BROOD

Louise's family origins contrasted with the spiritual and sacrificial course that her life later took. Her forebears had been too busy tilling the soil and trying to ensure enough food in their children's mouths to embark on spiritual search. But it was thanks to her father's industriousness and competence in business that she was able to plough her own furrow in life with remarkable results.

Her father, Michael Mathew, was a self-made man, a man of his times. From a humble beginning he built up his own company, fathered 12 children and employed most of them in his business.

In days gone by the Mathew family were farmers in Kent, the county known as 'the garden of England', which borders on the south coast. For generations they had farmed near Beckenham and it was later recorded that 'Mr Michael Mathew was a descendant of one of the oldest families of Beckenham, the name being traceable back for several generations. It is interesting to mention that a Michael Mathew in line for generations lived at Copers Cope Farm . . . and farmed the Beckenham lands.'[1]

Louise's father was born at Kent House farm which his father, also named Michael, leased as a tenant farmer. The three farms: Kent House, Foxgrove and the quaintly named Copers Cope farm were owned by the Cator family, wealthy landowners who had retired from running a timber merchant's business in London to a quieter life with cleaner air in Kent in the 18th century.

But farming proved a hard and unprofitable life for Louise's grandfather and he fell into debt in the 1840s. It is recorded that in February 1840 he appeared before the court for relief of insolvent debtors and was sent to the Fleet Prison. Again in July 1845 he appeared before the same court and one shilling was paid to his creditors.[2] Louise's father must have learnt early on that harsh punishment would follow insolvency and he resolved to avoid the shame of debt by applying himself to hard work.

By the time Louise's father was 13 years old in 1851, Michael senior had given up the farming life and, looking perhaps for something more congenial and profitable, had become the publican of the Crooked Billet public house on nearby Penge Green, originally a coaching inn. He remained a publican here until his death in 1863 when his wife took over the running of the public house.

Penge was originally a small hamlet on the Surrey/Kent border, an area of woodland and a common with poor soil where sheep were grazed, pigs were pastured and firewood was gathered. However, Penge was just 10 miles south of the growing city of London and its rural peace was regularly shattered as early as 1715 when a stage coach service from Beckenham to London passed through the hamlet. Its peace was further disturbed when, after years of wrangling, its common was finally enclosed in 1827 and local small-holders found themselves no longer able to exercise their rights of grazing and gathering there. The 19th century saw entrepreneurs embrace the plan of building a canal from the docks on the south bank of the Thames in London to the town of Croydon, situated to the south of Penge. The craze for canal building was at its height and the plan was to bring goods such as timber, cereals and vegetables into London by canal, a faster route than by road as the roads were poor and notoriously slow.

Unfortunately, the Croydon canal, as it was known, never thrived. Its construction was difficult and when completed barges using it had to negotiate 28 locks, a time-consuming process. The canal opened in 1809 but by 1836 it had closed because it was unprofitable. By then railways were being looked upon as the coming thing and the London & Croydon Railway Company promptly bought up the Canal Company's assets and used the dry canal bed for the new railway line between London Bridge station and West Croydon which opened in 1839. The arrival of the railway marked a total change in the character of Penge and the surrounding area. Developers of the new railway realized that it could be useful in transporting goods but they also saw that it was ideal for transporting people. Suddenly there was a new fast route into London and the area around Penge was viewed as a prime location for residential villas and family homes for businessmen who wanted to live in the suburbs and travel swiftly into town each day for their work. In the 1830s and 40s Penge began to be transformed into a suburb of London with neat roads of desirable property.

Another major change that came to the area was the rebuilding of the Crystal Palace in Penge. Originally the Crystal Palace had been built in Hyde Park for the Great Exhibition of 1851 but once the exhibition was over the Palace was no longer needed in central London. The building's designer, Joseph Paxton, saw his chance to rebuild the Palace on a much grander scale outside London where it could attract sightseers who could travel to it by railway. The rebuilding was much more grandiose with twice the area of glass, a bigger capacity and surrounded by elaborate gardens with fountains, terraces and a lake. It opened to the public in 1854 and for many years it offered concerts, firework displays, exhibitions and spectacles such as circuses and balloon rides. Visitors flocked to it in their thousands, it was a massive success and made a huge impact on the local district.[3]

This was the area where Michael Mathew grew up and he must have been aware as a youngster that the character of the locality was changing and economic development was rampant all around him. At a very early age young Michael was put into the office of tea merchants in the City of London where he received no salary and acted as 'amateur postman' or one of a number of boys who ran around the City delivering letters. He was very bright and was soon promoted to a 'traveller in tea trade' when one of the firm's established commercial travellers fell sick. He amazed everybody by bringing back more orders than the company's best commercial traveller. Michael was good at saving his money and although he was only earning £80 a year when he married Emma Collins in 1859 he soon bettered himself so that before long he was earning £160 a year and was saving money at the same time.

Using his savings he invested in a tea shop, 'spending every spare moment after his ordinary day duties were done to nurse the business'.[4] After he added another shop to his business he went to his employers and requested to be put on commission. This meant that he could run his two shops and still work as a commercial traveller for the tea trade. It proved extremely profitable for him and with his two tea shops paying well he soon amassed the princely sum of £1,000. The young married couple lived in Penge with their one-year-old son, Ernest, and employed a house servant, so clearly his business was doing well.⁵

Michael's father-in-law, William Collins, was born in Sussex but moved to Southwark, south London, when he established his grocery there. In 1851 he was living with his wife Betty in the eponymous Collins Yard in White Street, Southwark and employing one man in his business. By 1861 William and Betty had moved out of London into the country to Penge with William travelling into London to work at his grocery. However in 1862 William died at the age of 56, leaving a prosperous business to his widow, Betty. Meanwhile Michael's wife Emma had an uncle, Thomas Collins, an egg merchant of Great Dover Street in Southwark, London who, when he wished to retire, offered his egg business to Michael for a nominal sum and Michael was quick to take up his offer which, when combined with his deceased father-in-law's shop, proved to be the start of his very profitable provisions business.

A big change now occurred in the Mathew family circumstances. Their family was growing: a second son, Percy, was born to them in 1862, a daughter, Florence in 1864 and their daughter Louisa in 1866 while the family still lived in Penge. By 1868 when Michael and Emma's son Sydney was born they had moved to Great Dover Street in Southwark, the location of the egg importing business, and Michael was an egg and grocery merchant in his own right.

From now on Michael Mathew turned his attention to egg importing and selling and made his fortune. When he died in 1909 he left £65,745, making him virtually a millionaire by modern standards and he employed over one hundred people. It was said that the 'name of Mr Mathew is known throughout England and France, where there is a large business established'.⁶

It seems extraordinary to us now that eggs and dairy products had to be imported into Britain, but in Victorian times agriculture was in decline in Britain and huge amounts of foodstuffs were imported from the Empire and also from Europe. In 1901 it was recorded: 'Australian butter of excellent quality, to the enormous extent of 25,000 tons – a large proportion being destined for London – was imported during the eight months up to April 30 1900, beating even Denmark', and 'Eggs seemed to arrive in London from every country under the sun; from Ireland, Germany, France, Belgium, Italy, and would soon no doubt come in great quantities from the Antipodes.'⁷ Michael had seen an opportunity for business development and had prospered accordingly.

More children followed, all born in London, and the Mathew family moved from Great Dover Street to the Old Kent Road not far away and then to Albany Road, Camberwell. By 1891 they had moved out of smoky, densely populated London and back into Kent to Brackley Road, Beckenham, near to Michael's roots. By this time Michael was describing himself as a provision merchant and the family employed two servants who lived in.[8] The house in Brackley Road was very large and was able to accommodate the parents and seven or eight unmarried children as well as the servants in its 12 rooms. An indicator of its size is that when much later this house was demolished, a block of 16 flats was built on the plot with room for substantial grounds around it. Brackley Road was a new road built to accommodate the newly prosperous middle class. It was part of a development designed to resemble an Indian colonial town with broad leafy avenues and ample detached houses in spacious gardens. From the western end of the road Michael could see to Kent House Farm where he had been born in comparative poverty. It must have given him great satisfaction to glimpse the site of his modest beginnings once he had made a fortune for himself and his family.

And so it was a large and affluent family in which Louise Mathew grew up. She was born in Penge on 1 February 1866 and was christened Louisa Alice Maria but for all her adult life she preferred to be called Louise and only used Louisa on official documents such as her passport. She was the fourth child born to Michael and Emma and had two elder brothers, Ernest and Percy, and one elder sister, Florence, known in the family as Flora. Tragedy struck the young family in March 1871 when Louise's baby brother Sydney died aged three years.

Emma had given birth to a fourth son, Leonard, in October 1869 and a third daughter, Edith, barely a year later in November 1870. Four more sons followed – Horace in 1872, Ralph in 1873, Vincent in 1879 and Harold in 1881. A fourth daughter was born – Ethel in 1875. So Louise was a member of a family consisting of 11 children who survived into adulthood.

She spent her childhood and teenage years living in London. She would have visited Penge again as a child because her grandmother lived there. She stayed there for a short time in April 1871 when her grandmother Betty looked after her, Flora and baby Leonard while her parents attended little Sydney's funeral in Norwood Cemetery near Beckenham. So Louise knew Penge and the area around Beckenham as a child but after her family moved to London around 1868 when she was a baby she was much more familiar with the Camberwell district of south London.

The area around Camberwell had been farmland with woods and meadows until the 19th century when new roads into central London and several new bridges across the River Thames were built. The Old Kent Road which had always been one of the main thoroughfares heading south became a busy metropolitan highway in the Victorian era crowded with horse-drawn buses. Railways changed the landscape from 1862 onwards and rail transport speeded up the journey into London. The area became attractive for residential building to enable people who worked in the city to live further out and still travel into town easily. Some elegant houses were built in the area although slums developed in other parts.

It is not known exactly how the Mathew children were educated although there are records that several of them, including the two younger girls of the family, were sent away to boarding schools. As the Mathew children were growing up in London there would have been any number of schools for elementary education available for them to attend and their father would have been able to afford any expenses incurred by their schooling.

However, it seems that Louise did not attend school as a child. Many years later while she was resident in the United States she was required to complete a census return and one of the questions on it was 'Did you attend school?' to which she gave the answer 'No'. This may have surprised the census recorder because she also gave her profession on the census as 'private tutor' which implied that she was well educated, which in fact was true. It is possible that Louise did not attend school because she was a delicate child. The Mathew family would have been able to afford private tutors to come to the house to educate their children and it is likely that this was the way that Louise and her older sister Flora were educated. Emma Mathew, her mother, was a great book reader and she encouraged the education of her children, including her daughters. In her will she left her large book collection to be divided amongst her children.

The Mathew children were all christened in the Church of England but this does not mean their parents had a strong allegiance to this church. While they lived in London the children's christenings took place at several different Anglican churches in the same part of south London indicating that the family may not always have attended a preferred church. It was normal for children to attend Sunday school in Victorian times, so the Mathew children probably were given a basis of Christian education at Sunday school.

There is no doubt that all the children of the family received an education that equipped them for a useful life and for most of them the life they were destined for involved working in their father's business. The eldest son, Ernest, who was six years older than Louise, was sent to manage the French side of Michael's business, supervising the provision and transport of goods such as eggs and butter from France to London. Ernest settled as a young man in Les Aubiers in the Deux Sèvres department of France and lived there all his adult life. Deux Sèvres is still a mainly rural area, as it was then, and agriculture is the mainstay of employment. Ernest married a French girl, Gabrielle Aliette Banchereau, in May 1884 in the Church of England at St Stephen's church in Walworth, London and Louise was one of the witnesses at her brother's marriage. The newly married couple went back to live at Les Aubiers and Ernest ran several businesses there successfully until the end of his days. He was decorated by the French government in middle age and awarded the order of '*Chevalier de mérite agricole*' for his great services rendered to agriculturists of France because of 'his peculiar knowledge and talent' relating to agriculture.[9]

Percy was two years younger than Ernest and he began work in his father's business as a 'provisions importer assistant' as a young man, going on to set up his own firm as an egg and butter merchant in later life. Leonard, born in 1869, was described in the 1901 census as a 'traveller in provisions' and we can guess that the said provisions were mainly eggs and butter. He may have travelled to the continent given the task of facilitating the importing of these provisions to England. Later he also became a provision merchant in his own right and employed staff in his own business. A similar career path was mapped out for Ralph who worked in his father's firm as a provisions merchant's assistant and later in the accounts department until he also established his own provision merchant company in the twentieth century. Ralph may also have travelled to France for his work because in 1910 he also married a young

French woman named Marie Claire. Unlike his brother Ernest, Ralph did not move to France but he and Marie Claire settled in England and lived near Croydon, Surrey. Horace managed to escape the family business for a few years, initially training and working as an electrical engineer. But by 1911 he was a 'traveller in provisions' possibly working for his brothers.[10]

Vincent was destined for a quite different profession and became a solicitor's articled clerk in his early 20s. But by 1911 he had succumbed to the lure of eggs and butter marketing and was running his own provisions importing company and employing staff. The usefulness of having a solicitor in the family was not lost however on the Mathews and two of Michael's grandsons became solicitors. Of the seven surviving sons only Harold escaped entirely from the family business. Maybe as the youngest child he was indulged a little and allowed to choose his own career. He became a successful civil engineer and settled in the Birmingham area.

All the Mathew sons who went into egg and butter importing made a success of their careers. They seem to have inherited their father's business acumen and prospered, all leaving substantial sums in their wills.

Of the four Mathew daughters only the youngest, Ethel, appears to have worked in the family business. As a teenager she was sent to Hook House school near Taunton in Somerset where, in the company of other girls of her age, she was educated in English, French, music and mathematics. This education equipped her to work as a 'corresponding clerk' in her father's business where her proficiency in English, French and maths would have been a great advantage. Ethel married Charles Smith, an electrical engineer, in Beckenham in July 1903.

Flora, the eldest daughter, was still classed as a 'scholar' in 1881 at the age of 17[11] so it appears that her education continued into her late teens. However, we know no more about Flora's subsequent life or any career that she may have followed. She appears to have been close to her mother who named her as one of her executors and main beneficiary of her will. She never married and cared for her mother in her years of failing health and old age.

In contrast, Edith who was five years younger than Louise chose a very modern career for herself and became a professional photographer. She attended a girls' boarding school in Margate, Kent and in her teens she won a prize for photography in a competition organized by the

Girl's Own Paper. The prize was that symbol of female emancipation, a bicycle. Although Edith was still living in the family home at the age of 30, she was no doubt perfecting her skills at photography because by the age of 40 she was living in the Welsh seaside town of Towyn, North Wales, running her own photography business at the County Studio and employing staff. She may have had an interest in the suffragist movement and is recorded on one occasion photographing the National Union of Women's Suffrage Societies caravan.[12] She remained single and later moved to Peacehaven on the Sussex coast where she died in 1933.

By the time the family moved to Beckenham in the 1880s Ernest and Percy had both married and had set up their own family homes elsewhere with their wives and children.

3

LOUISE SPREADS HER WINGS

Given that Louise, as a young girl, never attended school she must have spent a good deal of time at home, at first in Great Dover Street in Southwark, then in the family's house in the Old Kent Road and later in Camberwell which in the 1880s was a suburb of London.

As the family home was within easy reach of central London and its many cultural amenities it was easy for Louise to receive the sort of education considered suitable for a young girl in Victorian Britain. She had a great love of music and was a trained singer, having 'a beautiful lyric soprano voice'.[1] Emma, her mother, owned several musical instruments[2] and these would certainly have included a piano, a most useful instrument for accompanying a budding singer and for family musical evenings. Throughout her life Louise loved to write stories and poems and it is possible to imagine her as a young girl, maybe confined to home because of delicate health, creating juvenile works of fantasy and imagination. Handicrafts, especially embroidery, were considered a suitable pastime for young ladies and would no doubt have constituted part of Louise's education as a girl.

When, during Louise's teenage years, her eldest brother Ernest took on the role of manager for his father's firm in France, becoming a francophile, marrying a young French woman and thoroughly immersing himself in the French way of life, he nevertheless married in London. Louise was 18 when she acted as a witness at Ernest and Gabrielle's wedding.

It seems likely that Michael Mathew, realizing the importance of the French branch of his business, may have arranged for his children to receive tuition in the French language in their early years. Louise was fluent in French, a skill which was to be of enormous use to her in later life, and this fluency may well have been acquired as a child at a time when a perfect accent would have come naturally to her. She may possibly have visited France as a teenager, once her older brother was established and working there. The fact that she was a witness at his marriage implies that she was close to her brother Ernest and may already have made the acquaintance of his fiancée Gabrielle before the wedding and that she wished the couple well. Certainly the Mathew family had many ties with France, and with Louise's younger brother Ralph also marrying a French girl it is possible that the French language may have been practised in the Mathew household throughout Louise's childhood. Later during her years of education Louise studied and mastered German fluently which was to be another great asset to her in her adult life.

The Mathew family kept on expanding with the birth of more and more children and it was not until Louise was in her early 20s that the family moved to its final spacious home in Brackley Road, Beckenham. So in her teenage years Louise would have lived in a rather confined house with many younger siblings. One can imagine that her younger brothers, Leonard, Horace, Ralph, Vincent and Harold (not to mention her younger sisters Edith and Ethel) would have been fairly noisy about the house, probably occasionally playing boisterous games.

Although she was christened in the Church of England and no doubt given a grounding in Christian scripture as a child, as Louise grew older she rejected the faith she had been taught in her early years. Many years later she wrote to her friend Pauline Hannen: 'I have been out of orthodox thought on religion since I was 16, been through so many stages from agnosticism to Theosophy . . .'[3] Louise was referring to the Theosophical Society which was founded in 1875 in order to form a universal brotherhood without regard to race, creed, sex or colour, to study comparative religion and to investigate the unexplained powers latent in humankind.

So it seems that, having rejected her early religious education as a teenager, Louise set out on a search for truth that was to take her into her middle years before she found and accepted the Bahá'í teachings.

As she grew up Louise developed a social conscience and became involved in philanthropic projects. Victorian Britain was a country of great extremes of wealth and poverty and although the Mathew family lived in areas of respectability and affluence, Louise would not have had far to travel before she saw parts of London where the working classes lived in slum conditions. As an intelligent young woman she would have realized that she was supremely fortunate that her father had created a prosperous business and amassed enough wealth for the family to live in comfort, but that there were many people who were not so lucky. She was particularly concerned at the lack of education for the poor, realizing no doubt that without education very poor people would be unable to help themselves out of dire poverty.

The 1870 Education Act which enabled elementary education and set up school boards was followed in due course by the 1880 Education Act which made school attendance compulsory for children aged between five and 10. The intention was to try to stop the practice of child labour but school attendance did not immediately become one hundred per cent because many poor families depended financially upon the income earned by their children. Another difficulty in making education universal was that until the law was changed in 1891 there were school fees to be paid and this excluded many families from the luxury of schooling.[4]

Louise's concern for the welfare and education of poor children led her to be actively involved in improving their situation and her altruistic activities on behalf of the poor were later commended by 'Abdu'l-Bahá. It is not known whether she worked as a school teacher before receiving qualifications in teaching but this would have been entirely possible, as in the late 1880s when she was in her early 20s teaching qualifications were rare. However, once teacher education became more widely available she soon took steps to become qualified in her chosen profession.

Once she reached her early 20s Louise studied at Maida Vale College in central London. This would have given her sufficient grounding to move on for further studies and in October 1891 aged 25 she enrolled at Royal Holloway College, Egham, Surrey. This College was founded by philanthropist and entrepreneur Thomas Holloway in 1886. From humble beginnings he had become a multi-millionaire through his patent medicine business, promoting Holloway's pills and ointment. He married Jane Driver in 1840 but the couple had no children and the problem of what would happen to their vast wealth after their deaths became a source of worry to them. They decided to fund philanthropic projects and their first undertaking was a sanatorium for the middle classes that Thomas built at Virginia Water, Surrey. It is thought that Thomas's wife, Jane, then suggested that he should do something to benefit women and Thomas decided to found a college for the education of women. This was a bold idea in late Victorian England. Oxford and Cambridge universities had begun to admit women students (although women were not able to receive degrees until the mid-20th century) and there was already a college for women, Bedford College, from 1849, but nevertheless it was controversial to promote the education of women and the idea was still frequently ridiculed and lampooned. However, Royal Holloway College's magnificent building was completed in 1886 and opened by Queen Victoria herself.[5]

Louise studied arithmetic, algebra, French and German at Royal Holloway and in December 1892 she passed the Oxford preliminary examination.[6] She left the college immediately after the examination and never returned for the Lent term in 1893. It is possible that she was suffering health problems which caused her not to take her studies any further at this time, or it may be that her father refused to continue paying for his daughter's education which at this point would not have led to a professional or vocational qualification.

However, by 1894 she had decided to take up teaching as a career and to become a qualified teacher. In 1890 'day training colleges' for the training of teachers had been established attached to universities. The Royal Commission on the Working of the Elementary Education Acts, known as the Cross Commission, had recommended the setting up of these colleges and Louise was quick to take advantage of what they offered. It may have been that her father was prepared to fund her further education once it led to a professional qualification. The college that Louise chose was Edinburgh Training College, known as St George's Training College, some 400 miles from her home.[7]

St George's Training College in Edinburgh had been founded in 1886 and was the only institution in Scotland where women could train to teach at secondary schools and receive a recognized qualification as teachers. The women students attended lectures at the University of Edinburgh and this would have been an important incentive for Louise to choose to train in Edinburgh. She studied under the ground-breaking educationalist Miss Mary Walker who, famous in those days but more or less forgotten now, campaigned tirelessly for women to have the right to attend university and receive a degree. At that time men who had graduated from university did not need any further training to work as teachers and there was no teacher training available for women, so Miss Walker developed a curriculum for training women to acquire the skills necessary to become teachers and St George's College became the first teacher training college in Scotland.⁸ Miss Walker's fame as an outstanding educationalist and champion of women's rights must have reached Louise's ears in faraway London and she decided to make the journey to Scotland for her further studies. Always a keen traveller, she would have revelled in the chance to explore Scottish culture and history in Edinburgh.

At St George's Louise followed a two-year course which included economics, languages (French and German) and voice culture. The first women graduated from the University of Edinburgh in 1893 and it was in this year that Louise began her two-year training course; in June 1895 when she was 29 years old she received her Certificate in Education qualifying her as a teacher. She took her teaching exams under the auspices of Cambridge University which had the power to examine and certify students studying elsewhere.⁹ She was registered as a student at Edinburgh Training College at the time and was never a student at Cambridge University itself.

After she qualified Louise may have worked as a teacher for a few years in Britain but around the turn of the century she yielded to her strong desire for foreign travel and went with a college friend to live and work in Luxembourg.¹⁰ Louise's proficiency in French and German would have been of great use to her there as both languages are spoken in Luxembourg as well as the local language Luxembourgish or Lëtzeburgesch.

Once she was settled in Luxembourg Louise would assuredly have loved the remains of the old fortress of Luxembourg City and its narrow winding streets. Encircled by Belgium, France and Germany, throughout its history Luxembourg had been ruled by many countries including the French, the Burgundians, the Spanish, the Dutch and the Austrian Habsburgs, only achieving its independence as a Grand Duchy in 1867. During her time living there she must have become familiar with the intricate layout of the city, enjoying the magnificent views from the cliffs on which the town was built and getting to know her way across the deep gorges of the rivers Alzette and Pétrusse by the many bridges and viaducts.

It seems that Louise liked living in Luxembourg where she shared accommodation with her college friend, because she stayed there for nine years. She taught English 'to private pupils for 9 years and 7 of these

[I] had the girls' Government class free to all the girls of the town'.[11] This meant that she came to know many of the townspeople very well as she would have met so many of the local girls and their families. She later wrote that Luxembourg 'is like a country town almost, where everybody knows everybody and their business'.[12]

Perhaps the small size of Luxembourg finally became irksome to Louise or possibly it was after her college friend married a Belgian and moved away to live in the city of Spa, Belgium where her husband ran a hotel, but for whatever reason, around the year 1908 Louise went to live in Paris. Ostensibly this was to continue her studies in music. Paris would of course have offered excellent opportunities for furthering her talent for singing and would have been like a magnet for someone seeking a life rich in cultural experiences: musical, dramatic and artistic.

Paris in the first decade of the twentieth century was still the vibrant centre of 'La Belle Epoque' or 'beautiful age'. Its streets of the medieval period had been transformed by Napoleon III and Haussmann into spacious, leafy boulevards, the Bois de Boulogne and other landscaped parks had been designed as breathing spaces for the Paris population and the Eiffel Tower had been completed in 1889 and become the symbol of the modern, dynamic city. In European culture Paris at the time was second to none. New movements in art had included the Impressionists, the Post-Impressionists, Fauvism and Expressionism. Art Nouveau became the style recognized as thoroughly Parisian when it adorned public places such as the Paris Metro stations. Literature flourished with the publication of French realist novels and symbolist poetry; popular theatre was pre-eminent with cabaret, operetta and farce. Composers such as Debussy, Satie, Fauré and Saint-Saëns were delighting audiences with their music, and 'salon music' with its large repertoire of songs was still popular. No wonder Louise was drawn to Paris like a moth to a dazzling light.

Unbeknownst to her when she arrived in the city, there was another movement that was taking hold in Paris at this time. The Bahá'í Movement came to Europe in the last years of the 19th century and Louise was in the right place to meet a number of eminent Bahá'ís of the early days. May Bolles, a young and beautiful American, had moved to Paris with her mother and brother so that her brother could study architecture at the prestigious Ecole des Beaux Arts. May was an invalid but when she was visited in her sick room in Paris by Lua Getsinger, one of the first American Bahá'ís, she immediately believed. She was invited to travel with close family friend philanthropist Phoebe Hearst and a group of western pilgrims to Haifa and Akka to meet 'Abdu'l-Bahá and despite her physical weakness she joined the group. After the visit May returned to Paris where there was a large English-speaking expatriate community and soon established the first European Bahá'í centre there. She left Paris in 1902 when she married the architect Sutherland Maxwell and settled in Canada but the Paris Bahá'í community continued to flourish. When Louise moved to Paris in search of music and culture she was not to know that she would be drawn into the circle of Bahá'í luminaries there including such spiritual heroes as Hippolyte Dreyfus and Laura Barney.

The Dreyfus family were in the habit of giving 'musicales' or musical evenings at their home in Paris to which they invited 'people of taste'[13] and it may well have been at one of these entertainments that Louise met Edith Sanderson, a Californian, the daughter of Silas Sanderson, the Chief Justice of the California Supreme Court. Edith had moved to Paris with her mother and sister, Sybil, to further Sybil's career as an opera singer.[14] Edith had been introduced to the Baha'i Movement in 1900 by May Bolles[15] who also taught Hippolyte Dreyfus, named by Shoghi Effendi as 'the first Frenchman to embrace the Faith'.[16] Hippolyte was recorded by May Bolles as saying: 'I have come to learn what it is you have done to produce so remarkable a change in Edith S. [Sanderson]. She is not the same – she has found joy, serenity and a deep purpose in life' – and with his charming smile – 'how did you do it?'.[17]

Before long Louise was introduced to the Bahá'í teachings by Edith Sanderson. In such an active community, no doubt there were other members of the Paris Bahá'í group who also helped her to receive the Bahá'í message. It was during these Paris years that Louise met her friend Marion Jack and Marion later wrote that she had acted as a 'nurse maid' to Louise, meaning that she had assisted her in her understanding of the Bahá'í Cause.[18]

Meanwhile back in England, in March 1909 Louise's father died. On 12 March about noon Michael Mathew was hurrying from his home in Brackley Road to Beckenham Junction station, no doubt anxious to arrive at his place of work in London. However, when he reached the station he collapsed in the station approach. He was carried into the station and a doctor was called but when the local physician Dr Giddings arrived he examined Michael and pronounced him dead.[19]

One can imagine the consternation that was caused by Michael's death. He was 72 years old and had made his will a few years previously, so he had realized he was no longer a young man. But he was still running his business despite his age and such a dominant figure must have seemed to many of his employees as irreplaceable. The local newspaper reported the following week that over 100 of his employees attended his funeral. His son Ernest, living in France, had been scheduled to preside over a banquet in Paris that same week at which French government officials from the Chamber of Deputies and the Senate were invited and at which the French Minister of Agriculture was to speak. Naturally he had to miss this honour and travel to England for his father's funeral and without a doubt Louise did the same. The local newspaper devoted half a column to Michael's obituary under the headline 'The late Mr. Michael Mathew: a remarkable career'.[20]

Michael had made a very lengthy and detailed will and in it he made provision for each of his surviving 11 children to receive an equal share of the interest from his considerable investments. This share was paid quarterly and Louise was to benefit from this regular payment for the rest of her life. Her brothers Ernest, Percy, Leonard and Ralph inherited their father's business which they continued to run.

At this time Louise was struggling with the grief resulting from her father's death and possibly some feelings of guilt because his legacy now set her more or less financially free. It was a time of great change for her. Having met the Bahá'í group in Paris and learnt about the Bahá'í Movement, she was probably encouraged by her new friends to write to 'Abdu'l-Bahá asking His advice. The new western Baha'is, like their counterparts in Persia and the East, turned to 'Abdu'l-Bahá for spiritual guidance and wrote to Him frequently, knowing that He would do everything in His power to reply and answer their questions.

The first Tablet Louise received from the Master was sent to her through the agencies of Marion Jack and Hippolyte Dreyfus but clearly addressed 'To Miss Louise Mathew'. Written in Persian, it was later translated into English for her to read. It addressed her as 'thou who art turning to the Kingdom of God' which implies that she was receptive to the Bahá'í teachings but had not yet committed herself fully to them. The Tablet went on to advise her to praise God because she had 'heard His spiritual Voice through the ears of your soul'. It commended her 'for having shown such a kindness to the children of the poor', a reference to her altruistic work attempting to educate poor children. It implied that through helping the poor she had obtained the results of this good action and she had been granted the bounty of hearing 'the Proclamation of the Kingdom'.

'Abdu'l-Bahá went on to advise her to continue to 'concern yourself with the Divine Commands' and to be 'also busy in spreading the Cause of God', adding that 'when you will find it possible in the future, you will open a school to teach the children . . . giving to the young ones the Divine education'.

The Tablet and Louise's letter to the Master can be dated after March 1909 because she wrote to Him about her father's death and forgiveness of his sins. 'Abdu'l-Bahá advised her to make 'an earnest supplication to the Kingdom of the Merciful One, asking for remission and pardon in favour of your noble father' and added 'I too will pray for him and ask for his remission'. We are given no insight into what Michael Mathew's sins might have been and why he needed pardon.[21]

Louise was by now searching earnestly for spiritual truth and she wrote again to 'Abdu'l-Bahá on 14 November 1909, a letter that He acknowledged in His reply to her. In this Tablet He commended her and stated that her letter 'showed thy sincere effort, the devotion of thy heart, the purity of thy soul'. He added: 'I hope that thou wilt soon be the companion of the true Bahais and that thou wilt understand the truth of all the questions of the Bahai Cause.' He continued: 'I pray God for thee, that thou mayest discover the mysteries of truth and become a true Bahai and be the cause of the manifestation of divine bounty. Praise be to God that thou hast been aided by God to care for the poor and to serve the feeble.' He wrote that although she did not expect an answer 'yet because of the extreme love and affection that I have for thee, I answer thee, in spite of so many difficulties and occupations.' He added, 'If it is the will of God the time for our meeting will come.' So it seems that Louise had already asked to visit 'Abdu'l-Bahá and yearned to meet Him even before she accepted the Bahá'í Cause. He concluded the Tablet: 'Give my greetings to the servant near to God, Miss Rouhieh [Edith] Sanderson and upon thee be salutations and benediction.'[22]

This Tablet from 'Abdu'l-Bahá seems to have satisfied and comforted

Louise because later that year (in December 1909 according to her own account) she wrote to Him again declaring her faith in Bahá'u'lláh as the Messenger of God for this age. In fact she wrote to Him on 30 December 1909 and again on 25 February 1910. His reply was addressed 'To the honourable maid-servant of God, Miss Louise Mathew' and 'O daughter of the Kingdom!'. It exhorted her: 'Praise be to God that thou hast heard the heavenly proclamation, hast torn the veils of doubt and imagination and hast heard the Glad Tidings. I hope that thou art entirely detached from all desires and art filled with the love of God.' 'Abdu'l-Bahá acknowledged Edith Sanderson as Louise's spiritual teacher, responsible for guiding her to the Kingdom: 'Thou must with all thy heart be grateful to the servant of God, Miss Sanderson, because she has been the means of guidance, directing thee to this great gift; assuredly she was the means of life eternal for thee. Thou hast become born anew and hast received the baptism of spirit and fire. If thou didst offer in every breath a thousand thanks thou couldst not thank her sufficiently for her effort.'

He went on to advise her:

> A mirror can reflect the rays of the sun though it is on this earth, a very great distance from the heavens. Therefore when the human heart is attached to the Beauty of the Merciful it becomes the source of knowledge and wisdom; the heavenly mysteries are unveiled and the tongue, becoming conversant, in clear and eloquent explanations is the means of guidance to others.

She had written to 'Abdu'l-Bahá about her further plans for helping poor children and He replied:

> The home for poor children which is in preparation, is most commendable; all good works, of whatever kind they might be, are accepted in the Kingdom of God and become the cause of the progress of souls and the illumination of heart[s].

Louise had already been seized with the desire to visit the Master on pilgrimage and had beseeched Him for this bounty and now He concluded this Tablet:

> In the winter season it will be possible to come to Haifa for a certain number of days, that is, a stay of nine days. Then return to Paris and London, because thou must become engaged in diffusing the breezes of the Holy Spirit and be the means of guiding the people. Here there is no occupation nor service for thee, only the encounter of nine days is sufficient for that.[23]

So Louise was granted permission for her pilgrimage already in 1910 by receiving this Tablet from 'Abdu'l-Bahá and was advised that a stay of longer than nine days would be of no benefit to her. At that time 'Abdu'l-Bahá was resident in Haifa and pilgrims expected to visit Him there. By the 'winter season' He had departed Haifa on His extensive travels to the West and when she received the Tablet Louise could not have imagined that Egypt would be her meeting place with Him.

Although her heart was yearning to meet the Master and seek further spiritual guidance from Him, she would have to wait another year before achieving her heart's desire. She returned to London and threw herself into serving the Cause and continuing her plans to help educate the poor. She continued to write to 'Abdu'l-Bahá and received further Tablets from Him. In one of these He commented that she had written that the propagation of the Divine Cause was going ahead well in London, better in fact than one could have imagined. She had intimated that Mrs Stannard and Miss Rosenberg were working hard and Louise herself had given the message to many people and was ready to serve the Cause. 'Abdu'l-Bahá instructed Louise to tell a fellow worker that she should be happy to care for children and the poor for this is service to the Divine Kingdom. He also sent His respectful greetings to Miss Sanderson, Louise's spiritual mother Edith.[24]

With what surprise must the Bahá'ís have learnt that 'Abdu'l-Bahá had suddenly left Haifa in August 1910 and taken the steamer from Jaffa, the port to the south of Haifa. His departure was unannounced and surprising even to the Bahá'ís He left behind. It appeared that He was embarking on a trip to visit the West and He left His sister Bahiyyíh Khánum in charge of His affairs and the affairs of the community in His absence. However, He was no longer a young man and ill health forced Him to stay for one month in Port Said, Egypt. After a month there He boarded a ship for Europe but again was forced back for health reasons, this time to Alexandria in Egypt where He resided in Ramleh.

'Abdu'l-Bahá's stay in Egypt would last until July of the following year when He would finally sail for Marseilles and commence His visit to Europe.

So it was some time in the winter of 1910 or the early spring of 1911 that Louise eventually received her invitation to visit 'Abdu'l-Bahá in Ramleh and with admirable swiftness and single-mindedness she joyfully made her travel arrangements to visit Him in Egypt. She was at last about to meet the Master in radiant humility and seek further spiritual guidance from Him. She could not know that this pilgrimage would change her life out of all recognition.

4

WITH THE MASTER IN LONDON AND PARIS

Louise left no written record of her pilgrimage but Louis's account alludes to her participation in their spiritual journey.[1] After her pilgrimage in April 1911 she was transformed and rejuvenated both in body and in spirit. She now prepared to commit her life to service of the Faith and to humanity. She may have returned to Paris to share with the friends there her experiences on her pilgrimage and offer them the gems of 'Abdu'l-Bahá's wisdom that she had been privileged to hear. But, ever practical, she must have been eager to return to the project for helping poor children in England knowing that 'Abdu'l-Bahá had told her this was 'a service to the Divine Kingdom'.[2]

It was on 11 August 1911 that 'Abdu'l-Bahá departed Alexandria and sailed for Marseilles, France. He then spent some time in Thonon-les-Bains on Lake Geneva where He was visited by Juliet Thompson, the American Bahá'í and artist who later painted a portrait of Him and recorded her meetings with Him in her diary. Hippolyte and Laura Dreyfus-Barney were now married and stayed at the Hotel du Parc in Thonon and had the bounty of meetings with 'Abdu'l-Bahá. Other visitors there were the American Horace Holley and his first wife, Bertha. Edith Sanderson, her mother and two friends were staying nearby and were visited by 'Abdu'l-Bahá and His party.

After resting in Thonon-les-Bains 'Abdu'l-Bahá set off on His travels and arrived in London on 4 September 1911. Although this was four days earlier than expected He was graciously received by Sara, Lady Blomfield who had His accommodation swiftly made ready at her apartment at 97 Cadogan Gardens where He was to spend most of His time during this His first visit to England. Lady Blomfield had become a Bahá'í in Paris in 1907 when she was introduced to the Faith by Miss Bertha Herbert, who later became Mrs Bertha Holley. Bertha was assisted in giving the message to Lady Blomfield by Ethel Rosenberg, one of the first British Bahá'ís, who had recently returned from her pilgrimage to meet 'Abdu'l-Bahá in the Holy Land. Lady Blomfield, who had been on a spiritual search for many years, realized that the Bahá'í Movement was the guidance she had been seeking and became one of the most steadfast pivots of the British Bahá'í community, so it was natural that her home should be chosen to be blessed by the presence of 'Abdu'l-Bahá while in London.

Louise later recorded that she 'met Him ['Abdu'l-Bahá] in Egypt, London and Paris'[3] so it is clear that she associated with the friends who gathered round 'Abdu'l-Bahá, met with Him and attended His talks during His visits to both London and Paris.

On Sunday 10 September 'Abdu'l-Bahá gave a talk from the pulpit of the City Temple in London to around 2,000 people during the evening service. This was His first public talk anywhere in the world,[4] a remarkable achievement considering that He had been a prisoner of the Ottoman Empire for 40 years and He had no previous experience of public speaking. He had been invited to speak at the City Temple by the celebrated churchman the Reverend R. J. Campbell whom He had met shortly after His arrival in London. 'Abdu'l-Bahá spoke animatedly for nine minutes and then an English translation of His talk was read to the congregation by Wellesley Tudor Pole.

His address included the theme of unity which was to be a subject He frequently returned to in many of His talks in the West:

> The gift of God to this enlightened age is the knowledge of the oneness of mankind and of the fundamental oneness of religion. War shall cease between nations, and by the will of God the Most Great Peace shall come; the world will be seen as a new world, and all men will live as brothers.
>
> In the days of old an instinct for warfare was developed in the struggle with wild animals; this is no longer necessary; nay, rather, co-operation and mutual understanding are seen to produce the greatest welfare of mankind. Enmity is now the result of prejudice only.
>
> In the *Hidden Words* Bahá'u'lláh says, 'Justice is to be loved above all.' Praise be to God, in this country the standard of justice has

been raised; a great effort is being made to give all souls an equal and a true place. This is the desire of all noble natures; this is today the teaching for the East and for the West; therefore the East and the West will understand each other and reverence each other, and embrace like long-parted lovers who have found each other.[5]

It seems likely that Louise was amongst the huge congregation in the City Temple on this remarkable occasion.

A week later another London church was the location for a stirring address and benediction from the Master. He was invited to speak to the congregation at evening service at St John the Divine, Westminster by Archdeacon Wilberforce, grandson of the campaigner for the abolition of slavery, William Wilberforce. 'Abdu'l-Bahá was seated in the Bishop's chair on the chancel steps and after His talk the Archdeacon himself read a translation of the speech. 'Abdu'l-Bahá gave a blessing to the whole congregation, 'his wonderful voice rising and falling in the silence with the power of his invocation'[6] whereupon Archdeacon Wilberforce and 'Abdu'l-Bahá walked hand in hand down the aisle of the church.

The headquarters of the Theosophical Society was another venue for a spiritual discourse while 'Abdu'l-Bahá was in London. He was invited to speak there on 30 September by the society's president Annie Besant. Louise had been an adherent of Theosophy at one time, so it is likely that she was amongst the audience at this talk. 'Abdu'l-Bahá here gave an exposition of some main principles of Bahá'u'lláh's teachings, introducing his main points with the words:

> It is the inherent nature of things on this earth to change, thus we see around us the change of the seasons. Every spring is followed by a summer and every autumn brings a winter – every day a night and every evening a morning. There is a sequence in all things.
>
> Thus when hatred and animosity, fighting, slaughtering, and great coldness of heart were governing this world, and darkness had overcome the nations, Bahá'u'lláh, like a bright star, rose from the horizon of Persia and shone with the great Light of Guidance, giving heavenly radiance and establishing the new Teaching.
>
> He declared the most human virtues; He manifested the Spiritual powers, and put them into practice in the world around Him.[7]

During His time in London 'Abdu'l-Bahá met with dignitaries such as the Lord Mayor of London, prominent churchmen and eminent professors but He also had time for people of humbler status. He made two visits to the village of Byfleet in Surrey, a short drive from London. The first was on 9 September to Vanners, a country farm house where women who worked at the Passmore Edwards' Settlement in London were enjoying a country holiday and break from their labours. The women gathered round Him in a circle and He addressed them saying: 'Are you happy? . . . I love you all, you are the children of the Kingdom, and you are accepted of God. Though you may be poor here, you are rich in the treasures of the Kingdom. I am the Servant of the poor. Remember how His Holiness Jesus said: "Blessed are the poor!" If all the queens of the earth were gathered here, I could not be more glad!'[8]

He returned to Vanners in Byfleet on 28 September and stayed overnight. His observation of the poor people He saw in London and in the country villages he motored through impressed Him greatly and He said: 'I find England awake; there is spiritual life here. But your poor are so *very* poor! This should not be. On the one hand you have wealth and great luxury; on the other hand men and women are living in the extremities of hunger and want. This great contrast of life is one of the blots on the civilization of this enlightened age.'[9]

'Abdu'l-Bahá spoke several times on the importance of education and the improvement of the lot of the poor and destitute, a subject very dear to Louise's heart. She may well have heard Him say:

> The girl's education is of more importance today than the boy's, for she is the mother of the future race. It is the duty of all to look after the children. Those without children should, if possible, make themselves responsible for the education of a child . . . You must turn your attention more earnestly to the betterment of the conditions of the poor. Do not be satisfied until each one with whom you are concerned is to you as a member of your family. Regard each one either as a father, or as a brother, or as a sister, or as a mother, or as a child. If you can attain to this, your difficulties will vanish, you will know what to do. This is the teaching of Bahá'u'lláh.[10]

'Abdu'l-Bahá also visited the city of Bristol for the weekend of 23 to 25 September, a visit involving a longer drive through the English countryside which He admired, commenting on the ancient trees and the greenness of the downs and valleys, the little houses each with a plot of land. It is recorded that 'Observing a young woman who rode by on horseback with her hair flying free and several who bicycled past on their bicycles unattended, he said, "This is the age of woman. She should receive the same education as her brother and enjoy the same privilege; for all souls are equal before God."'[11]

In Bristol 'Abdu'l-Bahá stayed at the Clifton Guest House which was owned by Wellesley Tudor Pole. A tour of the local beauty spots in the neighbourhood, which must surely have included the dramatic Clifton Gorge, was followed by a gathering of 90 people in the Guest House. His address to them included the exhortation: 'Look upon the people of your own race and those of other races as members of one organism; sons of the same Father; let it be known by your behaviour that you are indeed the people of God. Then wars and disputes shall cease and over the world will spread the Most Great Peace.'[12]

He walked around the whole Guest House and blessed it, saying it would become a centre for pilgrims from around the world and become a House of Rest. The building was subsequently acquired in the 21st century by the Bahá'ís of the United Kingdom so that visitors may 'draw upon its hallowed spirit of tranquillity and peace to inspire them in their building of [Bahá'u'lláh's] world embracing civilisation.'[13]

Private homes were also blessed by a visit from 'Abdu'l-Bahá during His stay in England. On 8 September He attended a Unity Meeting at Ethel Rosenberg's apartment where He spoke on the station of Bahá'u'lláh and His teachings[14] and on 13 September He visited the home of Mary Virginia Thornburgh-Cropper, an American who had been unhappily married to an Englishman and who had met 'Abdu'l-Bahá on pilgrimage in 1898. Resident in England, she had become one of the foremost teachers of the Faith in Britain. Between 45 and 60 people attended this meeting and His loving words to the assembled friends on this occasion included:

> I pray for all of you, that you may become celestial warriors, that you may everywhere spread the Unity of God and enlighten the East and West, and that you may give to all hearts the love of God. This is my utmost desire, and I pray to God that your desire may be the same.

I am very happy to be with you all. I am pleased with the English King and Government, and with the people.

You may thank God that in this land you are so free. You do not know what lack of freedom there is in the East. When anyone comes to this country he is content.[15]

On 22 September a Unity Meeting was arranged by Marion Jack and her friend Elizabeth Herrick at 137A High Street, Kensington, London which 80 people attended. As Louise counted Marion Jack as one of her close friends it seems reasonable to assume that she attended this meeting. She will have heard 'Abdu'l-Bahá talk on the subject of the origin and spread of spiritual teachings: 'In [e]very age of great spiritual darkness, a light is kindled in the East. So once again the light of the teachings of God has come unto you. Even as education and progress travel from West to East, so does the spiritual fire travel from East to West.'[16]

'Abdu'l-Bahá's last public talk on this visit to England[17] was at the Passmore Edwards' Settlement in Tavistock Square where He spoke to at least 200 people invited by Mrs Thornburgh-Cropper. The Settlement Movement of the late 19th century was intended to bridge the ever-widening gap between the poor and the middle classes. A purpose-built building would be constructed in a working class area and young solicitors, doctors, architects and other middle class professionals would be encouraged to live there while at the same time the working classes would be free to use the building and mix with them, using the building more or less as a community centre.

Mary Ward, wife of Oxford don Humphry Ward and granddaughter of Thomas Arnold, famous headmaster of Rugby School, was a leading proponent of the Settlement Movement and in the 1890s she planned to build a new Settlement centre in central London. She invited the MP John Passmore Edwards to donate towards the scheme knowing that he was a famous philanthropist of the time, interested in promoting the welfare of working people. Passmore Edwards donated £10,000 towards an architect-designed building in Tavistock Square and Mary delightedly named the new centre after him.[18]

Accounts of this valedictory meeting for 'Abdu'l-Bahá record that between 200 and 460 people assembled to bid farewell to Him.[19] Several eminent speakers, some of them Bahá'ís and others not Bahá'ís, expressed their joy and satisfaction at the success of 'Abdu'l-Bahá's visit to England. He spoke for some fifteen minutes reiterating the message of unity and peace that He brought with Him and saying:

> Praise be to God! the signs of friendship are appearing, and as a proof of this I, today, coming from the East, have met in this London of the West with extreme kindness, regard and love, and I am deeply thankful and happy. I shall never forget this time I am spending with you.

He then closed the meeting giving a blessing 'in undulating rhythmic tones'.[20]

On 3 October 1911 'Abdu'l-Bahá departed from England and arrived in Paris where He rented an apartment at 4 Avenue de Camoëns in the centre of the city near the Trocadero gardens and within sight of the Eiffel Tower. As always, He paid for His own expenses, declaring that 'This is my home and the home of my friends' and employing 'a little fair-haired, pleasant-faced French maid' who 'presided over [the apartment's] domestic functions and answered the bell'.[21]

Lady Blomfield accompanied 'Abdu'l-Bahá to Paris together with her two daughters, as did Ethel Rosenberg and Marion Jack and there is no doubt that Louise also followed Him there, as she later recorded.[22] She knew Paris well by now and would easily have found her way around. As well as a large party of Persians who came with Him and 'apparently camped in the home of Abdul-Baha during his stay there' there were other followers: 'French, Germans, English, Hindus, and a large sprinkling of Americans'.[23]

Here 'Abdu'l-Bahá received visitors and gave short talks every day. As had been His habit in London, He rose early and dealt with His correspondence, then started receiving people who had requested interviews with Him, often starting before 9 a.m. Subsequently, at no fixed time in the morning He would address the friends who had gathered in the apartment. The American Bahá'í Mary Hanford Ford reported: 'Sometimes he came joyfully, waving a good morning to all, or best of all, greeting each one with a warm hand clasp.'[24]

But on another occasion after the Italian invasion of Benghazi, Libya in October 1911 He entered the room with sadness and said:

> I hope you are all happy and well. I am not happy, but very sad. The news of the Battle of Benghazi grieves my heart. I wonder at the

human savagery that still exists in the world! How is it possible for men to fight from morning until evening, killing each other, shedding the blood of their fellow-men: And for what object? To gain possession of a part of the earth! Even the animals, when they fight, have an immediate and more reasonable cause for their attacks! How terrible it is that men, who are of the higher kingdom, can descend to slaying and bringing misery to their fellow-beings, for the possession of a tract of land! . . .

How many widows mourn their husbands, how many stories of savage cruelty do we hear! How many little orphaned children are crying for their dead fathers, how many women are weeping for their slain sons!

There is nothing so heart-breaking and terrible as an outburst of human savagery!

I charge you all that each one of you concentrate all the thoughts of your heart on love and unity. When a thought of war comes, oppose it by a stronger thought of peace. A thought of hatred must be destroyed by a more powerful thought of love. Thoughts of war bring destruction to all harmony, well-being, restfulness and content.

Thoughts of love are constructive of brotherhood, peace, friendship, and happiness.[25]

'Abdu'l-Bahá gave His first public talk in France at St Germain, Paris on 9 November at the Alliance Spiritualiste, an organization founded in 1910 to promote spirituality. The meeting was opened by the society's president Madame Jeanne Beauchamps and the writer Louis Le Leu, General Secretary, gave a short address extolling the Bahá'í Movement. 'Abdu'l-Bahá spoke to a packed hall and His words included:

I am happy to be present at a gathering such as this, assembled together to listen to a Divine Message. If you could see with the eye of truth, great waves of spirituality would be visible to you in this place. The power of the Holy Spirit is here for all. Praise be to God that your hearts are inspired with Divine fervour! Your souls are as waves on the sea of the spirit; although each individual is a distinct wave, the ocean is one, all are united in God.

Every heart should radiate unity, so that the Light of the one

Divine Source of all may shine forth bright and luminous. We must not consider the separate waves alone, but the entire sea. We should rise from the individual to the whole. The spirit is as one great ocean and the waves thereof are the souls of men.[26]

Albert Jounet, another of the founder members of the society, closed the meeting with an appreciation of the Bahá'í Revelation which was well received.

On Sunday 26 November 'Abdu'l-Bahá spoke at the Foyer de l'Ame or 'Home of the Soul', the Protestant church established by poet and orator Charles Wagner who campaigned for religious unity and was fêted by President Theodore Roosevelt when he visited America in 1904. 'Abdu'l-Bahá's address included the words:

> The natural law for man is to walk on the earth, but he makes ships and flies in the air! He is created to live on dry land, but he rides on the sea and even travels under it!
>
> He has learnt to control the power of electricity, and he takes it at his will and imprisons it in a lamp! The human voice is made to speak across short distances, but man's power is such that he has made instruments and can speak from East to West! All these examples show you how man can govern nature, and how, as it were, he wrests a sword from the hand of nature and uses it against herself. Seeing that man has been created master of nature, how foolish it is of him to become her slave! What ignorance and stupidity it is to worship and adore nature, when God in His goodness has made us masters thereof. God's power is visible to all, yet men shut their eyes and see it not. The Sun of Truth is shining in all His splendour, but man with fast shut eyes cannot behold His glory! It is my earnest prayer to God that by His Mercy and Loving Kindness you may all be united, and filled with the utmost joy.
>
> I beseech you, one and all, to add your prayers to mine to the end that war and bloodshed may cease, and that love, friendship, peace and unity may reign in the world.[27]

The Theosophical Society in Paris was privileged to receive a visit from 'Abdu'l-Bahá where He set out 11 Bahá'í principles including the unity of mankind, unity of religion and science, abolition of prejudice and the equality of men and women, stressing the equal rights of women: 'Women have equal rights with men upon earth; in religion and society they are a very important element. As long as women are prevented from attaining their highest possibilities, so long will men be unable to achieve the greatness which might be theirs.'[28]

'Abdu'l-Bahá did not ignore the poor whilst He was in Paris. On 15 October He invited all those present at 4 Avenue Camoëns to join Him in the afternoon in visiting a Bahá'í couple, Monsieur and Madame Ponsonaille, in a deprived district of Paris. The artist Edwin Scott had arranged this visit to see the 'real Bahai settlement work' carried on by the couple.

Alice Beede, an American Bahá'í who accompanied 'Abdu'l-Bahá to Paris, recorded the visit for *Star of the West* and wrote:

> They are poor people. He is employed as a collector for one of the large department stores in Paris. Having received the Message, he felt his work for the Cause of God was among the very poor children, waifs and those who had no parents; so with his wife, some years ago settled his home here and by going without their noon day meal (which to the French means much) they could give it to these little ones. They started in an old car where they met together to read the Tablets and the Word of Baha'o'llah. It was not long before many came and it grew so that the clergy of many sects desired to have it consolidated under them. Mons. Ponsonaille did not consider this the way to serve best and he declined all these offers. At last, they grew so very jealous that they, with the help of the priests, took the car from him. The Bahai friends in Paris offered to build a place for his work and Mons. Ponsonaille told them if they would furnish him the boards and nails that he would build it himself, which he did, and it was here that we went, and after three months spent going around Paris every day, I assure you I had never seen such a dirty, miserable quarter.

The visitors entered

> into a small board cabin about 20 x 25 feet. At one end was a raised platform and desk of rough boards. I can only say as my eyes fell first upon The Greatest Name hanging in a frame from this desk and I

saw the crowd of miserably poor, dear little ones gathered there, and as my ears caught the music of their voices (for they were singing), tears filled my eyes and a great lump choked me. Then I looked and saw we were but a half dozen who had come as guests, and all, like myself, were deeply affected. It was Madam Ponsonaille, a woman with a strong, kind and most intelligent face, who evidently had taught the children to sing and who with her whole heart was leading and keeping time for them, for they had no instrument.

'Abdu'l-Bahá addressed them:

I am very glad to be here with you. I am very glad to see you all here. I love you very much. I have been in many beautiful houses, but this is more beautiful to me than any of the others, for the spirit of the love of Baha'o'llah is here . . . I have seen many beautiful rich children, but to me you are more beautiful, and I love you all (as Christ loved little children) here.

To the Ponsonailles He said:

This is a great work you are doing for the love of God in this great day, through the power of Baha'o'llah. Your station is great. Your names will go down through all the ages. Kings and Queens have never been talked of and remembered as you will be. You are workers in the Kingdom of Abha and I am very happy and love you very much.[29]

Edwin Scott and his wife Josephine were early Bahá'ís in Paris and received 'Abdu'l-Bahá in their artist's studio at 17 rue Boissonade on 6 November. The couple had regularly opened their home to Bahá'ís and those investigating the teachings. Entering their home 'Abdu'l-Bahá exclaimed: 'This is in truth a Bahá'í house. Every time such a house or meeting place is founded it becomes one of the greatest aids to the general development of the town and country to which it belongs. It encourages the growth of learning and science and is known for its intense spirituality and for the love it spreads among the peoples.'[30]

'Abdu'l-Bahá gave several talks in private homes during His time in Paris. On Sunday 29 October He visited the home of Madame Gabriel Sacy where she served dinner before a meeting which 60 people attended.

It was felt that this event was very much in the French style and 'Abdu'l-Bahá appeared pleased with this. During the dinner He commented:

> I am from a far away country and here in Paris, at your table, I find in union, love and happiness, Persians, Arabs, Turks and French, which proves that we are of one race and that all men are brothers. The God of Persia is the God of France, of Turkey, of Italy, etc. He is One and the same, so in loving Him we are united. Paris is the universal centre of culture and learning, of science and the arts. She must also be the centre of spirituality. There are all sorts of fruits; some can only ripen in a cold climate; others need the warmth and others yet the tropical sun. So it is with Paris. The greatest efforts are necessary that she may blossom and bear fruit.[31]

The evening's events were later recorded for the Bahá'í newsletter *Star of the West* by Madame d'Ange d'Astre, considered to be the first French Bahá'í from a Catholic background.[32]

On 24 November 'Abdu'l-Bahá graced the home of Mademoiselle Gastéa where He spoke on 'The cruel indifference of people towards the suffering of foreign races' saying:

> I have just been told that there has been a terrible accident in this country. A train has fallen into the river and at least twenty people have been killed. This is going to be a matter for discussion in the French Parliament today, and the Director of the State Railway will be called upon to speak. He will be cross-examined as to the condition of the railroad and as to what caused the accident, and there will be a heated argument. I am filled with wonder and surprise to notice what interest and excitement has been aroused throughout the whole country on account of the death of twenty people, while they remain cold and indifferent to the fact that thousands of Italians, Turks, and Arabs are killed in Tripoli! The horror of this wholesale slaughter has not disturbed the Government at all! Yet these unfortunate people are human beings too.[33]

The home of Hippolyte and Laura Dreyfus-Barney at 15 rue Greuze was sometimes the venue for meetings including the last occasion when 'Abdu'l-Bahá addressed the friends on 1 December saying:

When I arrived in Paris some time ago for the first time, I looked around me with much interest, and in my mind I likened this beautiful city to a large garden.

With loving care and much thought I examined the soil, and found it to be very good and full of possibility for steadfast faith and firm belief, for a seed of God's love has been cast into the ground.

Clouds of Heavenly Mercy showered their rain upon it, and the Sun of Truth fell warmly upon the young seeds, and today one can see in your midst the birth of belief. The seed cast into the ground has begun to spring up, and day by day you will see it grow. The bounties of the Kingdom of Bahá'u'lláh shall indeed bring forth a wondrous harvest!

Behold! I bring you glad and joyful tidings! Paris will become a garden of roses! All kinds of beautiful flowers will spring up and flourish in this garden, and the fame of their fragrance and beauty will be spread in all lands. When I think of Paris in the future, I seem to see her bathed in the light of the Holy Spirit! Verily, the day is dawning when Paris will receive her illumination, and the Goodness and Mercy of God will be visible to every living creature . . .

Since my arrival a few weeks ago, I can see the growth of spirituality. At the beginning only a few souls came to me for Light, but during my short sojourn among you the numbers have increased and doubled. This is a promise for the future![34]

And so 'Abdu'l-Bahá's first visit to Europe came to an end when He set sail for Alexandria once again on 2 December. He would spend nearly four months in Egypt until at the end of March He left Alexandria for Naples en route for America.

In Europe He had met people from a vast spectrum of backgrounds ranging from professors and academics to the poor people of Paris, had spoken in churches and private homes, had been the source of interest to newspapers and had personally met followers of the Bahá'í Movement who would never have had the opportunity to visit Him in the Holy Land. Bahá'ís had travelled from the New World to meet Him and to try to persuade Him to visit the American continent. His words had been translated into English and French and His followers painstakingly recorded His talks and later published accounts of them in books such as *'Abdu'l-Bahá in London*, *Paris Talks* and Lady Blomfield's

The Chosen Highway.

But in none of the published accounts of His travels in England and France is there a mention of Louise Mathew who, we know, 'met Him in Egypt, London and Paris'. Nobody records that she was present at any of His talks, visits or the 'At Homes' that people gave for Him. She seems to have been invisible and unremarked in the crowd. Her friend Marion Jack described her as 'a quiet little mouse'[35] and Louise certainly was modest and self-effacing and appears to have been able to slip in and out of meetings unnoticed.

But there was One Who noticed her. 'Abdu'l-Bahá noticed her and He seems to have had a plan for her. From letters that Louise later wrote it is possible to discern that she met and talked with the Master on more than one occasion during His European travels. Years later she wrote to her friend Agnes Parsons and mentioned: 'He ['Abdu'l-Bahá] told me so often "I am your Father, you are my daughter", no doubt this was to reassure me under all difficulties.' This surely indicates that she had more than one private conversation with 'Abdu'l-Bahá on His travels.[36]

She journeyed down to Naples in March 1912 to be with 'Abdu'l-Bahá again before He sailed to America on the *SS Cedric*, so she must have either been in touch with Him again by letter or have learnt from others His exact itinerary. However quiet and shy she was, Louise was not abashed to seek further guidance from 'Abdu'l-Bahá while He was in Naples, and from their conversation on board the *SS Cedric* before it sailed it is apparent that they had already spoken together of the possibility of her accompanying 'Abdu'l-Bahá to America.

Louise had no scruples in putting her suggestion to 'Abdu'l-Bahá: 'at Naples I asked if I might go with Him and He answered "Why not go later, you will have difficulties."' However, the 'quiet little mouse' was not to be put off: 'But I insisted I wanted to go with Him. Looking a moment at me He said, "You are better, you may go, but I warn you you will have difficulties." I told Him I would rather have the difficulties and go with Him. Then He said "I will strengthen you."'[37] How often in the years to come must Louise have remembered that she was promised difficulties and been aware with all her heart of 'Abdu'l-Bahá strengthening her.

5

THE SEED IS SOWN

The early Bahá'í newsletter *Star of the West* carried the following special news item in its issue of 9 April 1912:

> SPECIAL:
> A report that Abdul-Baha and suite sailed from Alexandria, Egypt, March 25th on the White Star Line S.S. 'Cedric', due to arrive in New York City, April 10th, has been confirmed.
>   Plans are being made by some of the assemblies to send wireless messages of greeting and good-will to him as soon as the vessel comes into the zone of communication from the shore stations. On behalf of all the friends the *Star of the West* sends the following: 'Welcome! Welcome! Welcome!'
>   The eyes of the Bahai World are now centered upon this notable event of the visit of Abdul-Baha to America. The *Star of the West* will endeavor to give as complete an account of his sojourn in the West as its limited space will permit.[1]

The ship was due to call at Naples before setting out on her transatlantic voyage. With Him sailed His grandson, Shoghi Effendi, a 15-year-old who must have been excited to be making a trip with his Grandfather to the New World where he would meet the American communities and help give the Bahá'í message to North America. Also accompanying 'Abdu'l-Bahá were Siyyid Asadu'lláh-i-Qumí, Dr Amínu'lláh Faríd (a nephew of 'Abdu'l-Bahá's wife), Mírzá Munír-i-Zayn, Áqá Khusraw and Mahmúd-i-Zarqání, 'Abdu'l-Bahá's secretary (who kept a diary of his travels with 'Abdu'l-Bahá).[2]

When the ship reached Naples Louise Mathew and several western Bahá'ís were waiting. All seemed set for departure to the New World but Italian health inspectors boarded the ship and pronounced their

THE SEED IS SOWN

verdict that the eyes of three of the people on board were infected with trachoma and would therefore not be permitted to enter the United States. Shoghi Effendi was one of the three. 'Abdu'l-Bahá spent a whole day trying to persuade the authorities to reconsider their diagnosis but to no avail. It was always suspected that Dr Faríd had influenced the health inspectors in a jealous attempt to prevent Shoghi Effendi from travelling to the United States. Sadly his machinations proved successful and the young Shoghi Effendi was devastated to learn that he had to return to Alexandria where he understandably pined and lost weight in the following months, disappointed to have missed his chance of a lifetime to travel with his Grandfather.

'Abdu'l-Bahá was Himself heartbroken that His grandson was unable to accompany Him. Later at dinner in the salon He remarked, 'These Italians took us for Turks. They sent a report to this effect and stopped three of our party from proceeding. One was a secretary, the other a cook. If they had stopped only these two it would have mattered little. But why should they treat that tender youth Shoghi Effendi so harshly? They have treated us with injustice . . .'[3]

It was while the ship was docked in Naples that Louise had her conversation with 'Abdu'l-Bahá concerning journeying with Him to America. He joked with her a little saying: 'Just now you said it was too far but as soon as you hear of my going it gives you strength to go.' She wrote later to a friend that this was literally true and continued:

> Then Abdul Baha after a silence said 'I am going to walk on the deck if you like you may follow.' Several Bahais both oriental and occidental including Fareed [Dr Faríd] had heard all this but when I followed Abdul Baha on the deck He was alone with Mahmud. Then He turned round and said 'I said what I did because I saw a seed in your heart.' Then almost immediately added 'Now is the watering time.' I could not understand what He meant and only thought it must be something of a spiritual nature. A moment later He turned round again and said 'I saw one seed in your heart, I wish it to produce many seeds.'

In the same letter she wrote:

> On the boat before we started I told Abdul Baha I had written to

Mr. Gregory and repeated to Him what I had said which was the words Abdul Baha had Himself said to me about going to America in which He had indicated I should go with Him . . . Mr. Gregory's answer which I also told Abdul Baha was 'I feel impressed strongly that Abdul Baha meant you to go to America. If Abdul Baha tells us to do something however difficult if we obey the difficulties will be changed into possibilities.'[4]

At this time Louise regarded Louis as a good friend but had no inkling of the idea of marrying him. Likewise Louis was happy to exchange letters with Louise and considered her to be a friend. As he later wrote to Pauline Hannen, 'Last year we visited Abdul Baha at Ramleh and the Holy Tomb at Akka and although greatly attracted to each other not even dimly realized its future bearing.'[5]

However, the seed had been planted by 'Abdu'l-Bahá and it was destined to bear fruit.

When the *SS Cedric* sailed for New York on 30 March there were five western Bahá'í guests who accompanied 'Abdu'l-Bahá as well as Louise Mathew. They were Mr and Mrs Percy Woodcock from Canada and their daughter and Mr and Mrs Austin from Denver, Colorado. The other passengers were greatly surprised to see these westerners happily consorting with 'oriental' Persians and the whole group enjoying one another's company.

On the transatlantic passage which lasted ten days 'Abdu'l-Bahá spoke on spiritual subjects from time to time. He asked after the health of the people in His group and on the second day He sent a cable to Ramleh letting the Bahá'ís there know that He was in good health and enquiring after the well-being of His sister, Bahíyyih Khánum. On several occasions He invited the western believers to His cabin and at least once He spoke about the time in His childhood when He and the Holy Family accompanied Bahá'u'lláh on His exile from Tehran to Baghdad during freezing winter weather, saying, 'There was so much snow and it was so cold . . . that my feet were frostbitten. To this day my toes are affected by cold weather.'[6]

Another afternoon He invited the believers including the western ladies to take tea and sweets in the library and spoke about ships, trains and carriages, saying that 'They are . . . good for long and tedious journeys; but for recreation and holiday trips, horseback riding in the spring season in the country, which is full of flowers and green foliage and sparkling waters, is the best of all and gives a unique pleasure.' The conversation turned to airships and aeroplanes and He said: 'Those who have provided the means for transporting arms and ammunition and the instruments of wars and massacres on earth will do so in the air. There will come to exist such instruments as to cause all the means of destruction in the past to be looked upon as children's playthings.'[7]

The western Bahá'ís requested to 'Abdu'l-Bahá that the three Persians in the party should change to wearing western dress except for their hats and coats but 'Abdu'l-Bahá replied to the effect that this was not a matter of importance.

An American newspaper publisher was on board and on one occasion was amongst the passengers and Bahá'ís who gathered round 'Abdu'l-Bahá in the salon. The newspaper publisher enquired why 'Abdu'l-Bahá was travelling to America and was told: 'I am going to America at the invitation of peace congresses, as the fundamental principles of this Cause are universal peace, the oneness of the world of humanity and the equality of the rights of men.'[8] The passengers and crew showed ever greater respect for 'Abdu'l-Bahá and would doff their hats and bow when they passed Him. Some passengers brought their children to meet Him and He showed great affection for them saying that Bahá'u'lláh 'has taught us to love children and to be the lovers of the whole human race.'[9]

One day the Master felt unwell but after taking a little soup at dinner He felt better and particularly enjoyed the music which was always played after breakfast and dinner and sent a tip to the musicians in appreciation. He frequently suffered from tiredness but He nevertheless wrote Tablets to the Bahá'ís in Tehran and frequently revealed Tablets to others during the journey.

The ship's list or manifest of 'alien passengers' was duly completed and shows 'Abdu'l-Bahá as a 69-year-old Persian 'author' lastly resident in Ramleh, Egypt with the intention of 'Touring' in the United States. Similar information is given for the Persian gentlemen accompanying Him who are described variously as 'attendant' (Mírzá Asadu'lláh), 'doctor' (Dr Faríd) and 'scribe' (Maḥmúd-i-Zarqání). Louise Alice Maria Mathew is recorded as a 46-year-old single teacher of English nationality last resident in La Croix, France and she gives her mother's name and address in Beckenham as her nearest relative. She paid for her ticket herself, is in possession of at least $50 and is making her first trip to the United States. She is five feet two inches tall with dark brown hair and brown eyes and, most interestingly, she gives Louis Gregory's name and his address in Washington DC as the friend she is going to join.[10]

On the night of 10 April the *Cedric* reached New York and moored offshore for the night because there was sickness on board and the sick people needed to be quarantined. The *Cedric* sailed past the Statue of Liberty and 'Abdu'l-Bahá exclaimed, throwing wide His arms, 'There is the new world's symbol of liberty and freedom. After being forty years a prisoner I can tell you that freedom is not a matter of place. It is a condition. Unless one accept dire vicissitudes he will not attain. When he is released from the prison of self, that is indeed a release.'[11]

Newspaper reporters boarded the *Cedric* at the first opportunity and hurried to interview 'Abdu'l-Bahá Who made clear His views on western newspapers saying 'There are good and bad newspapers. Those which strive to speak only that which is truth, which hold the mirror up to truth, are like the sun . . . Those who play for their own little selfish ends give no true light to the world and perish of their own futility.'[12]

Finally the ship docked in New York harbour on 11 April where a crowd of American believers had gathered to greet Him. But 'Abdu'l-Bahá sent a message that they should disperse and would meet Him later at the home of Edward and Carrie Kinney. Disappointed, they left the quayside, allowing Him to disembark without fuss from the ship. Only a small group of women – Juliet Thompson and two of her friends – caught a glimpse of Him leaving the ship and getting into Mountford Mills' car.[13]

'Abdu'l-Bahá's arrival in the United States caused a stir anyway in the newspapers, many of which ran headlines referring to Him as a Prophet (a title which He always refuted, preferring it to be known that His Father Bahá'u'lláh was a Prophet, not He). Some greatly exaggerated the number of Bahá'ís in the world claiming 20,000,000 and that several hundred followers had met Him at the dockside.

It seems that Louise had stepped unnoticed from the ship that brought her to the United States. She arrived in New York with little more than a suitcase, unaware that for the rest of her life she would count herself an American citizen. She had left everything from her past 46 years behind in Europe. From time to time over the next nearly forty years she would visit her siblings, but she would never see her mother again. Although she could not know it, her life was about to change dramatically.

She had given Louis Gregory's name and address as her destination in America, so she was duty bound to leave 'Abdu'l-Bahá's party at this point and to make her way to Washington DC where she would be greeted by her friend Louis. Undoubtedly Louise would have had plenty to tell Louis about: being present at many of 'Abdu'l-Bahá's talks in London and Paris, being in the Master's company on board the *Cedric* and all about the ocean crossing to America, her first long sea voyage. But she probably also made time for some sight-seeing whilst on this her first visit to Washington. Louise loved to travel and here she was not only in what was to her a new country but on a new continent. Her first impressions are not recorded but America was so different from the European countries that she was used to that its architecture, vast landscape and modern, bustling cities must have been a source of great interest and curiosity to her. She will have glimpsed New York with its amazing skyscrapers briefly before travelling the journey of over 200 miles to Washington and will have had the opportunity to look at the countryside and towns that the train passed through, gaining a first impression of this new country.

Meanwhile 'Abdu'l-Bahá was greeting the Bahá'ís in New York, giving talks to packed assemblages and being interviewed by journalists. He gave His first talk in America in the home of Edward and Carrie Kinney, resident New Yorkers who had met 'Abdu'l-Bahá when they went on pilgrimage in 1907. He later gave Edward the name 'Saffa' which means purity or serenity in Arabic and He called Carrie 'Vaffa' denoting fidelity. Later He declared them 'Pillars of the Faith in the City of the Covenant' [New York] for their steadfastness in the Cause.

In New York 'Abdu'l-Bahá stayed in the Hotel Ansonia, at His own expense as always. Zarqání described the hotel in his diary: 'The Hotel Ansonia is one of the landmark buildings in New York and is 17 stories high. The Master's suite was on the seventh floor and had two bedrooms, a drawing room, a kitchen and a bathroom, all completely furnished.' He adds: 'The rent for the Master's apartment was £4 a day, exclusive of board and incidental expenses.'[14]

During His first visit to New York 'Abdu'l-Bahá met with many people including the president of the New York Peace Society, the Lebanese artist and poet Khalil Gibran and Bishop Birch of New York. He gave several talks in private homes which, even though somewhat informal, were attended by huge crowds of well-wishers and the curious. His first public talk was given on 14 April (the day of the *Titanic* disaster) at the Church of the Ascension where He was invited by the Rev. Percy Grant, a close friend of the Bahá'í artist Juliet Thompson, to speak at divine service before a congregation of 2,000 people. He entered the church from the vestry hand in hand with Percy Grant who led Him to sit in the Bishop's chair. After hymns from the choir and prayers, the minister respectfully described something of the history and teachings of the Faith and introduced 'Abdu'l-Bahá Who spoke about the Revelation of Bahá'u'lláh and the message of unity for the whole of mankind. It is recorded that the congregation was spellbound and the more so when 'Abdu'l-Bahá chanted a prayer in His powerful and resonant voice.

Later there was controversy and heated debate in the newspapers because 'Abdu'l-Bahá had sat in the Bishop's chair and addressed the congregation from the chancel, breaking the rule which forbids the unbaptised to sit behind the altar rail. Finally the Bishop himself went to visit 'Abdu'l-Bahá at the Hotel Ansonia in order to welcome Him to New York and the controversy died down.[15]

As usual 'Abdu'l-Bahá met people from all ranks of society. He visited the Bowery Mission where He spoke about poverty to around 400 destitute people. Zarqání described in his diary that 'His words were so penetrating that even those who were not poor became envious at 'Abdu'l-Bahá's description of the station of poverty'![16] After His talk 'Abdu'l-Bahá said He wished to serve the poor, so He stood at the exit and as the poor people passed by Him He gave them each some coins.

In contrast 'Abdu'l-Bahá also spoke at Earl Hall, Columbia University where He spoke to professors as well as students on the importance of education and knowledge. So many people wanted to meet 'Abdu'l-Bahá and the meetings took so long that the professors' plan to give 'Abdu'l-Bahá a tour of the university had to be abandoned.[17]

Zarqání comments in his diary that prejudice and hatred existed at that time between blacks and whites and 'it has been impossible for white people to invite black people to their homes'. 'Abdu'l-Bahá turned this convention on its head when a reception was held at the home of Carrie and Edward Kinney. He made sure that Bahá'ís and their friends, both black and white, were invited and sat down together without prejudice. The Master prepared and served the meal Himself and Zarqání recorded that He said that 'this gathering of blacks and whites is like the gathering of many colored flowers and that the variety of colors enhances the beauty of the garden and brings about the loveliness of each'.[18]

After nine days in New York, on 20 April 'Abdu'l-Bahá travelled by train from Grand Central Station, New York to Washington DC with the Persian members of His party and two westerners – John Bosch who had come from California to meet Him and Edward Getsinger, who had first met the Master in Akka in 1898. Joseph Hannen described the joy that greeted 'Abdu'l-Bahá's arrival in Washington in these words:

> The hearts of the friends in Washington were gladdened and their souls refreshed by the presence of Abdul-Baha from Saturday, April 20th, to Sunday, April 28th, inclusive. Words are inadequate to describe the joy imparted by this visit, nor can one yet realize all it has meant to us. Time will tell, as the seed germinates and develops into the plant, reproducing itself in turn until from each tiny lifegerm there shall come into existence a rose garden, which touching another, and that in turn still others, shall transform the world into the garden of Paradise!
>
> Days of waiting were rewarded when, at 1:33 p.m. on Saturday, April 20th, Abdul-Baha reached Washington on the Pennsylvania Railroad. In accordance with his expressed desire, there was no notice given of the hour of his arrival, and no delegation to meet him. The arrival was as simple as the Guest, and yet as memorable to those who were privileged to witness it, as the majestic simplicity of Abdul-Baha! The train was just on time. Among the usual crowd of travellers there was a quaint note lent by the party of Orientals, in the midst of whom, cool, collected and ever the Master of the situation, Abdul-Baha was seen.[19]

Agnes Parsons was a wealthy member of the upper echelons of Washington society. She went on a pilgrimage to the Holy Land in 1910 and became a Bahá'í there. At that time she asked 'Abdu'l-Bahá if He would stay with her in Washington if He ever came to America and He agreed that He would. On returning from her pilgrimage Mrs Parsons had had a house built especially for 'Abdu'l-Bahá so that He could stay there during His visit to Washington. Juliet Thompson described the beauty of this house in her diary:

> Mrs. Parsons [sic] house has real distinction. It is Georgian in style and in it is a very long white ballroom with, at one end, an unusually high mantel – the mantel, as well as the ceiling and paneled walls, delicately carved with garlands. At the windows hang thin silk curtains the color of jonquil leaves . . . In front of the mantel, a platform had been placed for the Master and every day it was banked with fresh roses, American Beauties.[20]

'Abdu'l-Bahá had made arrangements to rent a house for His stay in Washington but on learning that Agnes Parsons had prepared her house for Him and would be heart-broken if He did not stay with her He agreed to be her guest and his entourage stayed in the rented house instead.

With 'Abdu'l-Bahá's arrival in Washington both Louise and Louis could be with Him and accompany Him to many of His engagements. It is not recorded how often Louise was in His presence during His Washington visit, but we do know that Louis was instrumental in arranging at least two of the Master's talks in the city and that 'Abdu'l-Bahá was very aware of Louis and ensured that he was present on several occasions.

At this time Louis was a successful lawyer working in Washington. He had already started to make teaching trips on behalf of the Bahá'í Cause in 1910 when he travelled to eight cities in the southern states where he visited black colleges and schools to speak, and these teaching trips became a regular feature of his life. He had also been elected in 1911 to serve on the Washington Working Committee, an early committee for Bahá'í administration. So he was recognized by the Bahá'í community not only as a gifted speaker but also as an able administrator.

One person who would play an important part in Louise's life and with whom she would work and cooperate for many years met 'Abdu'l-Bahá in New York and followed Him to Washington. She was Martha Root, a journalist, working at that time for the *Pittsburgh Post* as its Society and Religious Editor. She had counted herself as a Bahá'í since September 1909, so 'Abdu'l-Bahá's visit to the United States in 1912 was a highly significant event in her life and she took every opportunity to hear Him speak and sought private interviews with Him on two occasions. In January 1915 Martha began the first of her world-wide teaching trips, spreading the message of Bahá'u'lláh to royalty, eminent politicians, professors and working people throughout the globe. It seems impossible that Louise would not have met Martha during 'Abdu'l-Bahá's sojourns in Washington and later in Chicago, although neither of them could possibly glimpse at this time that they would be close colleagues in teaching work in later life.

In Washington 'Abdu'l-Bahá embarked again on a rigorous programme of talks and visits. On the very day He arrived in Washington He spoke at the Orient-Occident Unity Conference at Washington Public Library. He spoke at the Universalist Church the following day and one evening He visited the Library of Congress. On 23 April He gave a talk at Howard University, an all-black university, to a mixed black and white audience of 1,000 people. As Louis had studied at Howard University's law school he had no doubt been influential in arranging this talk. 'Abdu'l-Bahá stressed the importance of racial harmony and the unity of humankind, saying 'There are no blacks and whites before God. All colors are one, and that is the color of servitude to God.'[21]

After the talk at Howard University 'Abdu'l-Bahá was invited to lunch with Ali-Kuli Khan and his wife Florence. Ali-Kuli Khan had served as a secretary to 'Abdu'l-Bahá and came to America in 1901 where he found employment at the Persian embassy in Washington as chargé d'affaires. His marriage to Florence, an American Bahá'í, was described by 'Abdu'l-Bahá as the first between the East and the West and a symbol of unity. At the lunch at the Khans' there were about 19 guests including many prominent early American Bahá'ís and leading members of Washington political and social life. Shortly before lunch was served 'Abdu'l-Bahá called for Louis to come and present himself at the Khans' for an interview. Louis arrived and there was time for discussion and for 'Abdu'l-Bahá to answer questions before lunch was announced. Following the social code prevalent in Washington social circles at the time Louis drew back and prepared to leave the building while the white guests proceeded to seat themselves for their luncheon. But suddenly 'Abdu'l-Bahá called out 'Where is Mr Gregory? Bring Mr Gregory!' Ali-Kuli Khan hastened to find Louis and bring him to the lunch table where 'Abdu'l-Bahá had rearranged the place settings and seated Louis at His side in the place of honour, saying that He was very pleased to have Mr Gregory there. He then spoke eloquently on the need for unity amongst the races of the world.[22]

In this dramatic way 'Abdu'l-Bahá demonstrated to those assembled round the lunch table that the custom of racial segregation was a thing of the past and that henceforth people of all races should mix together in harmony and friendship.

A few weeks later 'Abdu'l-Bahá spoke in no uncertain terms expressing His approval of marriage between the black and white races. The *Cleveland News* reported that He had said: 'Perfect results follow the marriage of black and white races. All men are progeny of one . . . They are of different colors, but the color is nothing.' And the *Cleveland Plain Dealer* ran the headline: 'Bahaist Approves Unions of Races: Persian Teacher Tells Cleveland Women Intermarriage Results Ideal.' That this idea was radical and apparently startling is evidenced by the prominence that the newspapers gave to it, with the *Cleveland Plain Dealer's* article running the length of its front page and continuing to its page three with several photographs. The paper reported:

> Abdul Baha, a venerable Persian now touring America as leader of the Bahaist movement for a universal religion, declared last night for an amalgamation of the white and negro races by intermarriage . . .
>
> 'All men,' said Abdul Baha, 'are progeny of one – Adam. They are of different color, but color is nothing. Men of all races are brothers. God is neither black nor white . . .
>
> 'Perfect results follow the marriage of black and white races. In my own family in Persia was a negro slave who was freed. She married a white man and her children married white men. These children are now in my household. The results of the union were beautiful. They were wonderful –perfect.'
>
> 'Humanity,' he said, 'will be bound together as one. The various religions shall be united and the various races shall be known as one kind.'[23]

After the luncheon at the Khans' they hosted a reception for 'Abdu'l-Bahá at which were, amongst others, the Turkish Ambassador, Admiral Robert Peary (who had recently returned from his discovery of the North Pole) and Alexander Graham Bell, the inventor of the telephone and hearing devices for the deaf.

As if this were not enough for a busy day, a further reception was held at Agnes Parsons' home later that day and in the evening 'Abdu'l-Bahá addressed a meeting at the Bethel Literary and Historical Society at the Metropolitan African Methodist Episcopal Church. Louis Gregory had been a leading member of the Bethel Literary and Historical Society for many years and had previously arranged several meetings on Bahá'í themes at the Society which had been founded as a forum for debating racial issues thirty years earlier.

Nine-year-old Rene Hopper and her widowed mother Marie had travelled to Washington accompanied by their black cook, Eurithra, in order to be there while 'Abdu'l-Bahá was there, and were staying at a friend's flat for the duration. Eurithra had had the opportunity to meet 'Abdu'l-Bahá briefly and had immediately recognized His station, proclaiming 'He is my Lord, He is my Lord!' They all three really wanted to serve 'Abdu'l-Bahá with their own hands and invited Him to take tea in their friend's flat. 'Abdu'l-Bahá graciously accepted their invitation but made it a condition that they should invite black friends as well. They were of course only visiting Washington and did not know many people there and the only black person they knew there was Louis Gregory so they invited him. As it happened all Eurithra's family were able to attend as well and Marie had the bounty of serving everyone there with her own hands on what turned out to be a most joyful occasion.[24]

On 25 April 'Abdu'l-Bahá spoke to the local Theosophists on various spiritual subjects and then gave a talk in the afternoon at a feast given by the Turkish Ambassador. The next day He gave three talks including one to a group of young women who were suffragists, in the imposing hall of the Daughters of the American Revolution. Many influential politicians and leaders of society had interviews with 'Abdu'l-Bahá while He was in Washington including President Theodore Roosevelt himself and the Secretary of the United States Treasury, Lee McClung. On 'Abdu'l-Bahá's last day of this visit to Washington, Agnes Parsons held a formal reception for dignitaries on behalf of the Orient-Occident Unity Society to which 300 people were invited and many were introduced to 'Abdu'l-Bahá, shaking Him by the hand.

The next day He left for Chicago in the late afternoon by train. Louise was again honoured to travel with Him and Louis, naturally, found time from his professional duties to travel to Chicago and be present at the historic events that would take place there.

6

THE SEED GROWS

Louise travelled with 'Abdu'l-Bahá on the train to Chicago along with several other friends including a stenographer, Mrs Moss, to whom He gave the Persian name Marzieh. She was one of several stenographers who had the honour of recording 'Abdu'l-Bahá's talks in shorthand and later transcribing them in typewritten format during His visit to America. As they journeyed, the train crossed the Potomac River and passed through green and fertile land which 'Abdu'l-Bahá admired enthusiastically. Then He sadly commented that the landscape reminded Him of Bahá'u'lláh's love for the countryside and His many years of imprisonment, saying, 'Whenever I see such scenes, I feel great sorrow, for the Blessed Beauty liked verdure and greenery very much. God shall never pardon those who imprisoned Him in that place.'[1]

It was on this train journey that Louise had one of her many conversations with 'Abdu'l-Bahá, as she recounted later in a letter to Agnes Parsons: 'Later 'Abdu'l-Bahá said before Dr Getsinger and Fareed [Dr Faríd] and others in the train to Chicago to me, "How are you and Mr Gregory getting along?" Startled I answered "What do you mean, we are good friends?" To which He replied emphatically and with His face[d] wreathed in mischievous smiles "You must be _very_ good friends."'[2]

Although earlier Louise was totally unaware of any plans that 'Abdu'l-Bahá might have had for her to marry Louis Gregory, she must surely around this time have started to have an inkling of His intentions for them. During her first days in America another encounter with 'Abdu'l-Bahá had turned out unexpectedly for her and would have lasting consequences. She wrote:

> In this country [America] 'Abdu'l-Bahá first revealed to me symbolically, through a white flower which He told me to give Mr Gregory

and by looking at me in a peculiar way conveyed His meaning to me, that He wished me to marry Mr Gregory. Curiously enough after this love began to grow in my heart and the desire for the marriage whereas before I only liked Mr Gregory as a friend.

Louise had come to America purely to accompany 'Abdu'l-Bahá, to be in His presence and to continue receiving guidance from Him. As she later wrote: 'My marriage as you know was entirely brought about by 'Abdu'l-Bahá. I had no thought of marriage when I came to this country . . .'[3] Her friend Louis also had no thoughts of marriage at this time, being thoroughly engrossed in his work and his Bahá'í service. However, the two of them were shortly to meet again in Chicago where important developments were to take place both for the future of the Cause in America and for their future together.

The journey to Chicago took a night and all the following day. 'Abdu'l-Bahá admired the cleanliness of the sleeping car and its electric lights but was unable to sleep because of the unaccustomed speed of the train. They finally arrived in Chicago only to find that the Bahá'ís there had been expecting 'Abdu'l-Bahá and His entourage to arrive that morning. The fourth Bahá'í Temple Unity Convention had been assembled in the Corinthian Hall of the Chicago Masonic Lodge in the morning awaiting 'Abdu'l-Bahá and had later anxiously waited at the train station expecting His imminent arrival on train after train. The *Chicago Daily News*'s evening edition reported: 'Bahaist Chief Missing: Abdul Baha, Head of Cult, Disappears on His Way to Convention in Chicago: Puzzles His Followers.'[4]

'Abdu'l-Bahá's train finally arrived in Chicago that night and 'When the friends saw the Master at the train station, they were filled with excitement, crying out "Alláh-u-Abhá" and "Yá 'Abdu'l-Bahá", their voices resounding throughout the station.'[5]

Mírzá Asadu'lláh – the same Persian gentleman who accompanied 'Abdu'l-Bahá on His journeys and sailed on the *Cedric* with Him – is reputed to have suggested the idea of Chicago Bahá'ís building a House of Worship when he wrote them a letter they received in 1903. In it he described the inauguration of the building of a Bahá'í Temple in Ashkhabad in Turkestan. The members of the governing body of the Bahá'í community in Chicago were thrilled with the suggestion and petitioned 'Abdu'l-Bahá for permission to build a similar Temple (or Mashriqu'l Adhkár – 'dawning place of the mention of God') in Chicago, saying:

> . . . we are enkindled with the fire of the love of God that burnt and melted all other thoughts and desires into one great desire:–
> That in these parts and regions there may arise a Mashrak-el-Azkar, built in the Name of the Glorious God, and that there may go forth from the shelter of its beauty, rays of brilliant light . . .
> . . . permit us to begin the blessed undertaking of the erection of the Mashrak-el-Azkar in Chicago. We pray for wisdom and strength; we pray for thy mighty assurance, knowing that thou art the helper, and in that help, God makes us strong.
> In joy and hope that thou wilt grant our supplication, the eleven members present raised among themselves, a starting fund of eleven hundred dollars.[6]

'Abdu'l-Bahá replied joyfully giving permission and encouraging the members of the Chicago 'House of Spirituality' in their enterprise: 'Exert your energy in accomplishing what ye have undertaken, so that this glorious Temple may be built, that the beloved of God may assemble therein, and that they may pray and offer glory to God for guiding them to His Kingdom.'[7]

The Chicago Bahá'ís began donating money to the Temple project and later invited Bahá'í communities around America and even around the world to donate. A key player in the early years of the Temple project was James B. Thornton Chase, honoured by 'Abdu'l-Bahá as the 'first American believer'. Thornton Chase was not only active in Bahá'í administration and a rallying point for the early believers (given the name Thábit or Steadfast by 'Abdu'l-Bahá) but he was also a prolific writer and encouraged the publication of Bahá'í literature. Having become a Bahá'í in 1894, he was subsequently elected to the governing board of the Bahá'ís of Chicago which in 1902 became known as the 'House of Spirituality'. Surprisingly only men were allowed to serve on this body but the Bahá'í women of Chicago, just as active as the men, formed their own 'Women's Assembly of Teaching'. Later 'Abdu'l-Bahá wrote to the American Bahá'ís and instructed them that women should be on the Bahá'í Temple Unity, as the committee for the whole of America was named. Three women were elected to the committee's executive.

In fact women played an equal part with men in the Temple project and were even in the vanguard in the search for a suitable location and in fundraising. Foremost amongst the members of the Women's Assembly of Teaching and its first president was Corinne True who came to be known as 'the Mother of the Temple'. Despite appalling personal tragedies – she was to experience the death of her husband and five of her children – she remained a fervent supporter of the Temple and spearheaded its development. In February 1907 she went on pilgrimage to Akka bearing a petition signed by nearly 800 American Bahá'ís asking for 'Abdu'l-Bahá's blessing on the project. He expressed delight with the progress already made towards building the Temple and advised it should be built away from the commercial district of Chicago in a beautiful spot near Lake Michigan. 'Abdu'l-Bahá provided her with a ground plan for the Temple and told her that she would suffer and be misunderstood in her pursuance of completing the project but she must pray for the necessary strength.

Soon after this Thornton Chase also visited 'Abdu'l-Bahá in Akka and was astonished when 'Abdu'l-Bahá told him, 'When you return consult with Mrs True – I have given her complete instructions.' Mr Chase and the two men with him were amazed at this responsibility given to a woman at a time when women could not even vote in public elections.[8]

When Corinne returned to Chicago she began searching the area for a suitable site for the Temple. She eventually found a heavily wooded area at Grosse Pointe, a promontory overlooking the lake, in summer 1907. A Temple Fund was formed with Corinne as its secretary and shortly afterwards a national meeting of American Bahá'ís was held in Chicago and the site was visited and approved. In March 1908 the House of Spirituality bought a small parcel of land at Grosse Pointe followed by two more small lots. These purchases met with 'Abdu'l-Bahá's approval.

Esther Tobin, known as Nettie, was a member of the Women's Assembly of Teaching. She was an ardent supporter of the Temple project but was a woman of very slender means, a widow who worked as a seamstress in order to support her family. She failed to see how she could contribute substantially to the enterprise. But later in 1908 Mírzá Asadu'lláh wrote again to the Chicago Bahá'ís encouraging them in the project and his words appeared to imply that a 'first stone' was necessary to energize the building of the Mashriqu'l-Adhkár: 'the glory and honour of the first stone is equivalent to all the stones and implements which will later be used there.[9]

This must have inspired Nettie because after praying that she might find something to contribute she visited a construction site near her home and with the permission of the foreman she claimed a damaged stone. Then with the help of a neighbour she wrapped it in a piece of carpet, tied clothes line around it and dragged it home. She must have presented an extraordinary picture, a woman tugging an incongruous bundle through the streets with great difficulty and effort but her satisfaction would have been enormous when she succeeded in bringing it home. However, the next problem was how to transport it all the way to the Temple site at Wilmette because she lived some way from it. For the journey Nettie, her brother and a Persian Bahá'í named Mírzá Mazlúm were able to manhandle the stone onto two horse trams but at the tram station they found themselves still a long distance from the Temple site. They attempted to carry the stone some of the way but it proved too heavy. Then Mírzá Mazlúm effortlessly carried it on his back for a short distance and staggered to a disused farmhouse where they left the stone overnight.

The next morning Nettie appeared with a small handcart that she had made overnight. A passerby helped her by repairing the handcart and loading the stone onto it after she had hurt her wrist and broken a handle of the handcart trying to load it. She set off again and eventually a newsboy helped her on the final leg of the journey to the western corner of the Temple site where the handcart fell to bits. But the stone had arrived and was destined to stay.

In 1909 the recently formed Bahá'í Temple Unity bought 12 more lots of land. By this time many donations were coming in from Bahá'ís all over the world and on the day after 'Abdu'l-Bahá's arrival in Chicago it was announced that the executive had bought 292 feet of land fronting the lake and giving an unobstructed view of it.

The arrival of 'Abdu'l-Bahá in Chicago in 1912 signalled the occasion for the ground breaking ceremony of the House of Worship. It was to take place shortly after the fourth Bahá'í Temple Unity Convention. 'Abdu'l-Bahá stayed at the Plaza Hotel in Chicago where as usual He was interviewed by reporters. He then travelled to Corinne True's home where her son Davis lay very ill from tuberculosis. 'Abdu'l-Bahá spent some time with Davis and then told Corinne that her son was a wonderful young man and that He had found him much better than expected. Naturally Corinne was overjoyed to hear this, believing that Davis would recover. 'Abdu'l-Bahá and Corinne were very busy all the rest of that day so it was only later in the day that she learnt that Davis had passed away. She then came to understand that 'Abdu'l-Bahá had been referring to Davis's spiritual state and not his physical health.

Corinne was with 'Abdu'l-Bahá that afternoon when He spoke at Hull House, a civic centre founded to give poor immigrants social and civic education. He spoke on the importance of the unity of all races and then went on to speak on the same subject at the annual convention of the National Association for the Advancement of Colored People. In the evening He greeted the closing public session of the Bahá'í Temple Unity Convention where more than a thousand people had gathered. When He was announced 'the vast concourse, as one person, arose, and in a breathless silence the one awaited by many there for years, entered and proceeded to the platform'. After He had addressed the assemblage the 'Temple Song' was sung by all present. 'Abdu'l-Bahá donated 2,000 francs to the Temple Fund before He left for His hotel.[10]

The next day, 1 May, was the day of the ground breaking ceremony. A large marquee had been put up at the Temple site and nearly 400 Bahá'ís had travelled to Wilmette where they gathered at the corner of Linden Avenue and Sheridan Road. Although 'Abdu'l-Bahá was expected at 11 o'clock it was nearly one o'clock before He arrived in a taxi. Amazingly, Corinne True had made her way to the Temple site even though her son had passed away the previous day. Naturally devastated at Davis's passing, she still did not want to miss the historic event. 'Abdu'l-Bahá invited Corinne to sit with Him in His taxi and it can be supposed that He comforted her on the loss of her son.

When 'Abdu'l-Bahá proceeded to the marquee a crowd of children excitedly accompanied Him. Nearly 300 people sat in three concentric circles in the tent with 'a broad open space in the center across which the friends could read the love in each other's eyes' and 'Abdu'l-Bahá stood in the centre and addressed them.[11] He spoke on the power of the Cause to unite the peoples of the East and the West through the Word of God and about the Temples in Ashkhabad and Chicago.[12] When He left the marquee He asked where the centre of the Temple land would be and was shown an approximate spot. Several people, including 'Abdu'l-Bahá Himself, had donated foundation stones but none of them had arrived in time, so He called for Nettie Tobin's stone to be brought and the honour was given to her stone to be used as the foundation stone.

A Bahá'í from New York had brought a golden trowel in a leather case to be used for the ground breaking and handed this to 'Abdu'l-Bahá but it proved not to be strong enough to break the turf, so someone ran to a nearby house and borrowed an axe which 'Abdu'l-Bahá swung and cut through the turf in several strokes. Two Bahá'í songs celebrating the occasion were then sung. Another man borrowed a shovel for completing the ground breaking and at this point Corinne asked 'Abdu'l-Bahá if women could be permitted to take part in the ceremony. He then invited Lua Getsinger to turn the earth with the shovel. She was reluctant to do so out of modesty but was finally persuaded to participate. Next Corinne followed suit and after her representatives of many races, both women and men, turned the earth. Dr Faríd announced the name and provenance of each person who in turn took hold of the shovel: 'Persia, Syria, Egypt, India, Japan, South Africa, England, France, Germany, Holland, Norway, Sweden, Denmark, the Jews of the world, the North American Indians were among the races and countries thus successively represented . . .' Louise is listed as delegate from London, England at the ceremony, so it is certain that she was present and presumably she took her turn with the shovel.[13]

Her friend Louis had travelled to Chicago a few days before 'Abdu'l-Bahá and His party and had attended the annual convention of Bahá'í Temple Unity as a delegate from Washington DC. He spoke on 27 April at the 'Feast of Rizwan' and also at a large public meeting on 28 April on the subject of 'The Reality of Humanity'. Louis is listed as a delegate from Washington present at the ground breaking ceremony so without doubt he would have taken part in the same way.

'Abdu'l-Bahá 'consigned the stone to its excavation, on behalf of *all* the people of the world'[14] and used the golden trowel to push earth back around the stone. Finally He said: 'The Temple is already built.'[15]

The building of the Chicago Temple became an ongoing saga fraught with difficulties and enormous tests including a fire in 1931 but the Bahá'ís persevered and eventually the Temple was completed and dedicated in 1953.

After the Temple ceremony 'Abdu'l-Bahá stayed four more days in

Chicago giving talks in churches and clubs and meeting the people of Chicago, reporters and local Bahá'ís. Following His visit to Chicago 'Abdu'l-Bahá was to travel to Cleveland. By this time Louise was naturally becoming anxious about 'Abdu'l-Bahá's intentions regarding herself and Louis. Had she correctly understood 'Abdu'l-Bahá's hints and veiled words concerning her and her friend? If so, was she expected to approach Louis herself with a proposal? If she had misunderstood 'Abdu'l-Bahá's plans for her this would be embarrassing in the extreme. So, as she later wrote to her friend Agnes Parsons:

> Before He left Chicago I asked Abdul Baha plainly one morning early if I had understood aright that He wished Mr Gregory and myself to marry. He said 'yes.' He did wish it. 'I wish the white and the colored people to marry' He added.
>
> Then on my intimating that as a woman I could do nothing to bring it about He asked 'Do you love him, would you marry him if he asked you?' and I replied 'yes'. Then He said 'if he loves you he will ask you'. Later in the morning as I learnt some time afterwards, He told Louis it would give Him much pleasure if he and I would marry, which came as an utter surprise to Louis who had no thoughts of marriage. Abdul Baha said 'What is the matter? Don't you love her?' 'Yes as a friend' Louis said. 'Well think on it' said Abdul Baha 'and let me know; . . . marriage is not an ordinance and need not be obeyed, but it would give me much pleasure if you and Miss Mathew were to marry.'[16]

With these decisive words their future together was sealed. 'Abdu'l-Bahá had made it plain to both Louise and Louis that He wished them to marry and as they both were always obedient to 'Abdu'l-Bahá there was no question for either of them of doing otherwise. Louise later wrote that 'Our marriage [was] made by 'Abdu'l Bahá at Chicago.'[17]

One can assume that the couple spoke together – possibly with some surprise and awkwardness at first – and subsequently with growing love and fondness, and agreed that they would be happy to acquiesce to 'Abdu'l-Bahá's desire for them to marry. They would have considered themselves engaged from that time although no formal announcement of their engagement appears to have been made until later that summer. Louis was bound to return to Washington to resume his work at the

US Treasury Department, having taken a few days out for his trip to Chicago, and he was also devotedly undertaking his teaching trips to the southern states which he had started in 1910. It is not recorded how Louise spent her time once she was engaged to marry Louis, but naturally the couple would have wanted to meet frequently.

However, it is certain that Louise spent some time that summer at Storer College in Harpers Ferry, West Virginia because Louis wrote to her there in July 1912. Storer College had begun in 1865 as a primary school for freed slaves who had no education or training and therefore no way of making a living or improving their circumstances. It was established by the Freewill Baptist Home Mission Society of New England and run by the Reverend Nathan Cook Brackett. This school, which started by providing a very basic education, later became a fully fledged college through the good offices of John Storer, a New England philanthropist. He became aware of the school in 1867 and offered a US$10,000 grant if the school became open to all races and religions and to women as well as men. He stipulated that the school must eventually become a college that granted degrees and that the Freewill Baptist Church must raise a further $10,000 within a year. This was achieved and the school became the Storer Normal School and was later known as Storer College, specializing in training teachers.

Louise, now engaged to be married to Louis, a black American, had nowhere to go now that she was no longer travelling with 'Abdu'l-Bahá. Having only arrived in America that spring she had no friends there apart from Louis. Although she had learnt about the Bahá'í Movement from American Bahá'ís they were largely resident very far away in Paris and although she would later go on to make firm and trusted friends amongst the American Bahá'ís these were early days and she had still to put down any roots in the American community. Her fiancé Louis worked for his living in Washington and she could hardly stay in Washington waiting for him to finish his work every day. Also the couple were keen not to draw attention to their forthcoming marriage which might have been considered not only unusual but sensational in some circles. The choice of Storer College as a place for Louise to stay before their marriage was ideal. It was easily reached by train from Washington and Louis would be able to visit her there most weekends. As the college was attended by all races Louise's presence there would have been unremarkable and it is likely that she spent her time there assisting with the teaching of summer courses.

In his letter to his fiancée Louis begins by reporting on his weekend teaching trip to Remington and Manassas, Virginia where he was able to address the students at a summer school preparing teachers for their state examinations and spoke to them on the Cause of Bahá'u'lláh. He answered their questions and eventually talked privately for an hour with the principal and his right hand man on the Bahá'í teachings. However, it is clear that he missed meeting with Louise over the weekend as he wrote, 'Of course it was a sacrifice not to be permitted to see my beloved Louise this week end. But as you unite with me in this sacrifice of our personal desires you shall also share, God willing, its precious fruits. May God cement our souls together and make us richer by the Divine outpouring of His Spirit and Love.'

He anticipates their next visit together saying, 'Have written to Chicago for some copies of the Hidden Words and hope they will arrive in time for our next visit.' Louise had clearly been in touch by letter with Neville Meakin, now dying of consumption in England, and had had a request for Louis which he was endeavouring to fulfil: 'Shall also hope to find time to make [a] copy of Enoch's Vision for Mr. Meakin. I am sure it will be a means of help to him in his present condition. It is very beautiful for you to mention it.'

Plans for their wedding were obviously very much on Louise's mind and she had communicated her anxieties to Louis so that he replied: 'I am sure that the details of our marriage will all work out naturally and logically at the proper time under the Benediction of our Beloved Abdul Baha', and he closes the letter 'With greeting and loyal love, Louis'.[18]

In August 'Abdu'l-Bahá spent three weeks in Dublin, New Hampshire, a picturesque village in New England that was an artists' colony and where various wealthy people including Agnes Parsons had summer homes. While members of His retinue stayed at the Parsons' house, He stayed at the Inn. During His time there He gave only one formal talk but met constantly with local residents and visitors, many of whom had come to Dublin for the purpose of meeting Him. On 4 August He spoke to a group of 28 black people on the importance of unity and friendship between the races and announced that Miss Mathew, a white woman, and Mr Gregory, a black man, both of them Bahá'ís, were shortly to be married.[19] As Zarqání reported: 'The white people in the audience were astonished to see the influence of the Cause and the blacks were pleased. Incidents like these are little less than miracles; in fact "splitting the moon in half" would be an easier accomplishment in the eyes of the Americans. This meeting was full of joy.'[20]

Louise received a Tablet from 'Abdu'l-Bahá in August 1912 in which He encouraged her. The Tablet, written from Dublin, New Hampshire, was translated by Ahmad Sohrab and refers to Louise's letter to Ahmad Sohrab:

> O thou respectful one! The letter that thou hast written to Mirza Ahmad Sohrab was read. It became the cause of happiness, for it contained the news of the union which will be realized in the month of September . . . The union that thou desirest to organise is blessed. God willing, I hope thou mayest become assisted and that union may become the assembly of the heavenly birds and the cause of the guidance of the souls. Upon thee be Baha El Abha![21]

From these words the engaged couple became assured that their marriage had 'Abdu'l-Bahá's blessing and that although they would need the assistance of the Concourse on High they would be showing the believers the way for the future. They realized their marriage was intended to be an example of interracial marriage. From the first days after they had met in Egypt they had heard 'Abdu'l-Bahá extol the virtues of different races marrying and, although they had no idea at that time that His words could possibly apply to them, with time and with very sure guidance in no uncertain terms from 'Abdu'l-Bahá they came to realize what was required of them and were happy to accede to His wishes, having found that they did after all love each other. As Louise had written, 'Curiously enough after this love began to grow in my heart and the desire for the marriage whereas before I only liked Mr Gregory as a friend.'[22]

Racism was rife throughout the world in the early twentieth century and was very much alive in the United States. In fact there were 'modern' scientific theories that supported the idea that intermarriage or 'miscegenation' was harmful and that different races should not marry. Marriage between the black and white races was anathema to many people to the extent that such marriages were against the law or not recognized in many states.[23] This was to have severe repercussions on the marriage of Louis and Louise, drastically affecting their life together. In most of the states where Louis travelled to teach the Faith their union was considered illegal and they faced arrest or worse if they travelled there together, with the result that it was impossible for Louise to accompany her husband on his travels. Unfortunately the Washington Bahá'í community was also deeply troubled by racial prejudices at this time and these attitudes would add to the difficulties that the couple experienced.

However, plans for their marriage went ahead. 'Abdu'l-Bahá wrote to Louis before the wedding urging him to ensure that the wedding did not incur unpleasant publicity. Certainly neither the bridegroom nor the bride wished for undue attention to be paid to their marriage. Louis wrote to Pauline Hannen:

> Some weeks ago, Abdul Baha, who has watched over Louise and me with the tender solicitude of a loving father, sent me a Message directing me to use the utmost judgment in order to avoid criticism in regard to our approaching Marriage. With me 'the utmost judgment' was prayer for Divine Guidance, in which Louise heartily joined me. Our prayers have been heard and answered and we are very happy. Every matter connected with the event went off without friction, although some things were quite difficult.[24]

Baha'i marriage ceremonies were not legal in those days but they were able to find a church minister who was happy to carry out the ceremony. He was the Reverend Everard W. Daniel, a minister of the Episcopal or Anglican Church who performed the ceremony in his parsonage. 'Abdu'l-Bahá had expressed the wish that they should marry in New York, denoted by Him as the City of the Covenant. Accordingly they were married in New York on 27 September 1912. 'Abdu'l-Bahá Himself was not present at the wedding because on 27 September He was in Glenwood Springs, Colorado en route for California. Photographs of the couple at the time of their wedding show them smartly dressed with Louise wearing a fashionable large-brimmed hat, high-necked lacy blouse with a light-coloured silky coat, fur wrap and gloves while Louis wears a dark jacket and pin-striped trousers.

Louis described the wedding ceremony:

> On last Friday at noon, at the residence of Rev. Everard W. Daniel, just nine persons were present, including the minister and his wife, the bride and groom. After the ceremony of the Church of England was completed, the groom said, 'Verily we are content with the Will of God.' And the bride responded, 'Verily we are satisfied with the Desire of God' [these were the Baha'i marriage vows at the time]. Then Mr. MacNutt read the Tablet of Abdul Baha on marriage. Mr. Braithwaite followed, reading a Tablet revealed to the groom three years ago of which the following is an extract: 'I hope that thou mayest become the herald of the Kingdom, become the means by which the white and colored people shall close their eyes to racial differences, and behold the reality of humanity.' Mrs. Botay closed with the Tablet of Baha'o'llah, *Protection*. Then the wedding party repaired to the wedding breakfast. In this small company were represented Christian and Jew, Bahais and non-Bahais, the white and colored races, England and America, and the three Bahai assemblies of New York, Philadelphia and Washington.
>
> During the ceremony there was a light rainfall. This, Mrs. Nourse says, was a Bahai sign, the Bounty of God. After the ceremony the skies cleared, the sun shone and everything and everybody seemed to be happy.[25]

Strangely enough, the *Chicago Defender* newspaper carried the following announcement on 28 September, the day after their marriage:

> Announcement is made of the engagement of Mr. Louis G. Gregory of the Treasury Department, and Miss Louise Mathew, of Kent, England. Mr. Gregory is an ardent believer in the faith of Abdul Hamid [*sic*], leader of the Bahai cult, and so is Miss Mathew. They met abroad some months ago en route to Persia [*sic*], where they were making a closer study of the history of the Bahai religion, and the acquaintance and sympathetic interest quickly ripened into love. The marriage takes place this month. Mr. and Mrs. Gregory will make their home in Washington, after a brief tour of the east.[26]

Possibly the editor of the *Chicago Defender* was doubtful whether the interracial marriage would actually take place and held back the announcement until news of the wedding was received.

The newly-weds proceeded to Atlantic City the same day for their honeymoon. Louis declared: 'We find ourselves very harmonious and very happy.'²⁷

On the surface, it was a most improbable marriage. Not only were they of different races, one black the other white, but they were also of different nationality and cultures and from differing social backgrounds. She was from an affluent upper middle class family, accustomed to comfort, servants and education while he, though well educated, was the son and grandson of former slaves. In addition, she was eight years older than her fiancé and at 46 was entering middle age whereas Louis was still in his 30s.

However, what they had in common was their deep abiding allegiance to the Bahá'í Cause and their devotion to 'Abdu'l-Bahá. Because of this they were content for their marriage to serve as an example of interracial marriage. They were both prepared to devote their lives to service of the Faith and this was to be their uniting strength and, despite their manifold difficulties throughout the years, theirs was to be an enduring, loving marriage of true soul-mates.

7

'A FORTRESS FOR WELL-BEING'[1]

What did 'Abdu'l-Bahá see in Louise (that others failed to see)? Why was she the one intended for an interracial marriage with Louis Gregory and not someone else? We cannot presume to look inside 'Abdu'l-Bahá's mind at that time or claim to understand His intentions but we know that He spoke many times about the necessity for the races to unite in harmony and for 'the black and white races' to marry.

The woman 'Abdu'l-Bahá first knew as Louise Mathew had certain characteristics that marked her out as especially suitable for such a difficult enterprise as an interracial marriage in the early 20th century. Before she ever became a Bahá'í Louise had shown that she was a caring person, as can be seen from her involvement in philanthropic projects for the poor and particularly for the education of poor children. Although she was from an affluent family herself, she was not one to ignore the impoverished state of a large sector of the Victorian population, but instead to try her hardest to help them. When she arrived in Egypt in 1911 to visit 'Abdu'l-Bahá Louise was an unmarried woman in early middle age and her letters to 'Abdu'l-Bahá had shown her to be sensitive to the plight of the disadvantaged. In the baldest terms it could be said that she was a caring woman needing someone to love.

But she was also persevering and not afraid to stand out from the crowd. In her life before she met the Bahá'í Movement she had, it appears, taken on herself the necessity of becoming educated (probably encouraged by her mother). An intelligent young woman, she had pursued a course of academic studies unusual in a woman in that day and age. Her attendance at Royal Holloway College and later at Edinburgh University, together with having completed her teacher training, show remarkable perseverance in the face of contemporary society's denigration of the importance of education for women. Perseverance and steadfastness were attributes that she would need in abundance during her married life and the years of her youth show evidence that she had these qualities in unusual measure.

In addition she possessed an ability to cope with difficulties – her health, for example, was often frail – and this ability to cope would be a talent she would need to call upon and develop in the years to come. She was a woman who was not set in her ways but was extremely adaptable. She had shown that she was able to uproot herself from a comfortable upper middle class background and go off to college and university and even to settle in foreign countries such as Luxembourg and France, relishing the differences in culture she found there. This ability to adapt would stand her in good stead in her married life in a new country. Add to these qualities her sense of adventure and pluckiness which enabled her to embark alone on her pilgrimage to Egypt and the Holy Land and one can see that this 'quiet little mouse' had the courage that would be necessary for the future that 'Abdu'l-Bahá envisaged for her.

Most important of all, she had a deep love and understanding of the Bahá'í teachings and moreover a 'personal connection' with 'Abdu'l-Bahá Whom she saw as a loving father. In her marriage she was able to unite with Louis in her devotion to the Bahá'í teachings and consecrate herself to creating with him a living example of a mixed race Bahá'í marriage.

After their honeymoon in Atlantic City the couple set up home in Washington DC where Louis had established himself as a lawyer. Louise was not unused to putting down roots in a strange land and creating a new life for herself there but nevertheless she must at first have experienced a certain culture shock in finding herself now living in a different country – a different continent even – where the way of life and many customs were different from what she was used to at home. She knew the cities of London, Paris and Edinburgh and must have enjoyed getting to know the bustling city of Washington DC. The newly married couple lived in the Cardozo-Shaw district of the city, near to the U Street Corridor which was famous as the home of America's largest urban African American community. In her leisure time she would have been able to take the metro or subway downtown and to familiarize herself with landmarks such as Capitol Hill, the White House and the National Mall.

Interestingly, in one of her first letters to Pauline Hannen only a few weeks after her marriage she herself drew attention to the different culture in which she was now living and wrote: 'You know I am not at all a public person though you seem very anxious to make me one. Please remember that if my marriage has made me legally American, I am still English by nature and not accustomed to publicity as you Americans are.'² In this case she was referring to a request to speak at Bahá'í meetings, something that at this stage in her life she was reluctant to do. However, in later years she overcame this reluctance so that she would give public talks, and sometimes even gave them in German.

There must have been many surprising aspects to Louise's new life in America that she would take some time to become accustomed to. The informality of the American way of life would have contrasted sharply with the more formal customs of Britain and France that she had grown up with.

Louise probably had a different way of looking at things from the local Bahá'ís and this is evidenced from a letter written to Agnes Parsons in the early Washington years: 'My husband and I are very truly one in all essential things . . . The only reason I did not commit him before writing to you was that he has been so afraid of me doing anything to make certain of the friends think I was putting myself forward too much as a newcomer as he knows some of them dislike this.'³

From her letters it sounds very much as if she was being pulled in two directions at once in these early days of her marriage – on the one hand being asked to speak in public almost as a celebrity, and on the other hand being aware that some of the friends disliked a newcomer 'putting herself forward'. The difficulties that 'Abdu'l-Bahá had foretold were, it seems, not long in making themselves evident.

Prejudice against white people and African Americans living together or even being together in the same building were sadly prevalent throughout America in those days. Even in Chicago, a northern city, such prejudice was rife. Mírzá Maḥmúd-i-Zarqání tells a story illustrating this in his diary of 'Abdu'l-Bahá's travels in America:

> There exists among the whites in America a marked animosity for the blacks, who are held in such low esteem that the whites do not allow them to attend their public functions and think it beneath their dignity to mix with them in some of the public buildings and hotels. One day, Dr Zia Bagdadi invited Mr [Louis] Gregory, a

black Bahá'í, to his home. When his landlord heard about this, he gave notice to Dr Bagdadi to vacate his residence because he had had a black man in his home.⁴

In the face of such prejudice it is small wonder that Louise and Louis found it difficult to have a home where they could live together.

Where the newly married couple was to live became a burning question and one which was to become an ongoing problem for them. There were not many parts of Washington where an interracial couple would be accepted. After beginning their married life at 1338 V Street North West, eighteen months after their marriage the couple were still not settled in suitable accommodation and Louise wrote in March 1914 still from 1338 V. St NW that they expected to move house that summer.⁵ A month later she wrote that they were looking for a house to buy.⁶ This purchase of a house of their own was eventually successfully completed and they enjoyed a brief period of living in their own home.

The Gregorys moved home many times in the course of their marriage and it is impossible to keep track of whether they were living in a house they owned or whether they were renting accommodation at any given time. Likewise, it is not clear when they sold the various houses that they did own because from time to time they would let a house they owned and receive rent from it until they eventually sold it and moved on.

The prevailing spirit of racial prejudice in Washington as a city was, unfortunately, mirrored in the Bahá'í community there. The Bahá'ís, all relatively new believers, were on the whole unable to accord their new Bahá'í beliefs in the unity of mankind with the deep-seated racial prejudice that they had grown up with and that they experienced day by day. The most troubling aspect of this manifested itself in finding a suitable venue where all the Bahá'ís, of whatever race, could meet together. Many of the white Bahá'ís were wealthy and owned large houses which, up to a point, they were happy to throw open to the holding of Bahá'í meetings. But several problems arose from this: the black Bahá'ís were not used to socializing with white people and felt uncomfortable about entering the large houses of wealthy Bahá'ís; in addition, it was felt that white people who were looking into the teachings of the Bahá'í Movement would feel awkward with sharing a room with black people and therefore would not attend. This appalling situation was not made any

79

better by the proposal that the Bahá'í community should rent a room or building for its meetings instead of using a private home because most hotels or public buildings would not accept mixed race meetings and, if they did, the black people might be subjected to the humiliation of having to enter and leave the building by a back door.[7]

Tragically the Bahá'í community in Washington began to split into several separate factions. These included those white Bahá'ís who clung to their earlier beliefs in racial segregation; a group of believers, both white and black who endeavoured to put into practice 'Abdu'l-Bahá's teachings on racial harmony; and a group of confused white Bahá'ís who simply did not know which way to turn under the pressure of the problem. 'Abdu'l-Bahá had given the Bahá'ís clear instructions on the issue of racial integration through His practical demonstrations of racial harmony, on several occasions inviting black people to join with the white people at social and religious events and frequently speaking unambiguously on the importance of the races being in unity, but it would take some time for their deeply held prejudices to be conquered.

'Abdu'l-Bahá had spoken on the beauty of racially integrated meetings when He gave a talk at the home of Pauline and Joseph Hannen, saying:

> This is a beautiful assembly. I am very happy that the whites and colored are together. This is the cause of my happiness, for you all are the servants of one God and therefore brothers, sisters, mothers and fathers. In the sight of God there is no distinction between white and colored; all are as one. Any one whose heart is pure is dear to God whether white or colored, red or yellow . . .[8]

The Gregorys, as that unusual example, for that time, of a mixed race couple were naturally thrown into the middle of this dilemma. The Washington Bahá'í community had welcomed the newly weds as can be seen from the letter signed by both Louis and Louise that they wrote to the community a month after their wedding, thanking the friends for their good wishes:

> To our Beloved Friends in El Abha: We humbly beg to thank you, each and all, for your token of love and well wishes, bestowed upon us so abundantly at the last meeting. We hope by striving to be more

worthy of your confidence and favor. Among the treasures of God are love and loyalty. Steadfastness in these is a sign and promise of immortality. May we all attain![9]

As a foreigner newly arrived in America, Louise must have particularly struggled to understand the many strands of difficulties and tensions in the racial problem. In December 1914 she wrote to Agnes Parsons about the intricacies of the difficult situation. She refers to the 'unfortunate state of affairs that is bringing the Cause into disrepute in the outside world as well as troubling the minds of believers, colored and otherwise'. A well-meaning white Bahá'í, Mrs De Lagnel, had invited both races to her home but 'many who were believers or on the brink of becoming so will have nothing to do with us'. It so happened that Laura Dreyfus-Barney, whom Louise knew of course from her days in Paris, was visiting Washington at the time:

> We therefore with great difficulty for she was on the point of leaving, got Mme Dreyfus to come and see us and talk over the matter. When we had explained the whole matter to her she agreed with us that no public meetings could safely be held for white people only besides being contrary to the teachings, but that meetings for prejudiced white people might be held at an apartment house and at people's private homes for that purpose. Mrs De Lagnel was so insistent that the Friday meetings could be held at her house and the Bahá'ís had not the money for a Hall and so the matter dropped . . . but in reality everyone felt the necessity of a public meeting place and I feel if we had had faith enough we could have obtained it and all this trouble would have been avoided as it would certainly have been open to <u>all</u> races. I do not say any of this from any personal motive, nor do I wish to criticise Mrs De Lagnel who has made great sacrifices and is liked by all i.e. the few colored people who go to her house and is exceedingly kind to them.[10]

Louise sympathized with the African American Bahá'ís and felt deeply their humiliation because of unjust treatment even meted out to them on occasion by the Bahá'í community. In 1916 she wrote about a recent Bahá'í meeting: 'The colored people have a real source of grievance because they were not really <u>represented</u> in that meeting for consultation

... That the "colored Baha'is" are "not expected to attend" was the part of that explanation that wounded most I think . . .'[11]

Louise and Louis found themselves in the extraordinarily difficult position of peacemakers to the troubled community, as Louise was aware:

> In regard to these disputed questions both my husband and myself have endeavoured to act the difficult part of peacemaker, explaining the difficulties of the white people to the colored and the point of view of the colored people to the white. What is needed is a better understanding of each other of a realization that in the Baha'i Cause there is <u>no color line</u> for Baha'o'llah [sic] has forbidden all distinctions and [there is needed] more consultation in the spirit of love.

She was treading a difficult path in danger of upsetting established practices and was probably aware that her sentiments may not at this point have been entirely endorsed by Mrs Parsons because she closes her letter: 'Please forgive me if I have taken up too much of your time and take this letter as I have written it, in an absolutely impersonal manner.'[12]

In addition to their efforts to bring all sectors of the Washington Bahá'í community together and to settle the problem of where Bahá'í meetings should be held, the Gregorys did not neglect donating to philanthropic ventures such as the Orient–Occident Unity. This charitable organization sponsored scholarships for poor children in Bahá'í schools in Iran. In 1914 the Gregorys received a Tablet from 'Abdu'l-Bahá in which firstly He stressed their role in trying to bring the races together: 'O ye two believing souls! Continually do I remember you. I beg of God that through you, good fellowship may be obtained between the white and colored races, for you are the introduction to this accomplishment . . .' He then praised them for their donations to charity: 'I am most pleased with your philanthropic activities, especially your contribution toward the final payment of the debt of the Orient–Occident Unity.'

In the same Tablet He acknowledged their attempts to teach unity of the races: 'I know also that your thought and mention by day and by night is the guidance of souls – white and black. Therefore be ye most happy, because you are confirmed in this great matter.'[13] The knowledge that they had 'Abdu'l-Bahá's abiding love and approval must have been a source of great comfort to both Louise and Louis during their manifold troubles.

Louise did not give up on her philanthropic endeavours and attempted to help the poorer section of the Bahá'í community in Washington, although this plan also ran up against difficulties of the racial kind. She wrote to Agnes Parsons that some Bahá'ís in Washington were hard up by reason of their age or ill health and that other better-off Bahá'ís donated money for them which in fact they would have preferred to give to the Temple Fund. To help this situation she suggested that Bahá'ís who did have money could rent a house and then rent rooms in it to poor Bahá'ís. (If the tenants felt bad about this she recommended they could always pay into the Temple Fund.) Louise herself was willing to pay $10 a month towards this project from her private income from England. Taking into account the problems she was only too aware of when white and black people tried to live in the same house, she suggested in this letter that only white Bahá'ís should be offered accommodation in such a rented house. Almost immediately she reconsidered and wrote to Mrs Parsons the next day that of course the Bahá'í Home must be for all races. But she was thoroughly aware of the reality of the situation and therefore concluded that such a project was not feasible at that time because of racial prejudice. Instead she suggested the community could give small pensions for poor Bahá'ís (of any race).[14]

Not content with taking on the problem of impoverished Washington Bahá'ís in general, Louise became very concerned about two elderly Bahá'í ladies of her acquaintance, Mrs Sargent and Miss Hudd, attempting to find paid work for them. She became particularly worried about the plight of Miss Hudd, an elderly lady who had worked as a nurse and as a kindergarten teacher and she conceived the plan that Miss Hudd could be sent to Haifa to serve in 'Abdu'l-Bahá's household. She was probably remembering how her friend Marion Jack had spent six happy months in the Master's House years before. There is no record of whether Miss Hudd ever went to serve in Haifa or indeed whether she was in favour of the plan. But Louise's concern for the elderly lady is yet another token of her desire to help those less fortunate than herself.[15]

Throughout all the difficulties of these early married years Louise could be sure of the love and support of her husband. They were both well aware of the racial tensions within the Washington Bahá'í community and the prejudice of many in the general population regarding the rights of black people. In particular, they realized many people considered their mixed race marriage to be scandalous, but Louise and Louis were constantly united in their love and respect for each other and their devotion to the Bahá'í teachings. Their fervent desire was to serve the Bahá'í Movement, as it was then known, and their lives were a day-to-day example of Bahá'í service and unity. Furthermore they were conscious that 'Abdu'l-Bahá had chosen them to be a living example of racial unity.

In their social life Louise and Louis mixed with both white and African American friends. Louis had a good friend in Roy Williams, a young newly-declared black Bahá'í with whom he would work extensively in the future as a travelling teacher. Roy considered 'Abdu'l-Bahá's designation of him as Louis Gregory's 'fellow-traveller' as a great honour.[16]

The newly married couple were often invited to dinner at Roy's grandmother's house where she would cook southern-style food which Louise enjoyed as much as her husband. Roy recorded that 'My grandmother was a very excellent cook and Mr Gregory always liked to . . . visit especially on the days when Grandma would cook her famous hot rolls.'[17]

Louis, already established as a prominent member of the Bahá'í community, was naturally involved in Bahá'í activities which frequently took him away from home. Having been elected to the Executive Board of the Bahá'í Temple Unity which was responsible for the construction of the Temple in April 1912, he was often required to attend meetings in Chicago and other cities. He was not elected again to the Bahá'í Temple Unity for a few years but in 1914 he was appointed to the committee responsible for auditing the accounts of the Temple Unity treasury. By now he was recognized as a brilliant speaker and he spoke regularly at National Bahá'í Conventions: in 1913 in New York, in 1914 and 1916 in Chicago and in 1917 in Boston and then again in Chicago in 1917 for the commemoration of the centenary of the birth of Bahá'u'lláh.

Early in their married life Louis was back at Storer College in Harper's Ferry, West Virginia teaching, when he fell seriously ill, possibly with typhoid. Louise hurried to be with him to care for him in his sickness. Pauline Hannen and friends in Washington sent bedclothes for him but it fell to Louise to wash his sheets. As she wrote to Pauline

Hannen: 'I washed all the things myself finally as well as I could in cold water and naptha [sic] soap and I had no means of ironing so had to let them rough dry.' Under her tender care Louis began to improve and she wrote:

> Louis is steadily improving though he often has a good deal of pain . . . I hear him now talking to nurse in quite his natural voice . . . Letters do him so much good when I read them to him. He needs a good deal of cheering and encouraging as he is mostly very depressed, quite contrary to his usual nature, but he is unused to pain and does not at all understand it . . .[18]

Louis's trips to the southern states in order to spread the Bahá'í teachings continued and, for example, in 1915 he travelled to Atlanta and Nashville. He was able to lecture at schools, colleges and churches in the south, particularly reaching large sectors of the black population and he made valuable contacts with influential people there such as Professor George W. Henderson of the Roger Williams University and others who became enamoured of the Bahá'í teachings and later helped to establish the Faith in the southern states. However, Louise, his wife, was unable to accompany him on these trips as, their marriage being deemed illegal in these states, they risked being arrested there or, even worse, being subjected to physical violence.

The 'anti-miscegenation' laws or laws forbidding intermarriage between people of different race were at that time enforced in all the southern states of America. In 1914 Alfred Lunt, a Boston lawyer and Bahá'í, looked into the laws regarding intermarriage following a query by Mrs Parsons who was worried about the involvement of Bahá'ís in such marriages.[19] He reported that at that time 25 states prohibited racial intermarriage. As late as the 1940s it was recorded that 'In view of the fact that Negro-white intermarriage is forbidden by law in thirty states and condemned by the mores throughout the nation it is scarcely surprising that such marriages seldom occur.'[20] And as late as 1965 the opinion was given that 'Today interracial marriage is opposed because of social considerations by the majority of both Negroes and whites. Even those who approve in principle would find it difficult to advise their sons and daughters to enter into such a marriage knowing the unavoidable social problems which confront an interracial couple.'[21]

Despite these widely-held views, the United States Supreme Court ruled in 1967 that laws forbidding interracial marriage were henceforth illegal.

However, throughout the years that Louis was travelling to give the Bahá'í message he was forced to endure humiliating restrictions aimed at segregating the races in the southern states. These laws were colloquially known as 'Jim Crow' laws after a character in a black and white minstrel show named Jim Crow who was a white man with a blacked-up face who capered and danced in a grotesque and ridiculous manner. The term 'Jim Crow' became a derogatory name for African Americans. Such laws decreed that black people must travel in special ill-equipped train carriages at the rear of the train, had to use separate public conveniences, must give preference to white people while walking along a pavement or driving a horse-drawn vehicle or car on the road and could only eat in designated restaurants or parts of restaurants away from white people. In a multitude of ways people who were not 'white' (and it became increasingly difficult to prove who was entirely of the white race and who had mixed blood) had to endure petty indignities and serious infringements of their civil rights. Louis, even though he was highly educated and qualified, was nevertheless subject to these laws.

His travels in service to the Cause were long, gruelling and physically punishing. They were made bearable by the joy he received in meeting with enlightened souls and in spreading the Bahá'í teachings and by the support that he received from Louise. Being united in their dedication to the Cause, they both saw his travel teaching as a bounty bestowed on them by 'Abdu'l-Bahá and Louis knew that his wife understood perfectly why it was necessary for him to spend long periods away from home. While he was away she wrote to him worrying about his long hours of uncomfortable travel and whether he was eating properly and when he returned – often briefly – she nourished him both physically with a healthier diet and emotionally with her abundant love and support. Years later he wrote of her as 'my angel wife, Louise' and wrote that 'We were supremely happy together in our quaint old home near the sea.' [22] Having returned from one of his extended travel trips Louis wrote, 'It is really very pleasant to be home once more and Louise, my wife, is doing all in her power to make me comfortable. She is truly one of the jewels of Baha'u'llah, so full of the spirit of sacrifice and service and so self-forgetful.' [23]

Louise Mathew in Luxembourg, c.1900

Louise on her wedding day

Louis G. Gregory on his wedding day

The Gregorys on their wedding day

So while he was away Louise was left at home in Washington, a city she barely knew in the early days and in which she had yet to make real friends. Louis certainly recognized that this was a hardship for Louise and wrote home to her frequently expressing his love: 'My Darling, Your letter . . . told of your being alone in the house and having a lonesome feeling'. He hoped she was feeling 'very close to the Beloved of all hearts, Abdul Baha [sic] and that His Great Love sustains you.' He closed his letter, 'Be happy, O my Darling, in the sacrifice you have made in the Path of God. It may be the means of Guidance to many souls.'[24]

She was constantly in his thoughts as he travelled and he wrote to her from Chicago, 'I often pray the rising prayer with you, my darling as well as the prayer before sleep, even though you are far away.'[25] He ends another letter to her, 'With my heart's best love and a tender caress, I remain Your husband, Louis.'[26]

8

'TWO BIRDS OF THE NEST OF THY LOVE'[1]

In 1920 Louise received a Tablet addressed to her from 'Abdu'l-Bahá in which He extolled her husband Louis, blessed again their marriage and commended them for serving the Cause together:

To the dear maid-servant of God, Mrs. Louise Gregory:
Unto her be the Glory of God, the Most Glorious.

HE IS GOD!

O thou revered wife of his honour, Gregory!
Do thou consider what a bounty God hath bestowed upon thee in giving thee a husband as Mr. Gregory, who is the essence of the love of God and is a symbol of guidance! How luminous is the face of this person! His character is (like unto) a rose-garden. He is always busy, together with thee, in the service of the Kingdom. Ye are serving together with Ella Quant, Mrs. Margaret La Grange and Mr. G. V. Williams with all your power, raising the Call of God.[2]

Any doubts that Louise might have had concerning the rightness of her marriage to Louis would have been swept away by receiving this wonderful Tablet, reading 'Abdu'l-Bahá's praise of her beloved husband and His commendation of them for their efforts to unitedly serve their Faith.

The eight years between their wedding in 1912 and the receipt of this Tablet had not been easy and the difficulties that 'Abdu'l-Bahá had hinted at had soon become evident. Louise's health was always fragile and coping on her own while Louis was away travelling must often have been challenging. A noisy environment was always a problem for her and city life was frequently full of clamour and hubbub and she would sometimes experience pains in her head in response. In a letter to Agnes Parsons which she wrote at the time when they planned to move to Portland, Massachusetts, she mentioned that it had seemed at first that she would be unable to join Louis 'because no <u>quiet</u> rooms could be found and <u>quiet</u> is essential for me in order to sleep and without sleep and surrounded with noise I quite lose my health and suffer agonies with my head'.

She continued: 'I am not sure this flat that Louis has just found is as quiet as I wish, but in any case it is better than Mrs Duffield's which is right on the car line [tramline] and a very noisy part. I fancy you do not like noise yourself and can perhaps sympathize with my troublesome head.' However, she continued, 'Abdul Baha has always found me some place that is at least endurable if not ideal, but usually it has looked hopeless when we have begun to search and it has always . . . been through Bahais that we have found what we need.'[3]

Over the course of several years of married life Louise had often pondered what 'Abdu'l-Bahá had meant when they spoke together on the ship before departing for America and He had told her: 'I said what I did because I saw a seed in your heart . . . Now is the watering time.' She later commented in a letter to her friend Agnes Parsons: 'I could not understand what He meant and only thought it must be something of a spiritual nature. A moment later He turned round again and said 'I saw one seed in your heart, I wish it to produce many seeds.'

The explanation for these words later suggested itself to her:

> Some two years after our marriage I suddenly realized what Abdul Baha had meant when He said 'I saw a seed in your heart etc.' The seed I realized was the attraction between Louis and myself, the watering time the ripening of this feeling into love leading to marriage, its fruit, the 'one seed producing many seeds' the attraction of the hearts of the white and colored races to be produced by our love and marriage.
>
> Our marriage therefore is important as Abdul Baha has indicated. He said I heard later that the importance of our marriage was not understood at that time but would be understood later. It was the first inter-racial marriage between these two races among

the Baha'is you know and known to be brought about by Abdul Baha Himself thus encouraging inter-racial marriage and letting the Baha'is know that He encouraged it. Since then I suppose you know there have been two of these marriages among Bahais neither of which I think would have taken place without the example of our marriage. Mr Taite's marriage is of course one and Mr Simpson's of New York who is to go to Africa, another.

The sensitivity of such marriages was of course known to Louise through first-hand experience and she adds regarding Mr Simpson's marriage:

I am not sure if it is known he has married a white Baha'i lately so I will not mention her name, their engagement was known to a few of us only and kept secret at their request.

As Abdul Baha told you He made our marriage I thought these particulars would interest you.[4]

Through all the difficulties and inconveniences of their married life Louise and Louis must both have taken great comfort from the fact that 'Abdul Bahá Himself had intended their marriage, that it was important in educating the Bahá'ís on the suitability of such a marriage and that it opened the door to the possibility of many other happy inter-racial marriages. She mentioned this again to Mrs Parsons in another letter describing how 'Abdu'l-Bahá 'showed us both He wished us to marry, also how He made it clear to me that He hoped the example of our marriage would encourage other inter-racial marriages. He told me also plainly: I wish the white and the colored people to marry.'[5]

Louise wrote frequent letters to Agnes Parsons and the two ladies formed a close friendship so that eventually Louise felt able to confide very personal information to her friend. Their friendship is interesting given that they came from such different backgrounds: Mrs Parsons, a wife and mother, a wealthy American woman used to being the doyenne of Washington high society where she mixed with diplomats, professors and politicians (who were never what she would have described as 'colored') and Louise, a reserved, highly educated English woman, recently arrived in America, who had married late in life to a black lawyer. Truly, if all three had not been Bahá'ís it is unlikely they would ever have met. But Louise and Agnes did form a close relationship. As

Louise knew virtually no one in Washington apart from Louis when she married him, it is perhaps not surprising that she often wrote to Mrs Parsons for advice at first, finding herself in a sadly divided Bahá'í community where racial segregation was a fact of life and she was suddenly in the thick of it.

It seems likely that Louise felt respect for Mrs Parsons whom she may have considered to be the 'mother' of the Washington community. Agnes Parsons, it has been noted, did not mix with black people in the normal course of events. It has been said that in her diary of 'Abdu'l-Bahá's visit 'there is scarcely a mention of any of 'Abdu'l-Bahá's talks at the homes of Andrew Dyer and Joseph Hannen, both of which were sites of racially integrated meetings for the Washington, D.C. Bahá'í community, or at African-American venues, such as the Metropolitan African methodist Episcopal Church, presumably because Mrs. Parsons did not attend most of these events. Such activities were not part of the social world in which she lived.'[6] However, it is possible that she was attracted to Louise because of her formal English manners and because she had lived in London and Paris, the great capitals of Europe. Also Louise was clearly very sincere and caring and these qualities may have struck a chord with Agnes Parsons. Whatever the reason, the two women formed a close enough friendship so that Louise felt able to share confidences with her.

One aspect of their marriage which had caused concern to both Louise and Louis was whether or not they would have children. Louise writes very candidly to Mrs Parsons about the agony of this question: 'I was 46 at the time of my marriage though no one guessed my age and Louis [was] over 8 years younger. He asked me not to tell people my age. I only tell you to show how impossible our marriage was from a human standpoint – sick and nervous as I was, these years older and of an age when I was not likely to have children while if he married he wanted them.'

Having described to Mrs Parsons how she had 'no thought of marriage' when she travelled to America with 'Abdul Bahá, she went on to relate her anxiety about the issue of child-bearing which caused her to consult a doctor on the problem:

> . . . from a physical point of view [I] was entirely unfit for marriage being in a very weak condition and on the verge of a nervous

breakdown, besides which there are things wrong with the formation of my body that made marriage unwise. This was told to me by a lady doctor a short time before my marriage which made things still harder, yet Abdul Baha Himself fixed the week of our marriage so I could only have faith in Him that all would work out right.

After our marriage I wrote to Dr Zia Bagdadi and asked him to tell the Master what the doctor had said to me and ask if I had cause to fear – that I knew Louis wanted a child. (She had told me that I was so narrow and delicate that it was practically impossible for me to have a living child born.) The answer came on a p.c. [postcard] from Zia. "Abdul Baha says not to fear – it will be all right.' The wonderful thing about this answer was that it satisfied both [of us], as Louis took it that it would be all right with me if I had a child and I believed I never should have one. I was right and at last Louis realized it and was content to have it so but in the early days of our marriage it was better he should not know this.[7]

Their undying faith and their obedience to the wishes of 'Abdu'l-Bahá saw them through this agonizing question of whether they would have children or not, although it clearly caused great anxiety to Louise and, in the early days, disappointment to Louis. Louise may have had mixed feelings on the subject but she seems to have accepted the fact that she would remain childless with some relief, understandably enough given the physical difficulties, while Louis took some time to reconcile himself to not having a family, finally accepting it because of his faith in 'Abdu'l-Bahá's wisdom.

As an educated woman qualified to work as a teacher, Louise often felt frustrated that she was not working and making use of her talents. In 1915 she wrote to Joseph Hannen suggesting that she could assist the Hannens in their business selling homeopathic medicines. Homeopathy was a popular form of medicine at that time in the United States and the Hannens ran a business selling 'Viari' homeopathic products. Although Louise never actually worked in the Hannens' business she and Louis trusted homeopathy and used homeopathic medicines throughout their lives. Louise wrote frequent letters to Joseph Hannen and his untimely death in 1920, knocked down by a motor car, must have been a serious shock to her, as it was to Louis and the rest of the Bahá'í community.

'TWO BIRDS OF THE NEST OF THY LOVE'

By 1917 Louise had taken steps to work again as a teacher and was giving private lessons, mainly in the French language. Having been educated privately at home herself this must have seemed like an obvious step to providing gainful employment, using her teaching skills as she was personally familiar with such a method. Louis wrote to her in November 1917 from Cleveland, Ohio saying he was glad she had taken up work which occupied her mind and also gave her the opportunity to teach the Faith. At first he had feared she would overtax her strength with this work but now he felt: 'Your success is a marvel' and she had 'made a sacrifice which few women would make, out of the purity of your beautiful soul, and for the advancement of the Cause of God. Because of this God is aiding you and rendering you victorious.'[8]

It is interesting to speculate on what Louis meant by her 'sacrifice'. Louise had given up her independence and her life as a full-time teacher in Europe, had left her family in England and France and no doubt many friends and acquaintances in Paris and other parts of France to start a new life and try to make new friends in America. She had probably never had to cook for herself or carry out domestic chores because she had grown up having servants to do this for her, and when she was older and lived away from home she would have received meals and accommodation in a *pension* or boarding house. After she married she must have had to learn to cook and keep house for herself and Louis. In marrying Louis she had embraced the many problems associated in those days with marrying a man of different race: the problem of finding a place to live where a mixed race couple was accepted, and no doubt facing the hardship of a certain amount of shunning from people who disliked their interracial marriage for one reason or another. From his letter and his use of the word 'sacrifice' it is clear that Louis understood what Louise had had to endure and he fully appreciated it.

In Boston in 1917 Louis gave a talk on the equality of men and women in which he courageously expressed this Bahá'í principle even though such ideas were way ahead of their time, because women did not receive the suffrage in the whole of the United States until 1920. In his address he asked:

> Are the sexes intellectually equal? Although in past ages women who arose to places of commanding influence were rare and exceptional, yet a number of such cases can be cited to prove their inherent

powers. In politics they have successfully ruled nations, inspiring their subjects to growth and freedom. Their contributions to literature, art and science have won fame and even in war time they have been forces to be reckoned with. Their right to vote grows in public favor throughout the world. Here again any seeming inequality of the sexes yields to those opportunities for education which the new cycle brings.[9]

Louis's innate sense of justice embraced the need for the recognition of the rights of women, be they black or white. His marriage, despite all its difficulties, was illuminated by this principle.

Resuming her career as a teacher and embarking on giving private tuition was one way of keeping herself busy while Louis was away, and avoided the feeling that she was wasting her considerable training. However, even the environment of the private lessons could be fraught with difficulties, as Louise commented a couple of years later in a letter to Joseph Hannen, referring to 'a lady here who is very friendly with me and would I think have me in her cottage in exchange for some French lessons if I felt able to stand the racket of her two excitable boys'.[10]

Louise never forgot that she was a teacher and she harboured the desire to found a school based on Bahá'í principles:

> I have another ambition; one which <u>seems</u> not likely to be carried out; to establish a school where <u>no</u> racial lines shall be drawn or recognized. One other is desirous of doing this with me. <u>Perhaps</u> Abdul Baha may permit us to join forces in this beginning to leaven the loaf of Humanity with the Principle of Oneness.[11]

It is not clear who she meant by 'one other' in this context – it may well have been her husband Louis – but she was correct in her assumption that this ambition would never be realized.

With her husband away travelling so much, Louise was ever looking for ways to keep herself occupied and if this activity could help her serve her Faith so much the better. She wrote to Agnes Parsons some time after the couple had moved back to Washington:

> I am wondering if I can be of assistance to you sometimes with your correspondence though I cannot use a type-writer. If so I would

gladly give you an hour or two from time to time, preferably of a morning. On account of a weak spine I cannot sit for a long time, but possibly I might take down in pencil a number of letters from your dictation as I did your letter to Louis on the phone today only at your house, and write the letters afterwards at my flat and then submit them when written to you, or write some at your house and others at home. I should be most glad if I could serve you in that way, and therefore the Cause which needs you so much.[12]

Throughout her life Louise enjoyed creative writing and this was an activity she greatly relished during these early years of her marriage, taking every opportunity that was offered to write, particularly if it could help spread the Bahá'í message. She wrote to Agnes Parsons in 1914:

It may interest you to know that I sent a few extracts of a story I proposed writing giving the Bahai Teachings to Abdul Baha to ask His permission and He gave His consent and all encouragement. Only about one tenth of it is at present written. It is to be called 'The Most Great Peace' and the story is placed in the year 1963. After giving an idea of the Bahai laws in operation then by the story, the grandmother tells the story of her life which gives an opportunity to describe life at Acca and Abdul Baha's visits to the West. Also in conversations the Bahai teaching is given.

This story, which appears not to have been finished, might have given fascinating insights into her own visit to Akka in 1911 and her personal memories of 'Abdu'l-Bahá's travels in the West. This letter to Mrs Parsons was written soon after World War I was declared in Europe and in it Louise was naturally conscious of the turmoil gripping Britain and other European countries: 'I have lately written a short story called "A Soldier's Vision of Peace" which gives the Message indirectly.' However, she was also familiar with publisher's rejection slips: 'When it was sent it occurred to me whether I ought to have submitted it to you first. It has been returned from two magazines and is now at the offices of a third, "The Atlantic Monthly".'[13]

Louise had more luck with writing for a young person's magazine called *The Boy Builder* published by her acquaintance and fellow Bahá'í, Dr Shaw, as she wrote a couple of years later to Mrs Parsons:

Dr Shaw asked Louis . . . to send him a story for boys. Louis said to me 'I can't write stories, you send him one you have written.' So I sent him a story I had heard as being quite true in all essentials, only names and other details being mine . . . Dr Shaw seemed delighted with my story and its teachings which were entirely in conformity with the ideas of his magazine.'

The magazine expounded Bahá'í principles 'and it is a most advanced magazine on education'. She closed her letter promising, 'I will send you a copy of "The Boy Builder" as soon as I can get one back I have lent.'[14]

In 1917 Louise's mother died at her home in Beckenham, England. It had been at least five years since Louise had last seen her mother and she must have felt grieved to think of the thousands of miles that had separated them during her mother's last years. Emma Mathew had been an invalid during her final years, living at the family home in Brackley Road, Beckenham with her niece Ethel, a nurse and two servants to care for her. She passed away at the age of 80 and was buried in Norwood cemetery, the final resting place of her husband Michael and their infant son, Sydney.

In her will which she had made in 1910 Emma named her sons Percy and Vincent and her eldest daughter Florence as her executors. She bequeathed three-fifths of all her household goods (including books, pictures, prints and musical instruments) to her daughter Florence and one-fifth of these household goods each to her daughters Louise and Edith with the provision that if they preferred they each could receive a legacy of 30 pounds instead. When she died she was the owner of 12 houses as well as the house in Brackley Road and these houses, which presumably were let to tenants, were to be let for a further five years after her death and then sold. The proceeds of these house sales were to be divided between all her 11 children, and after her funeral expenses had been paid any remaining money from sales of her property was to be divided equally between all her children.

Four months later Emma revoked the appointment of her daughter Florence as an executor and one wonders if this was because Florence felt inadequate to the task or if there was some other reason. A second codicil to the will revoked the arrangement whereby Florence would receive three-fifths of all the household goods and Louise and Edith one-fifth each. She changed this provision and instead 'whereas my children have at various times both individually and collectively presented me with numerous gifts some of which are of their own workmanship' she desired that 'such gifts . . . should at the date of my death be returned to my said children' and 'I give to my daughter in law Gabrielle Mathew [Ernest's wife] the chair which she worked for me many years ago'. Her 'wearing apparel dress material needle work lace jewellery trinkets and articles of personal ornament' were to be divided between all four of her daughters: Florence, Louise, Edith and her married daughter Ethel, while all her daughters-in-law were to receive some such article as a keepsake. All Emma's books (which seem to have been a considerable collection) were to be divided equally between all her children. After this was done Florence was to select three-fifths of the remaining items and one-fifth or the sum of 30 pounds each was to go to Louise and Edith.[15]

When the second codicil to Emma's will was made in March 1912 Louise was still unmarried. She most probably informed her mother that she was sailing to America with 'Abdu'l-Bahá on 30 March but the astonishing news that Louise was to marry and settle in America would not have reached her mother until later that summer. Interestingly, Emma made no further codicils to her will despite the drastic change to her daughter Louise's circumstances.

9

'DIFFUSE THE DIVINE FRAGRANCES'[1]

These were dramatic and troubled times on the world stage. Emma died at the beginning of 1917 while World War I was causing appalling casualties on all sides and a month before the Russian Tsar was forced to abdicate. Britain had declared war on Germany in July 1914 and over the next few years a war of attrition and bloody stalemate ensued with the Western Front's trenches changing little until 1917. News of the deaths of thousands of young men became an almost commonplace event in Britain, and Louise and Louis must have followed the news of the war in Europe with horror and dread. Louise's youngest brother Harold and her nephew Ernest both fought in the war and she must have worried constantly about them and prayed for their safety. Harold fought with the Royal East Kent Regiment, known as the Buffs, as an Indian Army Reserve Officer. He enlisted in August 1915 aged 34 and was married with a five-year-old daughter. Her nephew Ernest, son of her brother Percy, enlisted in January 1916 at the age of 18 and fought with the Royal Engineers as a Pioneer in the British Expeditionary Force involved in the Battle of Arras, responsible for construction of trenches and fortifications. Both were awarded the Victory Medal at the end of the war, so Louise's prayers for their safety were answered.

1916 witnessed the carnage of the Battle of Verdun from February to December and the first Battle of the Somme from July to November of that year with horrifying casualties to the British, French and German armies. At the close of the Battle of Verdun 130,000 unknown dead remained from both sides. The battle of the Somme saw a million casualties in four months with almost 20,000 British soldiers killed on day one, 1 July. Meanwhile the Battle of Jutland, World War I's fiercest naval battle, took place off the coast of Denmark from 31 May to 1 June of that year. The war in the Balkans, which had been smouldering since the first Balkan war in 1912, served to continue the breakup of the Ottoman Empire.

The old world order was being visibly destroyed with the war marking the end of the German, Russian, Ottoman and Austro-Hungarian empires and the maps of Europe and the Middle East changing forever. Against this backdrop of destruction and mayhem 'Abdu'l-Bahá steadily unveiled His plan for the spiritual conquest of the planet in the form of the 14 Tablets of the Divine Plan. The first eight Tablets were revealed by Him between 26 March and 22 April 1916.

The last six Tablets were revealed by 'Abdu'l-Bahá between 2 February and 8 March 1917, approximately a month before the United States entered the war on 6 April 1917. By this time the conflict had spread to the Middle East with the Sinai and Palestine Campaign raging between the British and Ottoman Empires. This resulted in the Bahá'í community in Haifa and Akka becoming isolated and cut off from most of the Bahá'í world. There was real danger of bombardment of Haifa by the Allied forces so that for a time 'Abdu'l-Bahá, His family and the local Bahá'í community were evacuated to a village in the hills to the east of Akka for safety. 'Abdu'l-Bahá was Himself personally in danger of His life when Jamál Páshá, the Ottoman Commander-in-Chief, threatened to kill 'Abdu'l-Bahá by crucifixion and to destroy the Tomb of Bahá'u'lláh. Shoghi Effendi later described how 'Abdu'l-Bahá had foretold the sufferings of the first World War:

> The war of 1914–18, repeatedly foreshadowed by 'Abdu'l-Bahá in the dark warnings He uttered in the course of His western travels, and which broke out eight months after His return to the Holy Land, once more cast a shadow of danger over His life . . .

and how He agonized over the war:

> He felt acutely the virtual stoppage of all communication with most of the Bahá'í centres throughout the world. Agony filled His soul at the spectacle of human slaughter precipitated through humanity's failure to respond to the summons He had issued, or to heed the warnings He had given. Surely sorrow upon sorrow was added to the burden of trials and vicissitudes which He, since His boyhood, had borne so heroically for the sake, and in the service, of His Father's Cause.[2]

Nevertheless, it was at this violent and critical time in the history of the world that 'Abdu'l-Bahá chose to reveal His plan for the spreading of Bahá'u'lláh's message and the global expansion of the Bahá'í Cause. Many years later the Universal House of Justice declared:

> How wondrous the vision of the Plan's Author! Placing before the friends the prospect of a day when the light of His Father's Revelation would illuminate every corner of the world, He set out not only strategies for achieving this feat but guiding principles and unchanging spiritual requisites.[3]

The Tablets were addressed to the Bahá'ís of the United States and Canada, conferring on them 'a signal mark of His special favor by investing them . . . with a world mission'.[4] From the first group of eight, five Tablets were sent to America and were published in the 8 September 1916 issue of *Star of the West*. Shortly after this, because of the conflict, all communication with Haifa ceased 'and the remainder of the Tablets were kept in a vault under the Shrine of the Báb on Mt. Carmel for the duration of the war. They were dispatched to America at the end of the war where they were unveiled in befitting ceremonies during the "Convention of the Covenant" held at Hotel McAlpin in New York City on April 26-30, 1919.'[5]

The editors of *Star of the West* in their issue of 8 September 1916 called the first five Tablets 'A Trumpet Call to Action' and continued:

> It is evident that Abdul-Baha in his love and wisdom is now giving each and all of the American Bahais a special opportunity to awaken to their responsibilities and to arise in love and sacrifice for this 'superhuman service'.
>
> A spontaneous uprising of the whole body of believers to this call is the first step necessary to the success of this great undertaking.
>
> We cannot over-estimate the effect of this united service. The spiritual and practical results of our efforts will depend upon our joyous, enthusiastic and prompt obedience to the command of the Center of the Covenant.[6]

After the remaining Tablets of the Divine Plan were revealed at the Convention of the Covenant in April 1919 (at which Louis G. Gregory spoke on 'The Power of the Holy Spirit') all of the Tablets were subsequently published in *Star of the West*.

The message of the Tablets of the Divine Plan was received by the Gregorys as a clarion call to arise for further service. By the autumn of 1916, inspired by the first five Tablets and particularly by the Tablet to the Bahá'ís of the Southern States, Louis had set off on a travel teaching trip to the south. In the Tablet 'Abdu'l-Bahá had lamented that 'In the Southern States of the United States, the friends are few' and had proceeded to list the states that should be visited, urging, 'A person declaring the glad tidings of the appearance of the realities and significances of the Kingdom is like unto a farmer who scatters pure seeds in the rich soil.' Louis wasted no time in sowing the seeds, speaking at colleges and meetings and giving 'the glad tidings of the appearance of the Kingdom of God'.[7]

Louise wholeheartedly supported Louis in his travelling for the Cause and saw how inspired he was by such a life. She had previously commented, 'Mr Gregory's work is almost purely mechanical at the Treasury and his talents in so far as his daily work is concerned are practically being unused.'[8] When Louis was travelling in the southern states, using his speaking skills to the utmost and meeting people who were attracted to the Bahá'í teachings, she would have known that he was using his talents for the benefit of the Cause and been thrilled that he had arisen to serve the Divine Plan.

There were practical difficulties in Louis's travel teaching to serve the Cause. By now he had given up his job at the Treasury Department and any other opportunities for advancement in his career, all sacrificed to becoming a travelling speaker for the Bahá'í Cause which he felt to be his calling. The couple had bought their own home a few years previously in Brentwood, Maryland,[9] a small town less than a mile from Washington DC, and now without his salary coming in it was a real problem to know how to finance his travels. One solution was to let the house so that they could receive money from the rent. With Louis away travelling it would be possible for Louise to rent a room on her own or to live with friends.

After the war was over and the second batch of 'Abdu'l-Bahá's Tablets of the Divine Plan had arrived, the Bahá'ís in the United States received another urgent call to teach the Cause in the south when 'Abdu'l-Bahá addressed a further Tablet to the 16 southern states, naming them all.

The Tablet goes on:

> Therefore in these sixteen states, because they are contiguous to other states and their climate being in the utmost of moderation, unquestionably the divine teachings must reveal themselves with a brighter effulgence, the breaths of the Holy Spirit must display a penetrating intensity, the ocean of the love of God must be stirred with higher waves, the breezes of the rose garden of the divine love be wafted with higher velocity, and the fragrances of holiness be diffused with swiftness and rapidity.

The Bahá'ís are urged to move rapidly:

> At this time and at this period we must avail ourselves of this most great opportunity. We must not sit inactive for one moment; we must sever ourselves from composure, rest, tranquillity, goods, property, life and attachment to material things.

The Tablet further called on the believers to 'sacrifice everything' and this is just what Louis and Louise did.[10]

Louis embraced 'Abdu'l-Bahá's call to action wholeheartedly, forgoing material comforts, and travelled to the southern states seeking waiting souls and speaking to high and low alike. But Louise was not able to accompany Louis on his trips to the south because of the anti-miscegenation laws that made their marriage illegal there. The resulting situation was like walking a tightrope both emotionally and physically for them both. Louise wrote to Mrs Parsons:

> We cannot bring harmony to others unless we have perfect harmony ourselves and this is difficult if we work beyond our powers of endurance physically and living such abnormal lives as Louis and myself. The year before this from April to April we were together only one week in Aug. and one day in Sept. It is not right as we both realized the next year and it nearly caused disaster.

She continued:

> You see now for almost two years he has been travelling continuously

and in all that time we have never had so long together at a time as this autumn and that was some days under 4 weeks.

The year before from Sept. to end of April he did not come back at all, then we had about 3 weeks together at New York under very trying conditions in one small room and having to get our meals out and New York too noisy for any comfort for me so that I was not well.

Their time spent together could be counted in days, not months: 'At Green Acre in the summer we had 16 days and there we were very happy, but we had our meals out and no real home life.'[11]

Their financial problems only became worse as time went by. In 1917 the Gregorys had consulted together on their financial plight and Louise had suggested they might sell their house to finance Louis's travelling. He wrote to his friend Alfred Lunt:

> My dear little wife, the Flame of whose spiritual love is aglow, suggested the sale of our home that a fund might be raised for the spread of the teachings. Negotiations for this are now in progress with signs of success. As a result I expect, God willing, to be able to spend the best part of a year in the field. Am very happy over the prospect.[12]

The drastic plan to sell their house was shelved, however, and they substituted the idea of letting it to tenants which helped their finances for a while. She wrote to Joseph Hannen in June 1919, 'I shall need the rent of that house to add to my income for living expenses and had better keep the money that is coming to me from England for travelling or other emergencies. . .'[13] The money coming from England amounted to the regular $50 a month which was from investment of the bequest left to her by her father. This money was a vital support to them for many years. In addition, in 1919 she was expecting a further sum from England, most likely from her mother's will but 'it is not wise for me to spend the few hundred dollars that are coming to me which I fear will be the last I am likely to receive unless something unexpected happens'. Furthermore, she wrote, 'I am warned by my brother that my income will be reduced from now on.'[14]

With their money worries becoming ever more pressing, eventually

Louis regretfully came round to the idea of accepting subsidization. By 1919 it was evident that the couple did not have the means to keep financing his travel teaching trips and he reluctantly agreed to accept financial help. His acceptance was aided by the statement by 'Abdu'l-Bahá in the Tablets of the Divine Plan: 'if a soul for the sake of God, voluntarily and out of his pure desire, wishes to offer a contribution (toward the expenses of a teacher) in order to make the contributor happy, the teacher may accept a small sum, but must live with the utmost contentment'.[15] It is recorded that in 1919 Louis's expenses amounted to about $100 a month including the expense of procuring Bahá'í literature to distribute on his travels.[16]

In September 1920 Louise was debating whether to sell their house:

> If I sell my house it is wiser for me to invest the money . . . as we are not likely to stay in Washington together again for some time and I expect I can do better work elsewhere when alone and keep in better health. I am hoping that by investing money . . . we may later have means enough of our own for both of us to travel and teach without Louis having to depend on the Bahai funds and also that we can buy a house later when we need it.[17]

In 1921 they had found a flat in Washington that they could rent and she wrote to Mrs Parsons:

> If Louis could be found work to do in and around Washington for a time while we have this flat with visits to not far distant cities it seems to me it would be well both for his sake and my sake and perhaps his future usefulness for the Cause as he is not strong enough to keep up that strain constantly year after year without longer and more frequent periods of rest and relaxation and our relations and their importance to the Cause would seem to me to make it necessary that we should be more together.

She always understood Louis's spiritual destiny and the importance of his work for the Cause in spite of the hardships it caused them both to suffer: 'I am purely stating my opinion knowing that Louis is the servant of the Assembly and of Abdul Baha and as such must be at your disposition, yet I feel you will be glad for me to express my opinion as I am his wife.'

She worried constantly about Louis's health as he was travelling the whole time and she particularly worried about him not eating properly:

> I have a feeling from his letters of late that he is getting nervous as he usually does after about two or three months' constant strain of travelling and lecturing and especially when he gets the wrong kind of food continuously. He has now been gone over two months. He can live here with me cheaper than when away as I cook for him and there would be no room rent so a part of the expense of the journey would be made up that way.

Whilst encouraging him to answer the call of the Divine Plan, she also longed to have some kind of home life together with her husband: 'For the first time in 2 years we have a place where we can live a real home life, have our meals together in our own home and I do not know when this will happen again as we have to give this up in April.' Previously she had enjoyed looking after her husband in a home environment and felt it had done him so much good: 'When we got settled down it was a wonderful rest to Louis to have his own home with me and relax from the strain of his travelling.'

The stress of Louis's travels with all the humiliation of the racial segregation he experienced took its toll on him, although he was always cheerful in his letters to her. But their not having a home together made them both feel ill, as she described:

> Louis wrote me lately that he never felt in better health in spite of the food etc., he wrote me the same just before I came home when his letters made me anxious but in reality his nerves were overstrained at that time and he did not know it . . . he tried to relax and could not, and was so nervous and irritable so unlike himself that I was in despair as I was feeling sick and nervous myself and we had many difficulties to overcome before we could get things at all comfortable here.

However she always trusted 'Abdu'l-Bahá and believed that in His wisdom He would help them:

> This difficulty of having a proper place to live in together when we

can be together will no doubt be solved for us by Abdul Baha in time and I feel He had a deeper meaning than that we should always be welcome in His Home when He said that. I think He meant . . . He would provide us with a home whenever we needed one as He really did this flat, but at the present time while things are as they are it is as you know rather a problem as we have no home of our own now and so I should be glad if while we have this temporary one we could have as much as possible of this time together if it can be managed without the Cause suffering.[18]

Little did Louise know at that time that it would be many years before the Gregorys would have a home of their own again. Meanwhile she lived in whatever accommodation became available. This varied from renting a room in someone's house or being fortunate enough to rent an apartment for a while, to staying in a sombre-sounding Boarding House in New York state.

However difficult it was for her to find somewhere to live by herself while Louis was travelling, she was always aware that racial prejudice made it even more difficult for black people to find somewhere to live where they would be accepted. But she looked forward to a better time: 'Perhaps by that time conditions will have changed and colored people will be as free as white people to live where they like through the influence of the Bahai Spirit in the world and as a result of their efforts under the blessing of Abdul Baha to remove race prejudice.'[19]

Louise sometimes wrote in her letters that she felt lack of faith and courage, but her faith must have been revitalized in June 1920 when she received a letter from Agnes Parsons informing her that she was to receive the gift of a handkerchief from 'Abdu'l-Bahá. It is believed that He gave five handkerchiefs to Mrs Parsons, probably while she was on pilgrimage, to be presented to various believers in the West. Louise was honoured to be a recipient of one of these precious handkerchiefs from the Master. She wrote to Mrs Parsons:

> Your letter of June 20, telling me of your conviction that I was to be one of the recipients of the handkerchiefs from the Beloved Master touched me very much. I feel very unworthy of such a gift but hope His Love and Mercy in choosing me as one to receive such bounty, added to all the bounty He has showered on me before and ever

showers, will give me fresh courage and strength to try to serve Him better.

She recounts how 'Abdu'l-Bahá's encouraging words had recently aided her to finally stand before an audience and address them on the Bahá'í message:

> Only His promise to transform the drop into the ocean and that we must not look at our own ability and capacity and that whosoever arises to teach will be assisted by Divine Confirmations gave me courage to face an audience on a platform . . . recently and speak to them when it seemed my duty as there was no experienced lecturer to take the work, which presented itself without seeking on my part.

The experience spurred her on to further service: 'I have resolved to make other similar efforts as we all felt the Presence of Abdul Baha was with us and this Gift of His is an added Confirmation of His approval of our humble efforts. . .'[20]

Increasingly Louise desired to serve the Bahá'í Cause in her own way. She undertook teaching trips herself in the United States during the early years of their marriage. In May 1914 she was on a trip to Kalamazoo, Michigan and wrote to Albert Vail, another travelling teacher, that she had 'stayed two days with a very delightful family of colored people'. There she spoke at a small gathering and 'telephoned to Mr. Patterson of "The People's Church" and took it upon myself to say that you may be coming . . . and to ask if he would care to have you speak. . .'[21]

Later, in September 1917, she visited Berkeley Springs, West Virginia where she was 'able to give the message to the visitors here and the butler (colored) . . .' She wrote to Joseph Hannen of her experiences there: 'The butler seemed . . . interested . . . I am to go and talk to his friends and family on Monday if the wife is back from a visit away somewhere . . .'[22]

Like Louis, she was inspired by the Tablets of the Divine Plan to travel and to offer the Bahá'í message to souls for the first time. She was proud of Louis's achievements and supported him in every way she could, but she loved to travel herself, and reading the lists of faraway places needing the message that 'Abdu'l-Bahá mentioned in His Tablets must have been torture to her, confined as she was in rented accommodation waiting for Louis to return home. Moreover 'Abdu'l-Bahá cited other heroic Bahá'í women who had travelled to exotic places for the diffusion of the fragrances:

> Consider ye, that Miss Agnes Alexander, the daughter of the Kingdom, the beloved maidservant of the Blessed Perfection, travelled alone to the Hawaiian Islands, to the Island of Honolulu, and now she is gaining spiritual victories in Japan! . . . Likewise Miss Knobloch travelled alone to Germany. To what a great extent she became confirmed! Therefore, know ye of a certainty that whosoever arises in this day to diffuse the divine fragrances, the cohorts of the Kingdom of God shall confirm him and the bestowals and the favors of the Blessed Perfection shall encircle him.[23]

Her letters to Joseph Hannen in 1919 expressed her desire to travel for the Cause: 'quite possibly I may want to go to Switzerland (Geneva) to teach the Cause' she wrote, probably giving the example of Switzerland because both French and German were spoken there and because she was fluent in both these languages.[24] Her travel plans soon became more concrete: 'I expect to travel to teach the Cause and pay my own expenses', although she was keeping her options open regarding where to go: 'I hope to travel to teach the Cause and am not sure where I may have to go.'[25]

But most of all Louise yearned to travel together with Louis so that they both could meet interested people, of whatever race, and could give them the Bahá'í teachings. It must have seemed to her that, as they were a living example of an interracial marriage and a loving, united couple this would offer many opportunities for talking about the Bahá'í beliefs on the unity of mankind and marriage between black and white in particular. Her longing for them to travel together as a couple and teach the Faith stayed with her over the years, but it was only very much later that this wish of hers was granted and they were finally able to make a travel teaching trip together. For now it seemed an impossibility.

Louise had no hesitation in writing to 'Abdu'l-Bahá asking for His advice – He had after all told her to consider herself His daughter. She wrote to Him in 1919 asking about places where she and Louis should go as a couple in order to teach the Cause. He replied on 25 August: 'To whatever city is deemed advisable by Mr Gregory and to which ye may go together and therein strive for the guidance of souls, that is acceptable.'[26]

Always fervently desirous of serving the Cause, but faced with what appeared to be unsurmountable problems in achieving a travel teaching journey together with her husband, and suffering loneliness, anxiety and frustration without even a permanent home where she could welcome Louis on his return from his travels, Louise was in a quandary.

10

THE FIRST TRIP

Since her marriage in 1912 Louise had experienced the happiness of sharing many joys with her husband Louis, but she had also had to struggle with the 'difficulties' that 'Abdu'l-Bahá had foretold for her. Nevertheless she had always clung to the belief that He would support and help her, including believing that He would help them find somewhere suitable to live. When she needed advice she would write to Him as His 'daughter' and He would respond by sending her a loving Tablet.

When news reached the West at the end of November 1921 that 'Abdu'l-Bahá had passed away, or ascended to the Abhá Kingdom as the Bahá'í community would express it, the news was received with immense grief and shock. Many of the Bahá'ís of both the West and the East had had the bounty of meeting personally with Him and for a large number of them He represented the rock on which they built their faith. For some of the believers it must have been impossible to imagine the Bahá'í Movement continuing without Him.

The Bahá'ís in America received a cablegram which stated: 'HIS HOLINESS ABDUL BAHA ASCENDED TO ABHA KINGDOM INFORM FRIENDS' shortly after He ascended on 28 November 1921 aged 77. 'Abdu'l-Bahá had expressed His desire to leave this world in a Tablet He sent to the American believers a few days before His passing saying: 'In the cage of this world I flutter even as a frightened bird, and yearn every day to take My flight unto Thy Kingdom. Yá Bahá'u'l-Abhá! Make me drink of the cup of sacrifice, and set Me free.'[1] His funeral in Haifa was held the next day, as customary in Middle Eastern countries. It is estimated that 10,000 people attended the funeral, thronging the narrow streets of Haifa and accompanying the coffin to its resting place at the Shrine of the Báb on Mount Carmel. His passing was lamented by ordinary citizens as well as by those in power and the heads of other religions.

'Abdu'l-Bahá was highly esteemed by the officials of the British

Mandate in Palestine and in 1920 He had been knighted by the British government, although He never used His title. On hearing of His passing, Winston Churchill, who was Secretary of State for the Colonies at the time, 'telegraphed immediately to the High Commissioner for Palestine, Sir Herbert Samuel, instructing him to "convey to the Bahá'í Community, on behalf of His Majesty's Government, their sympathy and condolence" ', while Viscount Allenby, the High Commissioner for Egypt, 'wired the High Commissioner for Palestine asking him to "convey to the relatives of the late Sir 'Abdu'l-Bahá 'Abbás Effendi and to the Bahá'í Community" his "sincere sympathy in the loss of their revered leader" '. A distinguished professor and scholar at the University of Oxford wrote concerning 'Abdu'l-Bahá's demise: 'The passing beyond the veil into fuller life must be specially wonderful and blessed for One Who has always fixed His thoughts on high, and striven to lead an exalted life here below.'[2]

His passing was reported in newspapers around the world and tributes were published in the *Times* of London, the *Morning Post*, the *Daily Mail*, the *New York World*, *Le Temps*, and the *Times of India*.[3]

Communication was of course much slower in those days than it is now, and it was nearly two weeks before a facsimile copy of the cablegram to the American believers, sent by 'Abdu'l-Bahá's sister Bahíyyih Khánum, was published in *Star of the West* in its issue of 12 December 1921 so that the majority of the American Bahá'ís could read it for themselves. The editors commented: 'With these words the Bahais of the whole world are stunned.'[4] Following this it was almost two months after His Ascension before Bahíyyih Khánum was able to cable again on 16 January 1922 with the news that Shoghi Effendi, 'Abdu'l-Bahá's grandson, had been appointed His successor and Guardian of the Bahá'í Cause in 'Abdu'l-Bahá's Will and Testament.

Shoghi Effendi himself sent a cable to the American believers in February 1922, expressing the appreciation of the women of the Holy Household for the American believers' 'unswerving loyalty and noble resolve'. He pronounced the sombre period of grieving to be a 'Day of steadfastness' and assured them of his 'loving co-operation'.[5] His first letter to the Bahá'ís of North America arrived the following month and appeared in *Star of the West*. With it the believers heard for the first time the inspiring call to action from their beloved Guardian. Over the course of the next 35 years they would be constantly encouraged, comforted and spurred on by his stirring letters. In his first letter he wrote:

> At this early hour when the morning light is just breaking upon the Holy Land, whilst the gloom of the dear Master's bereavement is still hanging thick upon the hearts, I feel as if my soul turns in yearning love and full of hope to that great company of his loved ones across the seas, who now share with us all the agonies of his separation.

He commends 'the friends on the American continent, who, in the past, have rendered so glorious a service to his Cause and will now, faithful to his special love for them, carry on their mission still more gloriously than ever before. . .' Victory will be ensured if they practise

> Unity amongst the friends, selflessness in our labours in his path, detachment from all worldly things, the greatest prudence and caution in every step we take, earnest endeavour to carry out only what is his holy will and pleasure . . . these – and foremost among them is the need for UNITY – appear to me as our most vital duties should we dedicate our lives for his service.

Concluding his letter, the Guardian signed himself 'Your sincere co-worker in his Cause'.[6]

Information had been slow to arrive because of the practical difficulties surrounding travel and communication in the early 20th century. Shoghi Effendi was living in England, studying at Balliol College, Oxford when his Grandfather passed away. He received the news in London and immediately collapsed with shock. Because of difficulties with his passport it was not until 16 December that he was able to leave England accompanied by Lady Blomfield and his sister Ruhangiz. It took 13 days for them to arrive in Haifa via boat to Egypt and train from Egypt to Haifa. Sadly there was not entire unity at this time of great sorrow, and the transition from the leadership of 'Abdu'l-Bahá to the establishment of the Guardianship was troubled. In Haifa some Bahá'ís refused to accept Shoghi Effendi's appointment as Head of the Cause and to make matters worse some people who had always opposed 'Abdu'l-Bahá took the opportunity to stir up more trouble.

Louise must have felt the loss of the physical presence of 'Abdu'l-Bahá keenly, devoted as she was to Him and reliant on His advice. However, she was above all steadfast in the Covenant and could no doubt see that the Bahá'í Movement was moving into a new phase which required maturity and utmost unity from its followers. In addition she was in the unusual position of having actually met Shoghi Effendi when he was in his teens and she was on pilgrimage in Egypt and, like Louis, had been impressed by him. She had almost certainly met him again the following year in Naples when she arrived to join 'Abdu'l-Bahá on the *Cedric* to sail to America. Shoghi Effendi had suffered bitter disappointment when he was unable to accompany his Grandfather to America and the Bahá'ís of the north American continent were deprived of the opportunity of meeting the young man, but Louise had done so and this was a bounty for her and may have somewhat alleviated the pain of the Master's passing for her.

However, in America many of the believers felt confused and frustrated. They had received 'Abdu'l-Bahá's Tablets of the Divine Plan and had prepared themselves enthusiastically to carry out His wishes regarding teaching the Cause and opening new territories to the Faith. They had braced themselves to challenge racism by planning a major Convention for Amity between the White and Colored Races to be held in Springfield, Massachusetts that December. Now with the news of 'Abdu'l-Bahá's Ascension they struggled with their grief and confusion. Louise's husband Louis clearly saw the way ahead and, on a travel teaching trip at this time of crisis, was able to counsel and comfort the believers he met. Arriving in Denver, Colorado just a few days after the fateful news had been received, he did not hesitate to reorient the Bahá'ís there, as reported by the secretary of the Bahá'í Assembly of Denver:

> Mr Gregory reached Denver just two days after we received the staggering news of our Beloved's Ascension. All were cheered and comforted by this dear brother, through whom the heavenly confirmations seem to flow uninterruptedly. The believers tried, in their deep sorrow, to appreciate more fully Abdul Baha's Words concerning the time when He would no longer be with us upon this earth. The hearts are filled with greatest longing to 'rejoice His heart, satisfy His cravings, comply with His request and fulfill His anticipations',

and the arrival of Mr. Gregory provided a blessed opportunity for service, in which privilege all have served most beautifully.[7]

The Convention for Amity went ahead in Springfield as planned and over a thousand people attended.

A few months later Louis wrote a report for *Star of the West* of 'The Feast of Rizwan' at the Fourteenth Annual Bahá'í Convention, in which he quoted the encouraging and inspiring words of Mountfort Mills describing Mills' meeting with Shoghi Effendi in Haifa:

> The Master is not gone. His Spirit is present with greater intensity and power, freed from bodily limitations. We can take it into our own hearts and reflect it in greater degrees. In the center of this radiation stands this youth, Shoghi Effendi. The Spirit streams forth from this young man. He is indeed young in face, form and manner, yet his heart is the center of the world today. The character and spirit divine scintillate from him today. He alone can today save the world and make true civilization. So humble, meek, selfless is he that it is touching to see him. His letters are a marvel. It is the great wisdom of God in granting us the countenance of this great central point of guidance to meet difficult problems.[8]

In 1921 Louise and Louis had spent a restful summer together in Green Acre in Eliot, Maine. Founded in 1894 by Sarah Farmer, daughter of local philanthropists, as a summer centre for the comparative study of religions, Green Acre had evolved into a Bahá'í summer school after Sarah put the property at the disposal of the Bahá'ís following her pilgrimage to Akka in 1900. Visited by 'Abdu'l-Bahá in 1912, Green Acre became the focal centre for development of the Bahá'í community in north America and a place for spiritual refreshment that Louise and Louis relished and to which they would return many times over the years.

Having enjoyed his period of rest in Green Acre, Louis set off on a truly phenomenal teaching trip criss-crossing the map of the United States in his travels and accomplishing an astounding number of talks and meetings at every destination. This was one of the longest teaching tours of his whole life, encompassing visits to the west coast as well as to the more familiar southern states. The National Teaching Committee commented in 1922 that his had been 'one of the most brilliant Bahai Teaching Tours we have ever been privileged to have in this country'.[9] Louis constantly attributed his success to the power of 'Abdu'l-Bahá but nevertheless he had emerged as one of the country's foremost Bahá'í teachers.

Early in 1922 Shoghi Effendi had called a meeting of trusted Bahá'ís from around the world to Haifa to consult on the possibility of electing the Universal House of Justice. After extensive consultation it became clear that the supreme international body of the Bahá'ís could not be elected until a number of National Spiritual Assemblies had been formed in various countries. These Assemblies would then elect the Universal House of Justice. The task therefore was clear: the believers would first need to form sufficient Local Assemblies so that they could elect their National Assembly. At that time no National Assemblies existed anywhere in the world. The American representatives at Shoghi Effendi's meeting returned to the United States and to their National Convention that April inspired by the Guardian's desire for the formation of National Assemblies, and at their Convention it was decided that there would no longer be an Executive Board of Bahá'í Temple Unity but henceforth a National Assembly would be elected. Louis Gregory was elected to this Assembly but the voting process was not conducted in an impartial way and not according to the Bahá'í principles which forbade canvassing and electioneering. Although the body the Convention elected was known as the National Spiritual Assembly of the United States and Canada, it was not until 1925 that Shoghi Effendi declared the National Assembly to have been elected by correct principles.

Serving on the National Assembly did not prevent Louis from making teaching trips and he visited Virginia after National Convention and before the National Assembly meeting in New York in June. Louise, always constantly worried about her husband's health, must have been relieved that he gave up this exhausting schedule for a few months so that they could spend the summer and early autumn together in New England, including spending some time again in Green Acre.

During their months together Louise began also making her own travel plans in consultation with Louis. It was now ten years since she had last been in Europe and since she had seen any members of her family, although she kept in touch with them by exchanging letters.

In addition, it was now five years since her mother's death and by the terms of her mother's will the 12 houses owned by her mother were to be sold after five years and the proceeds to be divided between her 11 children. A visit to England would be timely as it would enable Louise to reconnect with some of her siblings and their children and to collect the much-needed financial bequests from her mother. If she stayed with friends and family while she was away she would only need to have enough money for the Atlantic crossing and for travel between the places she visited. It was probable that she had been able to save up enough for this from the money she had earned from her private tuition lessons.

In 1922 it was necessary to have a passport to travel overseas, so on 18 September Louise made her application for a United States passport. In it she described herself as the wife of a native and loyal citizen of the United States born in Charleston, South Carolina and now residing in Washington DC. Louise affirmed that she had lived in the United States from 1912 to 1922 and her permanent residence was also Washington. Her trip was planned to take her abroad temporarily but could last up to one year. Required to list the countries she would visit and her purpose in visiting them, she wrote that she would go to France to visit her brother and also Belgium, England, Luxembourg and Germany to visit friends. She wrote that she intended to leave as soon as her passport was received.

In her application Louise used the name Louisa, the name given her by her parents. Her personal description, a necessary part of the application, disclosed that she was now 56 years of age, five feet two inches in height, with high forehead, brown eyes, straight nose, round chin, brown hair, dark complexion and oval face. These physical details were corroborated by the small passport photograph which showed a serious and much skinnier Louise than had been apparent in her wedding photographs ten years earlier. The application was verified by the couple's close friend and fellow Bahá'í William H. Randall who confirmed that he had known Louis for ten years and knew Louise to be Louis's wife. All these details were sworn before the Deputy Clerk of the US District Court at Boston and the application was accompanied by a letter from Louis written from Eliot, Maine in which he declared his place and date of birth and the date of his marriage to Louise.

In October the Bahá'í National Teaching Committee *Bulletin* informed its readers that Louis 'is at present serving in and around Boston where he will remain until Mrs. Gregory sails for England later in the month'.[10]

Louise's passport was successfully received, her passage was booked and towards the end of October she set sail from New York for Liverpool on the *RMS Ausonia* of the Cunard Steamship Company, a new ship which had been launched the previous year. After a crossing of five days she docked in Liverpool on 30 October and headed for Leeds in Yorkshire, her first destination of the trip.

As Louise had always been close to her brother Ernest, the eldest of the Mathew siblings, it went without saying that she would spend some time with Ernest and his wife Gabrielle in their home at Les Aubiers in the Deux Sèvres *département* of western France. It must have been a joyful reunion because it was at least ten years since the brother and sister had met.

After some time with her brother Louise moved on to Belgium to stay with her college friend who had married a Belgian hotelier living in the town of Spa in the Belgian Ardennes. This town, known as 'the pearl of the Ardennes' and famous since Roman times for its cool healing waters, had given its name to spas throughout the world and its mineral waters were renowned, being 'sparkling, easily digested, cheering' and containing 'carbonate of iron, soda, lime, and magnesia'. It was claimed 'they act on the bile, liver, stomach, and are efficacious in hysteria, anaemia, female disorders, etc.'[11] Normally a place for relaxation and elegant tourism, during World War I Spa had become the main convalescent hospital centre for German troops and in 1918 it was the headquarters of Kaiser Wilhelm II until November when he abdicated before going into exile in the Netherlands There must have been hair-raising stories from Louise's friend and her husband about their experiences during the war and interesting anecdotes regarding the Spa Conference of 1920 two years earlier which concerned the disarmament of Germany and reparations demanded by the Treaty of Versailles. No doubt Louise took the opportunity to talk to her friend about the Bahá'í Movement and to share the teachings of Bahá'u'lláh.

Another spa town that Louise visited on this trip was Wiesbaden in Germany and she may well have also visited Stuttgart, a city that Louis had visited in 1911 after his pilgrimage and where there was now a thriving Bahá'í community. But it was not long before she gravitated once again to her beloved Luxembourg where she was able to reconnect with many friends and former pupils from the years that she had lived in the Grand Duchy. It was from Luxembourg whilst she was staying in the Place d'Armes, a square in the centre of the old town, that she wrote to Shoghi Effendi on 23 June. This letter was the first of what was to become a long and devoted correspondence with the Guardian of the Bahá'í Cause.

Although Louise's stated purpose for acquiring an American passport had been to visit family and friends, it seems likely that spreading the Bahá'í teachings in Europe would have been another of her aims, particularly bearing in mind the inspiration that 'Abdu'l-Bahá's Tablets of the Divine Plan gave to the American Bahá'í community. Louis had travelled extensively and taught the Cause in America and especially in the southern states following the unfolding of the Divine Plan. We know that Louise was prevented from accompanying him to the south because of their interracial marriage, but nothing could prevent her from travelling in Europe where her knowledge of French and German were of enormous use.

In her first letter to Shoghi Effendi she wrote that she had found some souls who were interested in the Bahá'í Movement and that she felt they would benefit from a visit from a Bahá'í teacher after she left and returned home to the United States. Her letter arrived in Haifa after Shoghi Effendi had left for rest and recuperation in Switzerland. The shock of his Grandfather's Ascension and the news that he had been appointed Guardian of the Bahá'í Cause in 'Abdu'l-Bahá's Will and Testament had taken their toll on the 24-year-old Shoghi Effendi. Added to this unexpected and unhoped-for news, the machinations of the enemies of the Cause had resulted in the young Guardian leaving Palestine for Europe in April 1922. In the words of Bahíyyíh Khánum, his great-aunt:

> the Guardian of the Cause of God, the chosen Branch, the Leader of the people of Bahá, Shoghi Effendi, under the weight of sorrows and boundless grief, has been forced to leave here for a while in order to rest and recuperate, and then return to the Holy Land to render his services and discharge his responsibilities.[12]

He appointed Bahíyyíh Khánum 'to administer, in consultation with the family of 'Abdu'l-Bahá, and a chosen Assembly, all Bahá'í affairs during his absence'.¹³ 'Azízu'lláh S. Bahádur was to deal with Shoghi Effendi's correspondence while he was away. In fact Shoghi Effendi felt it necessary to remain in Europe for eight months, returning to Haifa in December 1922. In the summer of 1923 he had again departed for Switzerland in search of rest and it was during this time that Louise's letter arrived in Haifa.

'Azízu'lláh Bahádur replied to Louise in July 1923 commenting that

> Dear Shoghi Effendi is highly pleased with the sacrificial efforts you are putting forth in the service of the Kingdom of God. He would very often speak of your exemplary devotion, sincerity and inexhastible [sic] energy. All the friends here admire your faith and that of your dear husband, Mr. Gregory. By self-elimination and absolute submission to the will of the Lord you both have won the crown of glory in this age, a glory which will shine more and more as time goes on.

He advised her:

> As to the group you have interested in the Cause of God and the need of the visit of some noble soul after you leave that country, I think it would be advisable for you to write a letter to the National Spiritual Assembly of the German friends to pay attention to the services you have rendered and to water the seeds you have sown. Then their N. S. Assembly may send Frau Schweizer or Mr. Herrigel who are two wonderfully devoted friends and efficient teachers to look after the souls you have interested and led to the Abhá Kingdom.

Louise must have been happy to receive this letter even though it did not come from the Guardian himself, and especially on learning that 'Here at the Holy Shrines of the Blessed Beauty, the Báb and the Beloved of our hearts, 'Abdu'l-Bahá we remember you and supplicate heavenly confirmation and blessing for you so that you may become more happy and successful day by day.'¹⁴ She had spontaneously taken it upon herself to teach the Cause in Luxembourg, the first to do so, and had gathered a small group of people interested in the message of Bahá'u'lláh who could now learn more by receiving further teachers from centres of the Cause in Europe. With a feeling of satisfaction she could soon leave Luxembourg and prepare for her return journey to the United States and her beloved husband.

She made her way back to England that summer and before she sailed to America she spent some time with Sister Grace Challis at her nursing home, Ferndown Lodge on the edge of the New Forest. Grace Challis had worked as a nurse at the Home Sanatorium in Southbourne near Bournemouth where the Bahá'í Dr John Esslemont was Chief Medical Officer. When she began work at the sanatorium she was a practising Quaker but when Dr Esslemont gave talks on the Bahá'í teachings in his study at the sanatorium Grace attended and soon became attracted to the new message. At the time Dr Esslemont was writing his book *Bahá'u'lláh and the New Era* which went on to be translated into many languages and is still in print and widely read today.

In 1923 the owner of the Home Sanatorium died and the sanatorium was closed. This meant, inevitably, that both Dr Esslemont and Nurse Challis found themselves without employment. Grace responded to the crisis of the closure of her place of work by deciding to open her own nursing home, Ferndown Lodge, at West Moors not far from Bournemouth. Dr Esslemont was invited to Haifa the following year by Shoghi Effendi to serve as his secretary and it was there in 1925 that, terminally ill with tuberculosis and finally the victim of a stroke, Dr Esslemont passed away.[15] On his death he was granted the station of Hand of the Cause of God by Shoghi Effendi in recognition of his outstanding contributions to the Bahá'í Cause.[16]

When Louise arrived at Ferndown Lodge in August 1923 it was very early days for Grace Challis's nursing home and it is possible that Louise was one of the first visitors there. The first few years of running her own nursing home were very difficult for Grace and she had money worries and empty rooms. In order to fill the home she offered places there to Bahá'ís at a reduced rate and the London and Bournemouth Bahá'ís were helpful in sending her patients. She held regular Sunday meetings of the Bournemouth Bahá'ís at her nursing home and before he left for Haifa Dr Esslemont was a frequent visitor and gave talks there. It seems likely that Louise might have met him there during her stay. Other Bahá'í speakers such as 'Mother' George and Isobel Slade came down from London to give talks there. In later years Bahá'ís from all over the world, such as Martha Root from America, Effie Baker from Haifa and Margaret Stevenson from New Zealand, visited Ferndown Lodge.

THE FIRST TRIP

Grace Challis was a charming woman, dedicated to her patients and to her Faith. She served on the Local Spiritual Assembly of Bournemouth and in 1924 was elected to the National Spiritual Assembly of the British Isles which had been formed the previous year. She served on the National Assembly in various capacities for many years. Grace and Louise would have had plenty to talk about concerning the growth of the Cause in America and in Europe, but these pleasant days in the English countryside came to an end eventually and Louise travelled the short distance to Southampton where she embarked for New York, arriving there on 25 August.

11

'SPIRITUAL GLADNESS'[1]

After her European trip Louise returned to their current home in Albion Street in Somerville, Massachusetts, a city two miles north west of Boston on the west bank of the Mystic River. Her ten months away had given her a new perspective on her possible role in achieving the goals of the Divine Plan. Delighted as she was to be reunited with her beloved husband, nevertheless she had glimpsed a field of service in Europe that offered new possibilities of spreading the Cause. She and Louis spent some time relaxing in the peace and quiet of Green Acre that summer, having plenty to talk about comparing their various experiences. Louis, as a member of the national elected body, had had to restrict his travel teaching trips somewhat because of needing to attend meetings most months, but even despite his new duties he had managed to visit the southern states, stopping at Atlanta, Nashville and Chattanooga.[2]

Louise spent the autumn and winter in Albion Street and during that time she wrote to Shoghi Effendi's secretary 'Azízu'lláh Bahádur, replying to his July letter sent on behalf of the Guardian. She probably was unsure whether Shoghi Effendi had returned from his trip to Switzerland and thought it best to write to Mr Bahádur regarding her future plans. However, not receiving any reply from him, she wrote on 13 December to Shoghi Effendi himself. This time she received a reply from Mr Bahádur on behalf of the Guardian with a note in Shoghi Effendi's own handwriting at its close.

From this letter Louise learnt that 'Shoghi Effendi was highly pleased with your idea of going on another teaching tour. He leaves you at your own liberty as to which course of travel you may find more convenient. In this of course you have to seek the pleasure and advice of Mr Gregory too.' How thrilled Louise must have been to receive this letter encouraging her to take another teaching trip and to learn that the Guardian was not just acquiescent in her plans but was 'highly pleased' with her idea.

Although she was left at liberty to choose where to go on her next trip, the letter went on to comment on her proposed itinerary:

> Going to Luxemburg [sic] and Hungary seems more useful to Shoghi Effendi for at Luxemburg you have already sown the seeds of the divine teachings in the hearts of people and when you go back there, you will water those seeds and help those interested in the Cause grow in their attachment to the Holy Cause. You may visit Hungary where living is relatively cheap and with the assistance of the Holy Spirit of the Master you may establish a center [sic] for the Cause.

Returning to Luxembourg seemed a natural choice because of the group of interested souls that she knew was there. She had suggested Hungary because it seemed a cheaper place to stay for a few months than northern Europe, and also no doubt an exciting country to visit for the first time, with the opportunity to experience its culture and meet its people. In addition, the knowledge that 'Abdu'l-Bahá had visited Budapest in 1913, had spoken there and had been warmly received must have been an additional incentive.

The letter repeated that consultation with Louis was necessary before she completed her travel plans and promised her the beloved Guardian's prayers at the Holy Shrine, sending her and Louis Shoghi Effendi's 'affectionate greeting together with the love of the members of the Holy Family'. In his handwritten note Shoghi Effendi assured her he would always remember her in his prayers and wished her 'good health, prosperity and spiritual gladness', signing himself 'Your brother Shoghi'.[3]

This encouraging letter acted as a confirmation to Louise that she was to take another travel teaching trip, this time specifically for that purpose and with the blessing of Shoghi Effendi. So she made her plans, after consulting with Louis, but was not able to set out until summer, sailing at the beginning of July 1924 on the *SS Winifredian* of the Leyland Line from Boston to Liverpool. She spent the whole of the summer in the north of England this time, stopping near Liverpool for the purpose of deepening a friend whom she had introduced to the Bahá'í teachings more than ten years before when she had only recently become a Bahá'í herself. This friend had met 'Abdu'l-Bahá and several Bahá'ís but had not taken the step of declaring herself a believer. Louise hoped that she could revive her friend's interest and encourage her to investigate further. If her friend and her family could become Bahá'ís they could establish a centre of believers in the Liverpool area. Unfortunately Louise reported that to her disappointment this had not yet happened.[4]

Moving on in September, she travelled again to Luxembourg, where she stayed for six months, finding accommodation once more in the centre of the old city in the Place d'Armes where she made herself at home, using her lodging place as a base for visiting old friends and seeking out souls who might be interested in the Bahá'í Cause. In February 1925 she was still there and wrote again to her friend Agnes Parsons enclosing an item of handiwork that she had created for her: a piece of batik, a design created on fabric by using wax and dye, representing the Bahá'í symbol the Greatest Name. Always a perfectionist, Louise was not entirely pleased with the result and wrote to Mrs Parsons: 'The one I did and enclose did not satisfy me as to the outer design and color and so I intended making another, but as I have not found opportunity through other work, I do not like to wait longer and so send the one I originally made for you.'[5]

This present to her friend was intended as a gift between co-religionists but also partly as a thank you gift because Mrs Parsons, as chairman of the Race Amity Committee, had changed the schedule of Race Amity Conventions and thereby released Louis from his Amity Convention duties for a while to go on a teaching trip. Originally Louise had been making plans to return to the United States in time for the spring Race Amity Convention, something that she was unwilling to do because she wished to travel to Hungary in the spring. She wrote: 'I do not know if my letter to you at all influenced you in your decision or if you had already decided to let Louis go, but I truly believe in either case that you acted under divine Guidance.' Her concern for Louis's health, as always, was of paramount importance. She continued: 'I fear Louis would have been ill if he could not have gone [travelling] and I am most grateful to you for making it possible . . . I am expecting now to return in June some time (possibly early in June) and perhaps attend the Amity Convention at Washington in the autumn staying for a few days.'[6]

Agnes Parsons had made her second pilgrimage to Haifa and Akka in 1920 and had returned with an almost overpowering responsibility conferred upon her by 'Abdu'l-Bahá. One evening while she was in the Holy Land taking supper with the Master He had unexpectedly addressed her, as she later wrote:

> Abdul Baha suddenly turned to me, quite out of the blue . . . and said: 'I want you to arrange a convention in Washington for amity [friendly relations] between the colored and the white.' I thought I would like to go through the floor, because I did not feel I could do it. He said: 'You must have people to help you.' I waited for more instructions and he said nothing more. I then made an appeal. I said 'Mr. and Mrs. So and So will also help me.' This man was in official life and I thought they could help me, at that moment. He said[:] 'He is interested in his own people, but she might help you.' Well, then a very extraordinary thing happened. I felt suddenly the power of his creative words . . . I was really getting the confidence that of course was necessary, and Abdul Baha said absolutely nothing more to me. I was hoping every day that I would have some more instructions, but he did not give it [sic] to me.[7]

Although Agnes Parsons was active in the Washington Bahá'í community, inspiring respect because of her elevated status in Washington social circles, nevertheless throughout her life she had only moved in those circles and had no experience of communication with the poorer or the black inhabitants of that city. We know that she had entertained 'Abdu'l-Bahá in her Washington home and also in her summer home in Dublin, New Hampshire and had introduced Him to people of importance but she had no experience of organizing a convention or indeed of reaching out to people of other social strata with the message of Bahá'u'lláh.

The year before Mrs Parsons' second pilgrimage had been a time of intense racial discord in the United States with hundreds of deaths and casualties. In the summer of 1919 race riots had broken out in major American cities including Washington and Chicago. Soldiers who had fought in World War I returned home to find they were unemployed and in addition there were rumours of Bolshevik propaganda following the Russian Revolution of 1917. The Ku Klux Klan expanded in many areas and vicious lynchings became common. These fierce and violent disturbances, foretold by 'Abdu'l-Bahá, had resulted in political solutions such as the Commission on Interracial Cooperation which tried to educate white people on the importance of improving race relations, while the National Association for the Advancement of Colored People and the Equal Rights League put the case strongly to the government for the human rights of the black population to be observed, but none of these efforts engaged the attention of those most suffering from the racial strife. 'Abdu'l-Bahá's plan, however, stressed not a political solution but the principles of racial equality and the unity of the human family.

Louise had become aware of the violent riots and found the news intensely distressing. At the time she wrote to Joseph Hannen about them: 'I heard only yesterday of the terrible riots. I remembered how 'Abdu'l-Bahá said there was danger of a race war but Bahá'ís could avert it . . . [Bahá'ís] would do well to consult colored believers at this crisis . . . Hope you will excuse suggestions from me but times are so serious . . .'[8]

Mrs Parsons began to implement 'Abdu'l-Bahá's instructions for a series of Race Amity Conventions, and the first Race Amity Convention was held in Washington from 19 to 21 May 1921 with some 2,000 people, both black and white, attending the first session. Martha Root handled the newspaper publicity for it and 'Abdu'l-Bahá sent a message to the convention via Mountfort Mills. The second Amity Convention, held just a week after the Ascension of 'Abdu'l-Bahá from 5–6 December 1921 in Springfield, Massachusetts, was a success despite the tragic news. After a gap of a couple of years the third Convention was held in New York in March 1924, with a fourth being held in Philadelphia in October of that year.

As it turned out, Louise need not have worried about Louis not being able to take his travelling tours because of the demands of the next Race Amity Convention. The convention planned for autumn 1925 did not take place after all. The Race Amity Convention movement seemed to lose its impetus for a while because of lack of enthusiasm for it in Washington and growing financial difficulties and there was not another Amity Convention until 1927.

There were, however, other troubles playing their part in the Gregorys' lives. When Louise departed for Europe a second time there were those who spread rumours that their marriage was in difficulties and that she was fleeing to Europe to escape. As she explained:

> Believing that I must return to America and be present at the Amity Convention with Louis to set at rest the reports which were going

around among the colored people, so Louis told me, that we had separated, I was planning to return in April. This report about our separation bothered him somewhat and he was even ready to think we had made a mistake in my coming as he is very desirous of convincing the colored people that the Bahai Movement makes all things possible even inter-racial marriages and he knows Abdul Baha had said there was a special purpose in our marriage and he did not wish them to think I had gone to Europe because I found conditions in America on account of my marriage unbearable which is what the colored people had been expecting ever since our marriage and now they seemed ready to say to each other <u>'I told you so.'</u>

I was on the point of giving up the work in Hungary originally suggested by me and approved of by Shoghi Effendi, when [Shoghi Effendi's] letter came which made my duty very clear . . . Louis' letter telling me both Conventions had been put off, one till the summer [National Convention] and the other (the Amity Convention) till the autumn, came just a day before Shoghi Effendi's letter and told me that now he did not expect to be back home until the summer as he hoped to continue his teaching tour until then. This left me free to do Shoghi Effendi's instructions to the best of my ability. It made me realize how little our human reasoning can guide us. In this case I had thought my going to Hungary impossible and also any future work in Europe . . . Shoghi Effendi's letter however would seem to indicate not only two or three months' work in those countries but future work as it could hardly be possible to accomplish what he desires in that short time. So if it is to be no doubt the way will open up.[9]

The letter from Shoghi Effendi that Louise was referring to was written on 12 January 1925 on behalf of the Guardian by Dr Esslemont, who was at that time acting as the Guardian's secretary. As Louise had met Dr Esslemont in England it must have been a pleasure for her to receive post from him from Haifa. He wrote: 'I am enjoying the life and work here very much and am feeling much better in health – better, in fact, than I have been for the last two or three years.' Tragically Dr Esslemont had only another ten months to live and his service in Haifa would sadly be cut short.

In his reply to Louise's letter to Shoghi Effendi of 9 November 1924 Dr Esslemont wrote that Shoghi Effendi is glad to hear that it has been made possible for you to go to Hungary, and hopes you will go there, but he thinks it better to leave you to arrange the dates as you think best . . . It will be very interesting if you can visit your friends in Wiesbaden, Nuremberg, Spa and Brussels on your way home from Budapest. We greatly hope that you will be successful in establishing a permanent centre in Luxembourg before you leave.

This written encouragement was augmented by the handwritten note that Shoghi Effendi added to the letter in which he addressed Louise as 'My indefatigable co-worker' and praised her 'constancy and firmness of purpose as well as [her] heroic efforts'. He advised her: 'be sure to raise the Call in those promising countries and sow the seeds of the Teachings in their virgin soil'. He concludes:

> I will never never forget you in my prayers. May the Almighty spirit of Bahá'u'lláh enable you to set aflame the whole of Central Europe. May He bestow upon you health and strength and crown your work with marvellous success!

Small wonder that Louise felt inspired by this letter to persevere in her travel plans and dedicated herself to do her utmost to fulfil the Guardian's wishes.[10]

Throughout the many years of her travels Louise was constantly yearning for Louis to join her in Europe. In contrast to the rumours of the break-up of their marriage and the myth that she had fled to Europe to effect a separation between them, the truth was that what she wanted above all else was for Louis to join her. She wrote in her letter to Mrs Parsons:

> I have always hoped that Louis could join me in Europe during his rest time so that I could stay longer when here and not have to take that (to me) very tiring sea journey because of the difficulty I have in sleeping on account of people staying up so late and making so much noise and then the decks being cleaned at 5 a.m. giving only three or four hours' sleep for me. Louis is not troubled by noise and enjoys the passage and it is a rest for him. He however has not so far seen it possible to come though I would willingly contribute my

return passage money towards his expenses. Possibly after Shoghi Effendi's letter if I come again he may see the possibility of joining me if not coming over with me.[11]

Louise's months in Luxembourg had not been easy and she was disappointed that she had not seen her teaching efforts there bear more fruit. She wrote to Mrs Parsons:

> A number of people here are sufficiently interested in the Teachings to read Dr Esslemont's book 'Bahá'u'lláh and the New Era' but so far I see no prospects of forming a centre here. It is almost an impossibility (as yet at least) for Catholics to entirely accept the Cause and declare themselves Bahais and hold meetings. At present one can only sow and water the seed. I find Catholics easier to teach than Protestants in the <u>beginning</u> but difficult to get beyond a certain point. Even if they were ready to accept the Manifestation (and in one case at least . . . the person seemed ready to admit the <u>possibility</u>) they do not seem to realize that they would owe allegiance to this Being if He <u>is</u> the Manifestation. The <u>authority</u> of their church is too deeply rooted in their being for them to turn to <u>another</u> for spiritual Guidance. Their idea would be I think even if this is true and He is another like Christ, we have Christ so that is sufficient. You can only teach them at all too on stressing the fact that we are not trying to take them away from their church.[12]

She went on to give details of her difficulties in spreading the teachings there:

> There is one family who are . . . interested. Also a girl (or woman of almost 30 who was a pupil of mine when she was 12) who has entirely left her church and does not believe in prayer etc. These if they can get the <u>Light</u> could perhaps become the first believers here, but so far I am afraid . . . Mlle. Bourg's interest is intellectual only and chiefly to please me because she is fond of me.[13]

She described Luxembourg as being in those days like a small country town where everybody knew everybody else's business, 'which makes it more difficult for any one to declare themselves a believer or to have a centre here'.¹⁴ She later explained that 'a certain amount of interest was created with some dozen families and the Literature I gave or lent read, but it was not found possible to start a study class even or group of any kind.'¹⁵

Louise was naturally disappointed that no Bahá'í centre or group of new believers was possible as a result of her extended visit and despite all her efforts. The achievement of this fulfilment of the Guardian's wishes was to be granted to others who came later with the same message, but Louise had sown the seed and eventually it would bear fruit. Meanwhile she had Shoghi Effendi's letter to inspire her and could glimpse the delightful prospect of travelling to attempt 'to set the whole of Central Europe aflame' and the possibility of further trips in years to come.

Travelling on towards Central Europe, she later reported: 'In April however when I went to Austria it was very different.'¹⁶ In Vienna she met Herr Wilhelm Herrigel, who was at that time a very active German Bahá'í although he later unfortunately became a breaker of the Bahá'í Covenant. He asked her to accompany him to the city of Graz in Austria where he was going to give a couple of lectures on the Bahá'í teachings.

Graz was a most attractive city, with its medieval architecture, its old town centre and majestic Schlossberg, a heavily wooded mountain dominating the city and criss-crossed by steep walking paths. Louise would have been able to take the funicular railway to the top of the mountain to view the whole city, the River Mur below and the surrounding hills. She will have enjoyed the city's mild Mediterranean-type climate, protected from cold winds by its location south east of the Alps. The capital of the Austrian province of Styria, Graz was a university city where they readily found listeners keen to learn about the new religion.

Herr Herrigel suggested that Louise could carry on his teaching work there with those interested after he left the city. So Louise willingly agreed to his plan and after just over a month her work there resulted in a study class meeting weekly in the city. She always referred to her activities spreading the Bahá'í message either by lecturing or by meeting with individuals as 'work' and considered it as a duty or responsibility she had been given and was more than happy to undertake. She later handed the study class in Graz over to Herr Pöllinger from Vienna whom she described as 'a very self-sacrificing Bahá'í' with 'the probability that before long some at least of the twenty or more people who were attracted may become believers'.¹⁷

'SPIRITUAL GLADNESS'

Louise had by now completely overcome her nervousness about giving lectures and admired Herr Herrigel's system of teaching:

> Herr Herrigel's plan of first giving an advertised lecture and then inviting those interested at the end of the lecture to another more informal talk the next day or soon after, seems to me excellent. His custom is at this second meeting to ask those present to write their names and addresses on a paper he passes round so that future meetings may be brought to their notice through p.c's [postcards], gives any one doing follow up work good opportunities to get in personal touch with those interested. It was chiefly owing to these addresses that I was able to work at Graz both individually and by holding meetings from time to time and finally in establishing a regular meeting for study.[18]

Evidently Louise was happy to work with other Bahá'í teachers, to take their advice and to carry out 'follow up work' started by others. She also worked with other like-minded organizations, establishing contact with peace leagues, for example, whose members were prepared to supply introductions for her to their sister organizations across borders. As she wrote:

> The Women's League for Peace and Freedom at Vienna, Graz and Budapest were most kind and helpful to me . . . At Vienna I stayed with the president of the Women's League, Frau von Wettstein . . . for five days. Herr Pöllinger had interested her and given her Dr. Esslemont's book, 'Bahá'u'lláh and the New Era' and he wished me to stay a few days with her.

Louise always had an eye for the future and was willing to make suggestions for possible expansion of the teaching work:

> Frau von Wettstein seemed to me almost a believer and I think will be a very active worker for the Cause at Vienna. She is also able to be of considerable assistance through her connection with the League in many parts of the world. She knows acquaintances of the president of Austria too. The Vienna group is very small and young with no one capable of giving public lectures. Frau von Wettstein

says she is not a speaker, nevertheless should she become a believer, her home might become the centre of Bahai activities which could attract people the present group are unable to reach as Frau von Wettstein is highly educated and has many acquaintances among College professors etc.

Eventually Louise arrived in Hungary in May 1925 and with the help of the Women's League for Peace and Freedom she made contact with interested people there:

At Budapest I had to work entirely through the League[,] the president, Frau Szirmai (Jewish) of which had met Abdul Baha and heard Him speak on His visit to Budapest in 1913. Frau Szirmai became greatly interested and read all the Literature she could during the time I was there. She wrote me recently that she intended to study the subject further.

It was fortunate that Louise had overcome her reluctance to speak in public because in Budapest she was given an opportunity to lecture, with impressive results:

Frau Szirmai persuaded me to give an advertised talk at their Club Room at which she would translate and would introduce me. Three reporters visited me[,] two before and one afterwards for interviews and at least one account of the talk was put into a Hungarian newspaper. Some 35 to 40 people were present at a short talk on the History of the Cause and the Principles with readings from the Words of Baha'u'llah and Abdul Baha and some interest was aroused especially in regard to social questions.

Once again she looked forward to future opportunities that might arise out of her Budapest experience:

Frau Szirmai has promised to do anything she can to help a Bahai teacher in the future if one will go there to lecture etc. It was not possible in the three weeks I was there to start a study class but a number of people were anxious to read the Literature and a family of the name of Szántó (husband Hungarian Jew, wife Irish) father,

'SPIRITUAL GLADNESS'

mother and two daughters became quite interested and Frau Szirmai suggests their home might become a centre of future work to form an assembly and that lectures could be held at the Club Rooms of the Women's League. She said an American or English person, or a Persian would be the most suitable to give lectures etc. She would so much like Shoghi Effendi to come and speak. She was very kind to me entertaining me more than once at her country home. Many people were leaving for their country homes before I left Budapest May 30.[19]

This was Louise's first meeting with the delightful Szántó family, whose friendship would become a source of great pleasure to her on further trips.[20]

Returning to northern Europe for her passage home, Louise visited Bahá'ís in Germany again:

I spent five days at the home of Herr and Frau Schweitzer in Zuffenhausen on my way to Antwerp to join my boat. They were kindness itself to me. I met some of the Stuttgart friends personally but was unable to attend a meeting there. I visited the friends at Esslingen on their meeting day and attended a very spiritual meeting there . . . On my way from there to Antwerp I stayed a night at Frankfurt and was able to give a little further teaching to the Manager . . . at the hotel where I had stayed before two years ago and to whom I had then given the Message.

In spite of her usual fragile health and having been diagnosed with a 'weak spine' Louise seems to have covered considerable ground on her visit to Germany:

The day of my arrival I went also to Wiesbaden to visit a lady there to whom I gave the Message two years ago and who had been very attracted. She became extremely interested and will I think try to interest her son. She wished for a lecturer to come to Wiesbaden and offered to do anything she could. She said it would be best to have some one to speak [who is] able to contact with highly educated people because their acquaintances are chiefly among University people.

Embarking on the *SS Zeeland* for New York, Louise did not stop her teaching activities just because she was on her way home:

> On June 17 I sailed from Antwerp by the Zeeland from which I am writing this letter [to Horace Holley]. I have been able to arouse more or less interest in about half a dozen people one of these Jewish and one German, one being an English lady on her way to Canada to marry a minister there, an Englishman of the United church recently formed . . . This lady was I think the most deeply interested of all and will try to interest her husband.

Louise did not abandon her new contacts in Central Europe now that she had interested them, but instead she was quick to suggest Baháʼí teachers who could follow up for her, adding: 'I forgot to say I have Miss Martha Root's address in Switzerland and will write to her to ask her if she can possibly go to Budapest and Vienna in the early autumn. She could do excellent work there I feel sure. Perhaps Mr. Remey could also go there as I hear he is on his way to Germany. I will write to him in your care as no doubt you know his forwarding address.'[21]

Horace Holley was secretary of the National Spiritual Assembly of the United States and Canada for 36 years and editor of the *Baháʼí News* newsletter which he initiated.[22] He was destined to be the recipient of many very detailed reports from Louise of her travels in Europe and would mention her successes in the newsletter from time to time. Having received her long letter about her activities on this trip from July 1924 to June 1925 he wrote in the newsletter:

> Mrs. Louise Gregory returned in time to attend the 1925 [National] Convention after extensive travel and Baháʼí work in Europe. Mrs. Gregory passed six months in Luxembourg sowing seeds which will appear manifest later on . . . The Women's League for Peace and Freedom at Vienna, Grez [sic] and Budapest gave Mrs. Gregory cordial cooperation and support . . . There is splendid opportunity for follow-up work in Buda Pest [sic]. En route to take ship at Antwerp Mrs. Gregory had the privilege of paying short visits among the friends at Stuttgart and Esslingen.[23]

Louise was also an enthusiastic correspondent in her letters to Shoghi

Effendi. Before she sailed from Antwerp she wrote twice to him, once on 2 May and again on 9 May. The Guardian's secretary, Soheil Afnan, replied to her that Shoghi Effendi had been very interested to receive her letters about her 'pioneer work in Austria' which was 'really worthy of the utmost praise'. He went on to express the hope that the centres she had begun in Graz and elsewhere would be consolidated and not break up after she left and also that 'the German brothers and sisters will be able to visit these places more often and thus keep up and nurture the interest of all those who have been spoken to about the Bahá'í Movement'. Shoghi Effendi himself added his own note to the letter, expressing his satisfaction and joy at her success. Undoubtedly Louise would have been thrilled to read this and also his news that her letters were 'shared by the friends and the holy household and extracts from them are translated and [included] in the 19 day letters which the Haifa Assembly sends to the East'. He concluded, 'We all pray for you, admire your superhuman efforts and unquenchable zeal and cherish great hopes in you and your splendid contribution to the spread of the Cause in the West.'[24]

Arriving home, Louise was reunited with Louis and, in view of the unfounded rumours that they had separated, it must have seemed imperative for them to be seen together during the summer in order to allay the untrue suggestions that their marriage had not been a success.

By August Louise had written again to Haifa and enclosed a letter she had received from the friends in Graz. The Guardian's secretary reported that this had given great joy to Shoghi Effendi 'to learn of your work in Budapest and other places in Central Europe'. Once again he stressed the need for either Louise or other friends to follow on her work, saying: 'Yours has been the glory of pioneer work[;] there now remains the work of a permanent teacher or at least one who can stay long enough to make of the many interested people thorough Bahá'ís and real servants of the Master.' He commented that in Graz Herr Pöllinger 'is unceasingly working and he has won the deep affection and appreciation of Shoghi Effendi', and added that they were so glad that she was safely home again and sent 'deepest love to your dear husband'. Shoghi Effendi's handwritten note urged her 'to keep in correspondence with the friends in those regions and to convey to them each and all my fondest love and the assurance of my fervent prayers', signing himself 'Your fellow-worker Shoghi.'[25]

12

FIRST VISIT TO THE BALKANS

As a prolific letter-writer, Louise kept in touch with the new friends and contacts she had made in Europe. She did her best to 'follow up' with these souls and to ensure that they did not feel abandoned. She was also very keen to have news of the developments in Central Europe feature in the *Bahá'í News Letter* and wrote to Horace Holley in January 1926, giving him details of progress there since she had left. She wrote:

> Shoghi Effendi was very happy at the report of work done at Vienna, Graz and Budapest especially that a little group had been formed at Graz . . . letters from Graz coming to me signed by 14 and 15 people at Feasts three times within about two months or so, the names of which are nearly all known to me and several known personally. They had also been holding meetings regularly once a week.

It seems that Louise was acting as the go-between, forwarding letters from the new believers in Austria to Haifa and transmitting the Guardian's greetings back to them. She wrote: 'Shoghi Effendi to whom I sent the first of these letters sent them a beautiful message through me.' Acting as an intermediary was a task that Louise was happy to perform. She had been asked by Shoghi Effendi to keep in touch with the various people she had introduced to the Bahá'í teachings and, if she could not be there herself, to find someone to go on with the work.

Sometimes there were specific requests from the new Bahá'ís. She wrote to Horace Holley: 'Herr Adolf Fontana of Graz asks that his greetings and those of the little group be given to all the friends in America. Perhaps you can convey this message in a News Letter.'[1]

Accordingly, an item appeared in the February 1926 *Bahá'í News Letter*:

Herr Adolph Fontana of Graz, Austria, sends to all the American believers a loving greeting in behalf of the newly formed Bahá'í group in that city. This message was sent through Mrs. Louise Gregory, by whose efforts the group was attracted to the Cause. A special letter has recently been sent to the group by the Guardian, also through Mrs. Gregory. Shoghi Effendi is desirous that Mrs. Gregory, or some other believer, shall continue the teaching work she established in Graz, Vienna and Budapest.[2]

She also eventually managed to make contact by letter with Martha Root who was at that time in Europe. As these two Bahá'í women had known each other from the time of 'Abdu'l-Bahá's visit to America they had probably strengthened their acquaintance whenever Martha visited Washington DC while the Gregorys were living there. Louise recognized Martha's devotion to the Cause and especially admired her ability to reach people of prominence wherever she travelled. Louise, on the other hand, was happier working with individuals of modest background and with small groups when necessary. From now on she was destined to be a willing helper to Martha, who was described by Shoghi Effendi as the 'peerless herald of the Cause', and of whom he said that '[g]enerations yet unborn will exult in the memory of one who has so energetically, so swiftly and beautifully paved the way for the universal recognition of the Faith of Bahá'u'lláh'.[3]

Martha Root had arisen to travel and to serve the Cause immediately after the receipt of the Tablets of the Divine Plan. In fact there was a story that at the end of the 1919 Bahá'í Convention of the Covenant in New York where 'Abdu'l-Bahá's Tablets of the Divine Plan were presented Martha, who had attended the Convention, could not be found. Eventually she was discovered upstairs packing her bag to leave on a travel teaching trip inspired by the call to spread the Faith, and shortly afterwards she sailed for South America.[4]

Once Louise had made contact with Martha there followed a period of fruitful collaboration between the two women which was to last for many years. Louise wrote to Horace Holley:

I am very happy that after many difficulties I was able at last to contact with Martha Root who is now working in these countries and who is making use of addresses I sent her. She is doing a lot of public work in these countries no doubt. The latest news I had was from Vienna where she was to give several public lectures and then go on to Graz (3 days) and to Budapest (a month I think).⁵

Later that year Louise received a letter from Martha in which she encouraged Louise in her endeavours, writing: 'It is glorious that you are going to Europe.' And she also had suggestions and advice for her: 'Would it not be better to sail to Trieste, go up to Graz for a few days, then visit the Friends in Vienna for ten days, and then go to Budapest and stay in Budapest for some little time to try to get an assembly started there?' Louise had suggested she might move on further south but Martha advised otherwise: 'It would be a wonderful thing if you could get an assembly started in Budapest.' The friends Louise had made there were eager to see her again, Martha wrote: 'You will find Mrs. Szirmai and Mrs. Szanto heart and soul with you. They love you very much, and the Szanto children are devoted to you. Mrs. Szirmai hopes that you will come.' There was a good chance that these ladies could help Louise: 'If you go to Budapest perhaps Mrs. Szanto and Mrs. Szirmai would help you decide about getting a room. I feel they will help you in every way possible.' In addition to these recommendations there were the wishes of the Guardian to take into consideration:

> I think Shoghi Effendi is very eager to have you continue the great work you began in Budapest. You did wonderful work in all those cities and were the first to go and water those seeds planted by Abdul Baha. It makes my heart so happy to hear that you will go again. I shall always think of you and love you and pray for you in your great task.

Martha was busy working for the Cause in Britain: 'I work in Great Britain until November 15, then I go back to the Continent to work in other countries where I have not yet been.' The chances of her tying up with Louise in Hungary seemed slim: 'It does not seem as if I can be in Budapest again, but if you are there and I should be anywhere near I would try to come down and work a week with you.'

Having served on the committee tasked with assisting Agnes Parsons to plan the first Race Amity Convention in 1921, Martha knew Louis well. So Louis was by no means forgotten in her letter: 'Please give my love to Louis. I never forget our happy times altogether, and I always feel he is one of the greatest disciples of this new day. Perhaps in the Other World we shall all be working together.'⁶

Louise wrote to Horace Holley at the beginning of October that year while she was in the throes of preparation for her next trip to Europe. She was clearly experiencing the same stress and panic familiar to most travellers in the days leading up to their departure: 'Please excuse a hasty note in pencil as I am hurrying to get the 9 a.m. bus for Portsmouth [New Hampshire].' Her 'hasty note' which filled several pages concerned her financial arrangements for the trip as well as her plans for her Bahá'í work in Europe. Horace had raised the matter of Louise's travel expenses with the National Assembly but Louise, as usual, preferred to fund her travelling herself: 'I want just to thank you for your kindness in speaking to the NSA about Europe and to say that I can manage my own expenses by staying at Budapest most of the time as Frau Szirmai thinks with their assistance in finding a room in a private house for me I can get room and board for $1 a day.' So Martha's advice that Frau Szirmai and Frau Szántó would help Louise find cheap accommodation in Budapest had proved correct.

Hungary and Austria figured largely in Louise's plans for her next trip but, as ever, money was limited and it seemed that it might be more economical for her to spread her travelling tour over two years this time. She had considered this, no doubt in consultation with Louis, and was still weighing up the pros and cons of the idea of a two-year trip when she wrote the letter to Horace: 'But I think the work which I proposed to spread over <u>two</u> years for financial reasons, visiting not only Austria and Hungary but Rumania [sic], Bulgaria etc. where Martha Root has already opened the way, <u>could</u> be done in one year (i.e. before June [1927]) but my means will not allow of that extra travel . . .'

The idea of travelling further south to Romania and Bulgaria was clearly attractive to Louise but she realized her expenses would be greater there, 'especially in countries unknown to me and where I have no friends to arrange inexpensive places for me to stay, and would have to stay for a part of the time at least till I could find less expensive quarters, at hotels.' It was a problem for her to balance her desire to spread the teachings further south with the fact that her finances were limited, but nevertheless she was formulating a plan: 'Probably by March I should have done all that is necessary in Austria and Hungary and could go to other countries from March till May if my means would permit. This was the reason I wished to stay two years because I could then afford to work in those other countries the second year.' The cost of returning to America and then crossing the Atlantic again the same year would however also be a drain on her expenses: 'I do not see that I could afford to go back to Europe the same year as I returned, nor would Louis probably like me to go so soon again.'

Louise had her own limited income from investments in England, but all the same it must have been reassuring to know that friends saw the importance of her work and were willing to help financially, as she described: 'A Bahai begged me to let her know if I was short of money on my return or at any time and let her help me so perhaps I had better let her do so. I told her I just could not ask her . . .', but there again, 'I will tell that Bahai that if she likes to make it possible [for me] to go to Sofia I can accept it for her share in the giving of the Message.'

She was reluctant to accept money from the National Spiritual Assembly unless it was absolutely essential: 'Should I find that my work is hindered by lack of say $50 or so I will let you know.' Martha had lately written to encourage Louise to try to go to Bulgaria and visit the capital Sofia so this was also on Louise's mind at the time: 'As I told you I can get back on my own means but I am troubled to think I must leave work undone that I could do with either more money or more time as Martha would like me to go she says to Sofia if I have money enough and time enough.' However, in the face of the twin problems of limited finances and wanting to extend the scope of her teaching work, Louise realized that in the end she would need to rely on her faith, saying: 'It may be therefore that the way will be opened for me to go to these countries' and 'I think Abdul Baha will manage this matter for me according to His promises so do not ask anything for me from the NSA which has so much need of the money for work in this country.'[7]

So with these issues still on her mind, and regardless of Martha's advice to begin her European journey this time in Trieste, Italy, Louise set off once more on her travels, sailing again on the *SS Winifredian* from Boston and arriving in Liverpool on 28 October. She spent some time again in the Liverpool area and visited York where there was at least one Bahá'í, a Mrs Kinnethy who had been given the Bahá'í message by Louise and Ethel Rosenberg.[8]

Travelling through Belgium, she stayed for a while in Brussels before heading south to Austria. Back in the delightful city of Graz once more she was able to reconnect with the enthusiastic and active Bahá'í group there, meeting again with the various friends she had made there on her previous visit. Vienna was her next destination where she had many friends to greet once more, including Frau von Wettstein and the other members of the Women's League for Peace and Freedom.

It would have been hard for her to leave Austria except that she had equally devoted friends awaiting her in Hungary, so in Budapest, as Martha had suggested, she was able to benefit from the help and advice of Frau Szirmai and the Szántó family, taking advantage of their assistance in finding cheap and respectable accommodation that she could use as a base for her teaching activities. She found Dr Esslemont's book *Bahá'u'lláh and the New Era* of great use once again and lent it Dr Joi of Debrecen, a city in the Northern Great Plain region of Hungary. He returned it to her by post with thanks for her 'kind, long letter', promising that he would 'try to study on' and hoping to keep in touch with her, realizing that she was a woman whose work for the Bahá'í Movement caused her to be frequently on the move, asking: 'If I feel the need to apply to you later on, how am I to address my letters?'9

Dr Joi wrote and spoke excellent English but on the whole English was not very widely spoken in eastern Europe at that time and the Hungarian language is unrelated to any other European language except Finnish and Estonian and therefore difficult for Louise to master quickly. However, it is likely that she found German readily understood in Hungary where the Habsburgs had ruled the country as part of the Austro-Hungarian Empire until the end of World War I.

With the arrival of the spring weather she moved on again, arriving for the first time in Sofia, Bulgaria. Here the language was not only Slavic but it was written in the Cyrillic alphabet which is similar to the Russian alphabet. Undaunted by this, Louise discovered that her knowledge of French and German was useful in communicating with educated people who spoke these languages there. Martha Root had travelled to Sofia in February of that year and had stayed there for 12 days, meeting university students and lecturing in Esperanto. Local newspapers had printed her articles and she had sent books to King Boris II and his sister.

As Louise had foreseen, it was not possible for her to find cheap accommodation in Sofia where, at the beginning, she knew no one who could help her, so she based herself at the Hotel Union Palace. Sofia is unusual in that it has no major rivers that one might expect from a capital city but it has abundant hot springs, enjoyed by locals and travellers since Roman times. The city lies on a flat plain but the mountains can be easily glimpsed from it, especially the mighty Mount Vitosha which seems just a stone's throw away. In fact the city is surrounded by mountains on all sides and three mountain passes lead to Sofia, making it a crossroads of the Balkans. The main route from western Europe to Istanbul passes through Sofia and as the city is located on the western extreme of Bulgaria close to the Serbian border it is near to other Balkan cites such as Belgrade and Bucharest and midway between the Black Sea and the Adriatic.

The Balkan Peninsula at that time was in a state of ferment, having suffered a series of bitter wars, and during much of the 20th century the borders of its constituent countries were disputed and changed frequently. The Balkan states had been dominated for centuries by the Ottoman Empire and the Austro-Hungarian Empire, and nationalistic movements to take back control in the Balkan countries had flourished during the 19th century. When the Balkan League was formed in 1912, Bulgaria, Serbia, Greece and Montenegro united to fight against the Ottoman Empire, declaring war in October 1912.

This war, known as the First Balkan War, resulted in victory for the countries of the Balkan League and defeat for the Ottoman Empire which had been weakened by the Young Turk revolution in 1908 and war with Italy in north Africa. The First Balkan War ended in May 1913 with the Treaty of London but the Balkan League states could not agree the partition of various territories. Bulgaria and Greece disputed possession of the city of Salonika, while Bulgaria and Serbia wrangled over Macedonia, and Bulgaria and Romania could not agree over the disputed region of north-east Bulgaria known as Dobrudzha on the Black Sea coast. Increasingly isolated, Bulgaria declared war on Greece and Serbia in June 1913 and the Ottoman Empire and Romania took advantage of the conflict and invaded Bulgaria. This Second Balkan War lasted little over 30 days and resulted in defeat for Bulgaria which suffered very high casualties. Ten months later World War I began and the Balkans were again in turmoil.

The situation in the Balkans, constituting a prelude to World War I, was foretold by 'Abdu'l-Bahá on numerous occasions. He was in the

United States when the First Balkan War broke out in October 1912 and whilst addressing a meeting in Sacramento, California He said: 'The European continent is like an arsenal, a storehouse of explosives ready for ignition, and one spark will set the whole of Europe aflame, particularly at this time when the Balkan question is before the world.'[10]

Whilst He was in Washington DC in November 1912 'Abdu'l-Bahá had given a talk at the Universalist Church when, in all probability, Louise and Louis would have been present. On that occasion He implored the audience:

> Consider what is taking place now in the Balkans, what blood is being shed. Even the wild beasts and ferocious animals do not commit such acts. The most ferocious wolf kills but one sheep a day, and even that for his food. But now in the Balkans one man destroys ten fellow beings. The commanders of armies glory in having killed ten thousand men, not for food, nay, rather, for military control, territorial greed, fame and possession of the dust of the earth. They kill for national aggrandizement, notwithstanding this terrestrial globe is but a dark world of grossest matter. It is a world of sorrow and grief, a world of disappointment and unhappiness, a world of death. For after all, the earth is but the everlasting graveyard, the vast, universal cemetery of all mankind. Yet men fight to possess this graveyard, waging war and battle, killing each other. What ignorance! How spacious the earth is with room in plenty for all! How thoughtful the providence which has so allotted that every man may derive his sustenance from it![11]

'Abdu'l-Bahá foretold that the situation in the Balkans would not improve for many years:

> The Balkans will remain restless, and its condition will aggravate. The vanquished will not keep still, but will seize every means to kindle anew the flame of war. Modern universal movements will do their utmost to carry out their purpose and intentions. The Movement of the Left will acquire great importance, and its influence will spread.[12]

As 'Abdu'l-Bahá had predicted, the Balkans remained unstable and the region suffered humiliation and poverty. When Louise arrived in Bulgaria in 1927 the Balkans were still feeling the effect of the wars. Louis later wrote about the suffering there: 'Louise says that in the Balkans it is not unusual to see people literally in rags,'[13] and the situation was still volatile. Louis also wrote to a friend concerning his wife's work there: 'That Balkan region is where the world war started & it is still a seething caldron [sic] of unrest. Hence the importance of the Great Message reaching it[s] varied peoples so full of racial & religious & national hatreds, all of which spell tragedy these days.'[14]

While she was on this European trip Louise, aware perhaps that she was travelling ever further south and in the general direction of the Holy Land, wrote to Shoghi Effendi in April requesting permission to make a pilgrimage to Haifa. At the end of the month she received a letter written on behalf of Shoghi Effendi by his secretary commenting on 'the many wonderful chances you have had for serving the Cause'. The hope was expressed 'that as a result of your trip to the Balkan states some centres will be established there, and the region definitely opened up to the Cause'. Miss Root had sown 'some wonderful seeds' but they would need 'continuous rearing and watering before some fruit can be obtained'.

Sadly it seemed that this would not be a good time of year for Louise to make a pilgrimage because in Haifa 'from now on the heat is at times unbearable. It is least advisable for the friends to come here after April. After this date it becomes hot and malaria greatly increases.' According to his secretary, Shoghi Effendi advised that she should put off her visit until another more appropriate time. The letter ended with hopes that when Louise returned home she would find Louis in the best of health. The members of the Master's family were all well 'and join in wishing you a safe and happy return home'. A handwritten message from Shoghi Effendi conveyed the wish that, if Louise had already booked her passage to Haifa she should continue with her pilgrimage and 'risk the unpleasant heat of the summers in Palestine'. However, it would be preferable 'to visit the Holy Land in March or April, the best months of the year and the season of our Bahá'í Festivals'.[15]

Louise had apparently not yet booked her journey to the Holy Land so, disappointed no doubt that this was not the time for her pilgrimage, but hopeful nevertheless that another opportunity would soon arise, she returned home. The question of whether to stay in Europe for two years on this trip or whether to return home after less than one year was evidently solved and Louise decided to go back to the United States in June 1927 to spend the summer with Louis at Green Acre. She returned to America this time from Boulogne-sur-Mer, having travelled north through France which offered the possibility of visiting her brother Ernest again in Les Aubiers.

She wrote to Horace Holley when she had completed this travelling tour, sending him a report of her extended trip. Horace wrote several paragraphs about her European tour which appeared in the August issue of *Bahá'í News Letter* under the heading 'Mrs. Louise Gregory Returns From Eastern Europe', declaring 'During the past eight months Mrs. Louise Gregory has served most effectively in the teaching field.' He listed the cities and countries that she had visited and continued: 'Mrs. Gregory, who is now at Green Acre, reports that conditions in Sophia [sic] are exceedingly favorable for the spread of the Message among people of capacity, and expresses the earnest hope that some American believer can in the near future arrange to spend from three to six months in that city.' Horace went on to praise the work of Louise and other American travelling teachers:

> Consideration of the significance of the work accomplished by such devoted followers of Bahá'u'lláh as Miss Martha Root, Mr. Mountfort Mills, Miss Leonora Holzapple [sic], Mrs. Gregory and Mrs. Schopflocher indicates how America is endeavoring to obey the far-reaching program of teaching activity laid down by 'Abdu'l-Bahá in His series of Teaching Tablets revealed for the five regional divisions and also the general assembly of the friends in this country.[16]

13

CZECHOSLOVAKIA TO BULGARIA AND BACK AGAIN

Louise and Louis were living in Eliot, Maine at this time in close proximity to Green Acre and they enjoyed the peace and serenity of the New England countryside during the summer of 1927, participating in the Bahá'í activities there. The first of a series of Race Amity Conferences to be held at Green Acre took place there in the summer of 1927 and as Louis was a member of the Race Amity Committee together with Agnes Parsons, Dr Zia Bagdadi, the poet and professor Dr Alain Locke and Pauline Hannen he was naturally involved in organizing and running the conference.

Louis was elected to the National Spiritual Assembly again in April at National Convention held this time in Montreal, Canada, and he continued to be elected to the national body each year for the next five years. 1927 was in his own words 'that memorable year for amity congresses'.[1] The first Race Amity Conference since 1924 took place in Washington in April of that year, with other conferences held in New York state and Portsmouth, New Hampshire, monthly amity meetings in Boston and a second Amity Conference in Washington in November. Louis was busy with administrative work for the Amity Committee throughout that year but also managed to travel, mainly in the northern states.

Although he was away and Louise was on her own for much of the time, she was not without friends nearby. The McKinney family had moved to Eliot and were company for her. Edna McKinney had acted as one of the stenographers for 'Abdu'l-Bahá's talks during His visit to America and had travelled with Him. Her mother, Annie, was an early Bahá'í and had taught the Faith to her sister, Mary Revell, mother of the Revell sisters who were Edna's first cousins. In December 1927 Edna, having been unwell since the move to Eliot, was taken into hospital and Louise invited Annie to stay with her during Edna's time in hospital.[2]

By January, however, Louise was planning her next trip to Europe. She wrote to Shoghi Effendi on 11 January suggesting she could go again to Sofia, as Martha had suggested. However, at this time Louis had become ill and the Guardian's secretary wrote back to Louise that she should not consider going away while Louis was 'in failing health'. He wrote that Louis's constant travelling 'must be a great strain on him, so that it is perhaps necessary that you should stay in America and help in his complete recovery'. Reassuringly, he wrote that Shoghi Effendi would never fail to pray for him 'that our precious Master may strengthen and aid him in the great task that He wanted him to undertake, and He will surely provide for such a dear, devoted servant as he is'. He went on to say it was necessary for Louis to attend to his health in order to keep up his travels. A handwritten note from Shoghi Effendi said he desired Louis to take into consideration the interests of his health and subordinate every other consideration. Shoghi Effendi would pray for Louis to be guided and recover entirely, adding 'I wish him to be happy contented and assured for I realize fully how precious an asset he is to our beloved Faith.' Although Louis's health and his teaching services were of the utmost importance, Louise's travels were not forgotten and the Guardian would pray 'most fervently that the way be opened to you to travel in Europe and resume your valuable work'.[3]

Both Louis and Louise took Shoghi Effendi's advice seriously and Louis was rested and recovered sufficiently for Louise to write again to the Guardian at the end of January with the good news that Louis was feeling much better. Towards the end of that month he travelled to Chicago where he spoke at Chicago's first Race Amity Conference and then in mid-February he was again in Montreal where he addressed a conference there. In a letter in late February the Guardian's secretary wrote that Shoghi Effendi was delighted to hear of Louis's improved health. He advised Louise to 'keep good care of him when he is with you so as to strengthen him physically for the great and useful task that he so well accomplishes. This is a service well rendered and greatly appreciated and surely he would want your help and loving care.'

Shoghi Effendi's secretary wrote that the Guardian was pleased to learn of her plans for Europe next autumn, going back to the Balkans 'to pick up the loose threads you have left in the Balkans and to keep up your work of seed-sowing there, all of which is very valuable and from which Shoghi Effendi expects great results'. He advised:

> You would naturally keep in touch with Martha Root so that perhaps you could visit some of the places she has also visited and there by meeting people she has met and interested, aside from those you have met already, draw them into the Cause and help them establish permanent centres. This he feels is very important because it means a point of reference for many . . . who have need of and are interested in the Cause.

Louise's desire for a second pilgrimage was not forgotten: 'Assuring you always of our Guardian's good wishes and prayers and the loving greetings of the entire family who would be delighted to meet you in Haifa.' In a handwritten note Shoghi Effendi sent his 'warmest assurance of my heartfelt appreciation of the continued and valiant services of dear Louis and yourself, and the expression of my best wishes and prayers for your happiness, good health and success, your well-wisher and true brother, Shoghi.'[4]

The Gregorys could now be viewed as a team, working for the Cause, with Louis spreading the Bahá'í teachings, travelling widely in North America and working to heal the rift between the black and white races while Louise endeavoured to introduce the Faith to eastern Europe. They both realized the importance of the other's work and never failed to encourage each other in their chosen field of service even though for much of the time they were working thousands of miles apart and on different continents.

With Louis well again and departing on his American travels, there seemed to be nothing to stop Louise from embarking on her second trip to eastern Europe and she made plans to travel before the autumn date that she had mentioned in her mid-February letter to the Guardian. She wrote to him again before the end of February telling him that Louis was now completely recovered. The Guardian's secretary wrote back expressing Shoghi Effendi's pleasure at the news: 'He was glad to know that you were well and happy and that your dear and precious husband was well enough to keep up his tireless work for the Cause. To his services, you know, has Shoghi Effendi always attached the greatest importance.'

As for Louise's work, that could also now go full-steam ahead: 'You must be very happy now that you are able to leave for Europe and resume your work in the Central countries [sic] where you had already some acquaintances.' Martha Root had led the way and Louise was advised to follow her:

> It is a splendid idea to be in touch with Martha as she can direct you and may be able to point [out] the more promising countries . . . The Guardian hopes very much that you will succeed in your efforts and that you will try to establish permanent Bahá'í centres in Prague and some other towns in Central Europe. Once a permanent centre is established they can then be fed and supported by other European and also American centres through correspondence and encouragement, which would be also forthcoming from the Guardian.

Once again Louise's desire for another pilgrimage was mentioned: 'The family all send you their greetings and trust that you will come to Haifa where you would be very welcome'⁵

By early spring Louise was back again in Europe. This time she sailed direct to Germany and went first to Dresden where she spent 11 days. There she found a small Bahá'í group of three souls and was able to encourage them and work with them, giving talks in German at three meetings they organized that were attended by 20 to 30 people each time. From Dresden she moved on to Prague to join Martha Root.

Arriving in Prague, Louise at first intended to assist Martha by carrying on her work there after she left, and

> Martha hoped we could start a study class but it afterwards seemed to us both that the people were not ready and that I could do more good now by going to Sofia[,] also Shoghi Effendi in a former letter received while at Prague spoke chiefly of the Balkans as my work. So Martha and I being perfectly agreed about the matter I came on here [to Sofia] after almost 2 weeks spent with her meeting people and attending two of her talks in Esperanto etc.

Both Martha and Louise had learnt Esperanto, the international language devised by Dr Zamenhof to enable peaceful communication between peoples. They found that many Esperantists in eastern Europe sympathized with the principles of the Bahá'í Cause and became interested in learning more about the teachings. Martha had met Dr Zamenhof's daughter Lydia Zamenhof in Geneva in 1925 and had stayed with the Zamenhof family in Warsaw the following year. She became fluent in Esperanto and attended many Esperantists' congresses and meetings, giving talks in this expressive and sonorous language.[6]

By the middle of April Louise was back in Sofia, Bulgaria, staying once again at the Hotel Union Palace. She wrote in great detail to Horace Holley about her success in forming a study group in Sofia. A Theosophist friend, Mrs Zlatarova, kindly put her flat at Louise's disposal and because she spoke English she helped with translating for the study class. She had helped Martha the first time Martha was in Sofia and always translated for her. As Louise wrote to Horace: 'We began the class last Sunday evening in an attic room with a ceiling so low I could almost touch it. I have thought of the Apostles of Christ who gathered in an upper room and am encouraged to hope that such a humble beginning may later have great results otherwise the world would despise such a centre of Bahá'í activity.'

Five people had attended the two meetings of the class the previous week and once again an interest in Esperanto spurred more than one participant on to join the group. She wrote that of the class members one was an Esperantist, two were Jewish men (the very helpful Dr Binder and his best friend, both 'very much in earnest' and intently reading Dr Esslemont's book in its German translation), a young girl who had previously been in contact with Louise and also with Martha and finally another Esperantist who had heard of the Bahá'í teachings from a Japanese Bahá'í Esperantist by correspondence and who was reading *La Nova Tago* (*The New Day*, a Bahá'í book in Esperanto). Louise hoped that this small group could become the centre that Shoghi Effendi had asked for in his last letter. Dr Binder was most enthusiastic about the Bahá'í message and had written to Shoghi Effendi himself. He was spending all his spare time either reading Bahá'í literature or helping her with classes and she described him as 'invaluable' and 'almost a believer'. She hoped to continue the classes twice a week as they all seemed to enjoy them very much. In this way she planned to work with the group for the rest of May and part of June and hoped that 'we have really got the centre started for which Shoghi Effendi in his last letter asked me to try to form'.

Another development in Sofia was the interest of a university

Louise's passport photo for her trip to Europe, 1922

National Convention at Green Acre 1925

1 Louise Gregory
2 May Maxwell
3 Stanwood Cobb
4 Miss Barbara Fitting
5 Marion Jack
6 Mrs L. Boyle
7 Rowshan Wilkinson
8 Dr Youness Khan
9 Elizabeth Greenleaf
10 Lorol Schopflocher
11 Doris Lohse
12 Dr Susan Moody
13 Mary Maxwell (later Rúḥíyyih Khánum)

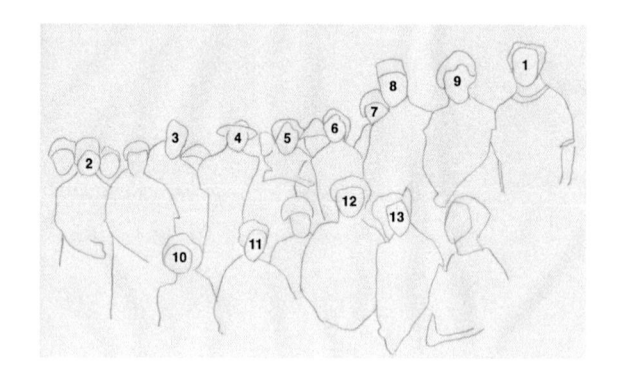

The Balkan Peninsula: A schematic map showing the countries of the Balkans

THE OVERLAND DESERT MAIL
THE DIRECT ROAD TO THE EAST

HAIFA—BEIRUT—DAMASCUS—BAGHDAD
by the
NAIRN TRANSPORT C°.
Pioneers of the Cross-Desert Motor Service
BEIRUT, SYRIA.

Chief Agents: THOS. COOK & SON, Ltd.
LONDON, BAGHDAD, AND BRANCHES

For List of Agents see page 15

Advertisement for the Overland Desert Mail from a Thomas Cook brochure. Louise travelled by this 'autobus' service to reach Haifa for her second pilgrimage in 1929 professor of Romance languages who had come to visit her. Martha had given Louise his address and so she had written to the professor. She intended to ask him to translate at her next public talk on Saturday. The previous day another university professor who was an acquaintance of Martha's had come to visit together with Dr Binder. He had promised to announce Saturday's public talk to his students and Louise would also try to advertise the talk in local newspapers.

Unexpectedly, there had been a major problem which was affecting attendance at lectures and which had caused the editor of one local newspaper ('a very nice man and speaks English') to hold back her article on the Bahá'í Faith until less troubled times. There had been a major earthquake which had been felt in Sofia and which had caused great destruction in Bulgaria's second city, Plovdiv. She wrote to Horace: 'It is difficult to get people to come to lectures etc. now they are in such a nervous condition from the earthquake shocks and can think of nothing else.' She believed that most of the city of Plovdiv had been destroyed. However, Louise appeared to have taken the effects of the earthquake in her stride, writing:

> I don't think there is any real danger from the earthquakes at Sofia which is built on rocky ground . . . Of course the shocks were rather alarming here when the whole room rocked like a boat. Even at Sofia to this day the Professor told us last evening, many people sleep in their clothes for fear an earthquake shock should come in the night and the night of the second shock which occurred at 9.30 pm April 18, half the population passed [the night] in the streets or in their gardens.

Louise, on the other hand, showed remarkable resilience: 'I went to bed at 11.30 pm and slept all night – on the 6th floor (the highest) of this hotel however, and knew nothing of another slight shock at 1 am.' And added hopefully: 'I am told this hotel is very solidly built.'

It would be impossible now for her to go to Plovdiv. Shoghi Effendi had mentioned in a letter that he wanted her to also go to Prague and other cities but she felt it would depend how firmly the Sofia group was grounded in the Cause and whether they could continue alone. Some more Bahá'í literature translated into Bulgarian would be most valuable but they could not afford to print and publish it locally. She wondered whether financial help might be forthcoming from the United States for a booklet in Bulgarian? In a note written as a postscript she asked Horace to give her love to his wife Doris.[7]

The Guardian's response to Louise's report on her activities in Sofia was very positive. His secretary wrote to her: 'He is greatly pleased and encouraged with the news of the possibility of establishing a Bahá'í centre at Sofia. That puts your work at once on a fruitful and permanent basis and renders all future activities whether on your part or that of any one else easier and more useful.' He continued that the Guardian 'prays that the small centre at Sofia may be firmly and soundly established, may grow daily in activity and in faith and may ultimately become a radiating centre of light and spiritual guidance throughout all the Balkan states.'

Shoghi Effendi himself added in a note to 'My dear and precious Bahá'í sister' that he was

> so glad and gratified to learn of the resumption of your valiant and strenuous labours in Europe. I feel you should concentrate for a time on the Balkans. Do not dissipate your energies along too many lines. Make a special effort to win entirely and unreservedly to the Cause a few whom you think are genuinely interested and spiritually receptive. What we need in these so newly-opened countries is a small nucleus of trusted, devoted and active believers upon whom we may rely to carry on the work of the Cause. I pray that you may be guided and strengthened to accomplish this most important task.

A separate letter was being sent to Dr Binder in reply to his letter to Shoghi Effendi.[8]

Upon receiving this letter from the Guardian Louise completely changed her plans. She had viewed this trip to Europe as brief but necessary and had planned to avoid the heat of a central European summer and return to spend summer in Eliot, Maine. She had actually booked her passage to sail back to America and had written to Horace Holley from Sofia that she was sailing for the United States on 31 May from Bremen.[9] But, as she later wrote, Shoghi Effendi's letter 'made me change my plans and stay on in Europe on the evening before I was to start for U.S.A. and had booked my passage.'[10] Shoghi Effendi's desire for the small group in Sofia to become firmly established and for Louise to concentrate her efforts on the Balkan countries dominated her desire to return home for the summer and her complete obedience to the Guardian's wishes proved stronger than her need for rest and home comforts.

Immediately upon receiving the Guardian's letter, Louise wrote to inform him that she would be changing her plans, cancelling her booking for the transatlantic crossing and staying on in Europe in the hope that she could continue working with the group in Sofia. However, she felt that the heat of the summer would be too intense for her if she stayed in Sofia and people there were still disturbed by the recent earth tremors and too troubled to come out to study classes. So she preferred to go temporarily to a mountainous area far away from the effects of the earthquake and where the temperature would be cooler. She had already visited Czechoslovakia when she worked with Martha in Prague and she decided to visit another part of that country.

She may have been influenced in her choice by the favourable descriptions in tourist brochures available at the time which stated that:

> Czechoslovakia is a progressive country, and improved facilities for travel and residence have done much in recent years to enhance its attractions for visitors. Railway communications between the chief centres are good; the trains are both comfortable and well organized; and visitors in search of new experiences and impressions will find endless interest in the varied grandeur of the scenery and the glamour of historical romance which still clings to the towns and villages . . . The health resorts of Czechoslovakia have a deserved reputation, both for their health-giving mineral springs and natural scenic beauties.[11]

Her choice for summer lodging was Trenčianske Teplice in the Carpathian mountains of Slovakia, a spa town nestling in the valley of the river Teplicka where the thermal springs had been enjoyed by visitors since the 14th century. She wrote to Louis from the Villa Viktoria, Trenčianske Teplice, in June worrying about his welfare back home in Eliot on his own and suggesting various family members or friends who could be invited to Eliot to stay in the lower part of the Gregorys' cottage and cook and look after him.[12]

The next letter that she received from the Guardian's secretary informed her that Shoghi Effendi had received 'a nice letter' from Louis letting him know that Louis was 'well and happy', so it seemed that Louise need not worry any longer about her husband's domestic arrangements in her absence. Shoghi Effendi was saddened that Louise had lost money by cancelling her ship's passage but nevertheless hoped that she would now be able to establish 'a flourishing and promising centre at Sofia'. He suggested that she should write to Martha and 'ask her for plans' and if Martha was able to join her she would be a great help 'and you will not feel so lonely'. His secretary intimated that the Guardian would soon be leaving for a well-deserved rest and Shoghi Effendi himself added a heart-rending note saying: 'I feel worn out as a result of my continuous and exacting labours and I feel the need for a prolonged rest. I will not cease however to pray for you and supplicate the Beloved's imperishable blessings upon your valuable work for our sacred Cause.'[13]

As a seasoned and enthusiastic traveller Louise would not have minded the long journey to the mountains of Slovakia and no doubt relished seeing new places en route. Once arrived in Trenčianske Teplice she found it suited her so well there that she spent all of June and July and most of August in the fresh country air. Naturally she did her best to give the Bahá'í message to those she met there but, as she later wrote to Horace Holley, 'I spent the summer, giving the message where, and to the extent, possible, but not finding many opportunities nor very favorable soil . . .'[14]

14

FROM CENTRAL EUROPE TO THE HOLY LAND

Towards the end of August Louise sent Louis a postcard featuring a picture of a Czech village wedding in the country that was then Czechoslovakia. She wrote that she had so far put off the journey to Vienna and thence back to Bulgaria because of the heat in those places but she was expecting to go in three days and arrive back in Sofia at the end of August. She would travel first to Vienna and knew of a boat that would leave Vienna on 26 August, sailing down the Danube, which would arrive in Ruse, Bulgaria on 30 August. Franz Pöllinger of Vienna, whom she had met three years previously, was happy she was coming, so presumably there would be opportunities for spreading the Bahá'í teachings there in Vienna. She had also heard from Mrs Zlatarova in Sofia who had found new accommodation for her there – a flat with a room for her that would no doubt be cheaper than staying in the Hotel Union Palace. She gave Louis a forwarding address for his letters to her care of the American Consul in Sofia and asked him to send her one or two Foye's linen handkerchiefs.[1]

After her pleasant few days in Vienna and the exciting novelty of sailing down the Danube to Ruse, Louise had a gruelling overland journey back to Sofia but was warmly received there by her friend Mrs Zlatarova and cosily installed in the new flat which she shared with her. Before long she wrote to Shoghi Effendi again in a letter which he received on his return from his summer rest in Switzerland. Louise was diligently carrying on her study classes in Sofia but it was uphill work. However, the Guardian's secretary wrote in his reply that 'Shoghi Effendi trusts that your noble endeavours will soon mature into rich fruits and you will succeed to accomplish the establishment of some permanent centre there'. The chance of a pilgrimage for Louise was again alluded to: 'Both he and the family are much pleased with the possibility of your visit to Haifa, which they hope will be made possible. They wish me to assure you of a hearty welcome.'

Louis, in the United States, was also not forgotten: 'The Guardian was also glad to learn that your dear husband was in good health and that he is extremely busy in his much-valued services. He has always the prayers and good wishes of the Guardian with him.' Louise herself was similarly remembered by the Guardian who wrote: 'My prayers will continue to be offered for you from the depths of my heart. Do not lose heart. The Supreme Concourse is watching over you and aiding you. You are not alone and helpless. Your loving brother Shoghi.'[2]

When Louise returned to Sofia at the end of August she found that her small study group had continued to meet without her once or twice a week until nearly the end of June when it became far too hot – the summer had been intensely hot in Sofia, she reported to Horace Holley – and she had started the class up again around the middle of September. But numbers attending the class had been disappointing with mostly only one or two people turning up, although the faithful Dr Binder was however 'a regular attendant'. She wrote to Horace in November: 'We hold the study class on two evenings a week, originally arranged so that it might be in English one evening and German the other, but now we find it better to adapt our language to the needs of those who come so chiefly we speak English and read English Literature often without much of translation.'

She had some 'hopeful news' concerning the arrival of a new member of the group, 'a master at the Gymnasium [High School] and a young man comparatively, probably not much over 30. His wife is also beginning to get interested.' Louise had put advertisements for English conversation lessons in the local papers – 'two papers three times each' – and this young man, Mr Nachev, had been the only person who responded 'and he is becoming deeply interested in the Cause, has translated Dr. Esslemont's pamphlet "What is the Baha'i Movement" into Bulgarian (of which I have had 2000 printed) and translated for me on this last Sat. at an advertised talk to which about 20 came, only very few of whom knew any English. I can only feel', she wrote, 'that he was sent by Bahá'u'lláh both for his own sake and to assist the teaching of the Cause here in Bulgaria.' She added that in future she would refuse to accept any money from him for his English lessons because of his help in translating.

There had, however, been difficulties: 'So far no one has come to the class through the talk. I fear I chose the day badly, it proved to be the Day of the Dead. As people stand at graves in the cemetery for 2 or 3 hours waiting for the priest at each grave, I don't suppose people were inclined to turn out again to a meeting in the evening.' Probably because of the unfortunate timing, the audience was not very responsive, except for the five friends already known to her, but 'one young man who had come back from a visit to Geneva and Paris . . . said he had met Martha at Geneva and attended talks and also seen Miss Edith Sanderson at Paris. He said he would try to come some time to our class but was very busy. I think he is a student'.

So although there had been disappointments, she was not inclined to give up hope:

> There are now four at least who are seriously interested and who are either coming regularly or studying at home in fact three are certainly reading at home and the fourth comes regularly again now but is elderly – certainly 65 I should think – and has much literary work to do so is unable to read Bahá'í Literature at home. He was 30 years a teacher in an American College at Samokov and now has the drawing up of the Sunday School lessons for the Protestant community so I think it quite wonderful that he is so interested though I feel doubtful if he can accept wholly because of his age and previous training.

Two of the first members of the group to have been attracted were Dr Binder and his friend Mr Schapira, 'both Jews and very good men, quite Bahá'í in spirit . . . (I gave Dr. Binder the Message and he gave It to Mr. Schapira)'. Dr Binder had read Dr Esslemont's *Bahá'u'lláh and the New Era* and Mírzá Abu'l-Faḍl's *Baha'i Proofs* and constantly used the *Hidden Words* in German. Unfortunately Dr Binder had already 'become a convert to Christianity through a Jewish Christian pastor' and 'he believes Bahá'u'lláh was a great prophet but that He could not be equal to Christ . . . He is however very sincere and a Bahá'í at heart and a worker and gives the Message whenever he can.' Mr Schapira 'is quite enthusiastic about the Message as far as he knows it, but business and family affairs have prevented him from frequent attendance or from much reading'.

Louise did not let her desire for a successful and continuing class blind her to the true motives and interests of some of those attending and wrote: 'A young girl of 22 comes sometimes and has read a fair amount of Literature but so far I think her interest is chiefly social and the pleasure of hearing English which she knows well.' Likewise Louise's helpful friend Mrs Zlatarova 'with whom I live and who used to translate for me is so absorbed in Theosophy I have no hope of her becoming a believer'.

Having reviewed the current members of the group in her letter, Louise continued:

> So you see there seems hope of the study class continuing after I leave and as Shoghi Effendi wishes me to spend all my time at Sofia and not try to work in other countries I am hoping by April when I must leave this country as my permission from the police expires then, that the centre may be firmly established and at least one or two become entire believers without reservations which Shoghi Effendi told me to concentrate on trying to work towards as far as possible.

In addition to the study class, Louise continued her series of public talks in Sofia and tried to give one public talk on the Bahá'í Cause a month. She was in contact with local newspapers and knew their editors: 'The editor of "*Mir*" (meaning Peace) who put in articles for Martha written by her and who put in one for me in the spring, kindly put in a resumé of my talk I gave him before the talk so it did reach a larger audience than 20.' Another newspaper had started up and seemed suitable:

> The editor of a new paper (quite small) and I think weekly called 'International Spirit' which was 'an organ for Esperantists, vegetarians, abstainers, quakers [sic] and similar liberal organisms [sic] and societies of this and foreign countries' by its title in Esperanto as well as Bulgarian though the subject matter is in Bulgarian, came to see me through Dr. Binder . . . and says he has put in an article on the Bahá'í Movement giving the principles and I think intends to reproduce 'Abdu'l-Bahá's photo Dr. Binder sent him.

Louise also followed up the possibility of attracting likeminded people to her classes through the local Esperanto society and wrote:

I attended the Esperanto meeting the leader of which I know well and she will some time give me the opportunity to read to them Martha's talk to the International Esperantist Conference of 1927. I intend to join their society and attend regularly both to get practice in Esperanto and to make contacts with them. Possibly I may arrange to have the use of their room (in a restaurant) which only costs them about $1.50 a month for weekly use.[3]

As usual Louise corresponded regularly with Haifa and received encouragement in her work from Shoghi Effendi. His secretary wrote to her in December that the Guardian had been glad to receive her news of the recent addition to her circle of Mr Nachev and his wife and hoped they 'may soon become the nucleus of an active . . . and enthusiastic Bahá'í centre in Bulgaria'. He added:

You should never be discouraged by such slow work, because we must realize that with all the demands of the teachings [on] any one who wishes to call himself a Bahá'í, you do not expect people to change their faith and follow the teachings in the twinkling of an eye. Your perseverance will surely have rich and lasting fruit.

He also added that he felt Louise would be interested to learn that Dr [Susan] Moody and Miss Sharp were in Haifa and 'will be soon leaving for Persia where they expect to work'. Shoghi Effendi himself wrote a note requesting Louise to send him a few copies of the Bahá'í booklet in Bulgarian 'and in any other language you may have'. He was sending her a copy of the *Bahá'í World* 'which I trust will be of help to you in your work'. Regarding her intended pilgrimage to Haifa, the Guardian wrote that he left the date and the route she should take entirely to her discretion, advising: 'Do whatever is most convenient and feasible.' Finally he assured her he would 'continue to pray most fervently for you, supplicating from the Beloved to guide every step you take, protect you, sustain you, and comfort you in your historic and valued labours.[4]

Louise stayed at her pioneering post throughout the winter of 1928 to 1929 despite many setbacks and severely cold weather. She wrote to Horace Holley in February: 'Things seemed for a long time at a standstill. Only Dr. Binder has come to the study class for the greater part of the winter and he always very late and often in a hurry to be gone to visit a patient or something.' There had been a lot of sickness in Sofia and this had been preventing her students from coming to the class: 'The few who are sincerely interested were kept away from illness themselves or in their families and other causes but now three come most weeks. It has been a dreadful winter here, so much intensely cold weather that it seemed useless to try to give public talks especially as there was so much illness in Sofia, epidemics of scarlatina and flu etc.'

But recently things had been looking up and she reported that

> the Saturday before last I gave a talk which was well advertised on the front page of "*Mir*" one of the best papers and an article of about a column or more written by the editor on late events in Persia and Turkey from information I gave him from copies of letters to the Bahá'ís of the West Shoghi Effendi sent me direct himself. The editor gave them as news of the Bahá'í Movement in Persia and Turkey after announcing the talk on 'The Awakening of the Orient and the Effect of the Union of East and West' and at the end advised those who felt interest about what he had written and wished further information to go to the talk. Some 15 or more came in spite of extreme cold, including a nice Bulgarian priest and a disputatious professor of the Theological College, as at the end he proved to be, and had a long talk afterwards with Mr. Natchev [sic] my interpreter who is very interested in the Teachings . . .

She felt that this talk had created much more interest than her previous one and several people had taken her address and said they would come to the class 'but so far no one has'.

Undaunted, Louise now had another plan – to read from the published talks of 'Abdu'l-Bahá: 'Now I am going to try to arrange to give readings and explanations that may be necessary each Saturday that remains of this month if I can get the room and Mr. Natchev to translate.' She added that there remained three more Saturdays in February and wrote that she was just going to see the editor of *Mir* 'to see if he will put in something for me again this week before Saturday and advertise the readings of talks given by 'Abdu'l-Bahá in Paris. This editor is such a nice elderly man and very friendly to the Cause. His paper "*Mir*" means "Peace" and gives very little politics and much about broad humanitarian questions I am told. I am hoping also to give a talk to the Esperantists by reading a talk which has been translated [into Esperanto].'⁵

Louise's plans for her pilgrimage were occupying much of her time and she was waiting for confirmation of her reservations – 'they are so slow here'. Her plan at this time was to leave Sofia at the beginning of March, travelling via Constanta on the coast of Romania, but this plan would change shortly when she discovered what seemed to her to be a more interesting route to the Holy Land.

Horace Holley wrote a paragraph about Louise's endeavours that appeared in the *Bahá'í News Letter* for April 1929 under the heading 'Study Class in Sofia' and went on to say:

> An interesting communication from Mrs. Louise Gregory brings details of her important teaching in Sofia, Bulgaria. The class she started last year has been resumed this fall and winter, with a few deeply attracted students of the Cause. Dr. Esslemont's pamphlet '*What is the Bahá'í Movement?*' has been translated into Bulgarian by one of these new friends, and an edition published by Mrs. Gregory. Through articles in newspapers, a series of monthly public talks and contact with the Esperantists, Mrs. Gregory is accomplishing the great task of founding the Cause in that country.⁶

Just a few days after writing her letter to Horace, Louise wrote to him again, this time on a postcard crammed with the exciting details of her revised travel plans. She wrote that she would stay in Sofia until 19 March because she wanted to work a little longer. She had arranged to give three more talks before she left and possibly a talk to the Esperantists. The latest news was that she had discovered she could travel overland to Haifa by the Simplon Orient Express as far as Tripoli (the port of Tripoli in northern Lebanon, not the Tripoli in Libya), 'except for 20 min. crossing the Bosphorus into Asia, and from Tripoli by autobus to Beirut and Haifa – 2 1/2 hrs. to Beirut and 3 hrs. later Beirut to Haifa . . . The connection with Tripoli and Haifa is twice a week and the Fabre Line boat only goes once a month.' The thrilling anticipation of this journey outweighed for her the moderate increase in cost: 'The expense of the overland route seems not to be much more than the Fabre Line boat to Haifa [from Constanta] and less than other boats or not more.'

This change of plan would give her longer in Sofia, necessitated by the extreme cold weather there which had delayed her work: 'By this change I can work here about 2 weeks longer and still stay about 2 weeks at Haifa. I did not know of this overland route possibility when I decided to leave by the March boat for Haifa and wrote you so.'[7]

The autobus route that Louise had chosen was styled the 'Overland Desert Mail: the Direct Road to the East', a service run by the Nairn Transport Company based in Haifa. It ran a fleet of specially built Cadillacs which travelled in pairs on ancient caravan routes, one car fitted with comfortable seats for passengers and another a van carrying the mail and the passengers' luggage. All the drivers were 'British ex-Service men with long experience of motor transport and of the East.' The service had been started in 1919 by the Nairn brothers as a mail and passenger motor service between Haifa and Beirut and was later extended to Tripoli in Lebanon with another longer service available from Beirut via Damascus across the desert to Baghdad. The company's brochure boasted: 'Never once have they been held up through mechanical inefficiency.' The drive from Beirut to Haifa took six hours and cost around £2. This pioneering cross-desert travel could not fail to appeal to Louise's spirit of adventure.[8]

She wrote to her husband Louis about her travel plans, which he lovingly endorsed. He wrote to her before she left for her pilgrimage:

> According to your latest advises [sic] tomorrow is the day selected for your start to Haifa . . . Bahá'u'lláh has revealed [a] very wonderful Tablet about the happiness of those who make the pilgrimage . . . And now you will have the joy of meeting the Guardian mingling with the Holy Family and the relations and also with those who have the station of martyrs through service. I hope that a great confirmation and true guidance will be yours . . . Hope you will realize your brightest dream and find eternal harmony through this effort.[9]

The overland trip to Haifa went smoothly and afforded Louise the chance to see and experience Turkey and Lebanon, new and exciting Middle Eastern countries for her. When she arrived in Haifa she found many changes since her previous visit 18 years before. Haifa itself had grown into a busy port with a much larger population and now boasted such modern amenities as a sewerage system, water supply and electricity.

From the German Colony at the foot of Mount Carmel nine terraces now rose in splendour up to the Shrine of the Báb. Louise did not leave any record of her pilgrimage but there are accounts of visits to Haifa and Akka by others in the same year as her visit. Isabel Rives, a Bahá'í from Washington DC and London, who was also on pilgrimage in early 1929, described the beauty of the terraces and surrounding gardens in her report for *Star of the West*:

> There are nine terraces with steps leading from one to the other. All the walks and paths are strikingly red; that is, they are evidently constructed of tiling reduced to a fine gravel consistency. Each path or walk is bordered with small red plants; inside that another border of taller plants with green leaves; while within this enclosure there is beautiful green grass – a rare thing in the Holy Land; and then again more of the tiny red and green plants arranged in designs reminding one of an exquisite Persian rug. There are also many palms and curious trees the names of which I do not know. Then there are pomegranate and orange trees, and a very distinctive group belonging to the cedar variety.[10]

For Louise it would have been especially poignant to visit the Shrine of the Báb where the mortal remains of 'Abdu'l-Bahá were now interred in the northern room. Electric lighting had been installed by Curtis Kelsey in 1919 and a particularly bright electric light shone out from above the door of the Shrine of the Báb. According to 'Abdu'l-Bahá's plan three more rooms were to be added to the Shrine to make it square in shape and in 1928 Shoghi Effendi had caused excavation of the rock behind the Shrine to be commenced with this extension in mind. The additional three rooms were completed during the course of 1929 so there may well have been signs of this building work being carried out during Louise's pilgrimage.

She stayed at the new Western Pilgrim House in Haparsim Street which had been completed three years before and was also lit by electric light. She would have been welcomed there by Effie Baker from Australia who served for 11 years in Haifa together with her colleague Fujita, a devoted Japanese Bahá'í.

The road to Akka was still by way of the beach and it is to be hoped that on this later pilgrimage Louise was able to visit the House of

'Abbúd and the prison. Isabel Rives wrote, 'It was a privilege, too, to be able to visit the place where Bahá'u'lláh was living at the time He wrote the '*Kitab-i-Aqdas*' (Book of Laws) [the House of 'Abbúd]; and to see the Garden of the Ridván where He spent much time.' At Bahjí the Mansion was finally rescued from the hands of the Covenant Breakers in 1929 but this did not happen until late in the year, so Louise would not have entered it, although like Isabel Rives she will have seen it in a serious state of disrepair. Isabel wrote, 'This house needs repairing very much, but I was told it is to be fully restored and preserved as far as possible.'[11]

Another visitor to Haifa and Akka in the spring of 1929 was Dr John Haynes Holmes, pastor of the Community Church in New York, who visited the Shrine of the Báb and the tomb of 'Abdu'l-Bahá and then

> In the afternoon, under the escort of a cousin of Shoghi Effendi, also grandson of 'Abdu'l-Bahá, we started for this ancient city [Akka]. Our way led us first along the hard, clean beach of sand which stretched across the roadstead . . . Fishermen were busy, as high winds and dark skies drove in the fish . . . At intervals among the fishers walked long caravans of camels, each patient beast contrasting strangely with the background of sea and sky. Far ahead loomed the ancient city, its ridge of close-packed houses surmounted by the huge bulk of the mighty citadel and a minaret so graceful as to suggest a dream of paradise.

Holmes also visited Bahjí:

> Another fifteen minutes, and we were in the Bahá'í garden where lay the remains of Bahá'u'lláh. Huge cypresses and palms were close about; the same red-tiled walks threaded their way through luxurious grass and flowers. A strange peace again dropped down upon us from the encompassing atmosphere of beauty. With eager reverence we once more removed our shoes, and stepped into the sacred presence of the Prophet's tomb . . . Here, appropriately, was not darkness, but light; not gloom, but glory. These Prophets' shrines are truly among the sacred spots of earth.[12]

Marvellous although it was for Louise to visit again the holy Shrines and the Riḍván Garden and to enjoy the beauty of the newly developed terraces, the highlight of her pilgrimage must surely have been meeting again with Shoghi Effendi. She had met him when he was a remarkable teenager but now she met him again as the Guardian, Head of the Bahá'í Faith. There are many descriptions of pilgrims' meetings with the Guardian and they frequently recount the emotion pilgrims experienced when greeted by the Head of the Faith, who welcomed each pilgrim separately and made them feel at the same time humble and loved and appreciated. The latest pilgrim to arrive in Haifa was always seated opposite Shoghi Effendi at the dinner table and received the bounty of his attention and warm conversation. Louise would no doubt have been the recipient of such a heartfelt welcome and would have listened spellbound to his discourse. In her first pilgrimage in 1911 Louise had been a very new Bahá'í, although already devoted and eager to serve the Faith. She arrived in Haifa this time a married woman, a deepened Bahá'í and an experienced travelling teacher.

Another joy for Louise on this visit was surely meeting again the women of the Holy Household. Bahíyyih Khánum, the Greatest Holy Leaf, was now 83 years old and very frail, although still as active as her age and health permitted. Munírih Khánum, widow of 'Abdu'l-Bahá, was almost the same age and it is recorded that the two women were close companions and intimate friends.[13] By 1929 all of Munírih Khánum's daughters were married and most had children. It is to be hoped that if Louise enjoyed the company of the younger women she had no suspicion of their Covenant-breaking that would later emerge.

At the close of her pilgrimage Louise was able to sail from Haifa by the Fabre Line boat *SS Asia* all the way to Providence, Rhode Island. The French Fabre Line ran a fleet of cruise ships which also transported emigrants to the New World and pilgrims to the Middle East. The *SS Asia* was part of their service of single-class ships designed to meet 'the wishes of patrons of limited means' and 'providing real comfort at greatly reduced rates'. There were 130 airy outside cabins and room for 1,350 third class passengers. It seems likely that Louise would have taken a cabin for such a long journey. The ship made its leisurely way through the Mediterranean and across the Atlantic en route to North America, allowing Louise the opportunity to see Lisbon, Madeira and the Azores as it called at these destinations. Such a protracted journey also permitted her to make friends on the trip and to offer them the message of Bahá'u'lláh and the chance for them to take Bahá'í literature.

She arrived in Providence on 13 May. Sadly, Louis was in Kansas City when she disembarked, still on his travelling tour. He had written to her apologizing for not being able to meet her, writing: 'sorry to be so far away when you are landing after so long an absence, also realizing that perhaps more than a month must pass before we can again greet each other in person'. Louise was heading for their cottage in Eliot and he wanted to warn her that she might not find everything as she liked it at their home: 'Since you will soon be on your way to Eliot I hope you will make the most of the situation there and not let it depress you.' He wrote about the problems they were having adding a bathroom to their cottage and difficulties with the water supply there. It seems the roads were inadequate for bringing the timber they required for the building and he suggested she might need to find other accommodation until he was able to come in a month's time.

In a more positive light he told her he was grateful for her letters from her pilgrimage telling of her meetings with Shoghi Effendi and added: 'May Maxwell and Mrs True have told me some marvellous things about Shoghi Effendi . . . I am anxious to hear more about your pilgrimage and am sure others will gladly hear you. Your prayers at the Sacred Shrines have greatly refreshed and helped me.'[14]

So Louise travelled up to Eliot from Rhode Island alone and it was not until June that they were reunited. Louis wrote happily to Edith Chapman later that month:

> And now with my dear wife . . . I am united once more after nearly a year of separation [in fact it was well over a year] and we are happy in our little nook in the heart of the woods. Green Acre activities proper will not start until next month, so that meantime we are getting some rest. The good wife seems greatly improved by her services abroad and especially by her visit to Akka and Haifa . . .[15]

15

'YOUR NAME WILL BE GRATEFULLY REMEMBERED...'[1]

Unusually, the Gregorys were now able to spend several months together, establishing a normal home life as a married couple in Portsmouth, New Hampshire. Louise now enjoyed cooking for her husband and they grew vegetables in their small garden. They made firm friends with neighbours, both black and white, and rejoiced in having guests visit them. Some time in 1929 or early 1930 Doris and Willard McKay came to visit. Years later Doris remembered their visit clearly, recounting how they had exclaimed: 'There he is!'

> Yes, there stood Louis Gregory waiting for our bus with a look of boyish eagerness. We walked briskly with him to a small house on a side street... When we stepped into the kitchen, Louise, small and dark and with a red scarf wound around her head, was bending over the stove and stirring the contents of an iron pot. 'I hope you like okra,' she said anxiously as we shook hands.
>
> The hospitality was southern. The stew, featuring the okra, was a blend of meat and vegetables. Time passed dreamily, while we floated on Louise's solicitude and Louis's gaiety...
>
> The neighbours, both White and Black, came and we sat in the neat little parlour which must have come furnished with the house. The intimacy we had known at dinner was extended now to the guests. We sat there, somewhere beyond our usual selves, secure in love.

Doris relates that 'Louis and his wife Louise had been married for eighteen years; yet, only occasionally had they lived together in a place they could call home.' She describes their meeting for the first time in the presence of 'Abdu'l-Bahá and how He had suggested their marriage.

> In spiritual attune, they did [marry], through devotion to Him. Soon they were to discover the bounties of intellectual compatibility and the growth of human affection. They were truly married on every plane. But, by agreement, they had, for months of each year, gone their separate ways: Louise to teach in Europe and Louis to promote racial unity in the United States. Here, in Portsmouth, New Hampshire, they were together for a time.

The conversation that evening turned to spiritual matters, prayer and tests. Louis showed his keen sense of humour which he used to illustrate a spiritual principle: ' "let me tell you that, in my youth, my greatest sin was pride," ' he announced.

> We were amused to hear this admission, for Louis was a most humble and self-effacing man. So humble was he that we all laughed heartily at the 'monster of self' that we imagined him to have slain. Louis laughed too, and mocked the situation by getting down on his knees and begging for help. He continued, in a more serious vein. 'We have to look at ourselves first and bring ourselves to account so that we will know when we are "standin' in need of prayer".'
>
> We slept that night in the Gregorys' house, deeply aware of the privilege that was ours.[2]

First-hand accounts such as this of the Gregorys' home life, their loving marriage and welcoming hospitality to neighbours and Bahá'í friends alike serve to emphasize the scale of the sacrifice they both made in so often leaving the home they had made together and setting out separately to teach about racial harmony and the oneness of God and humanity.

A couple of years later Louis would go travel teaching with Willard McKay in Alabama, Tennessee and Ohio, forming what was then the unusual partnership of a black man and a white man travelling together and propounding the same teachings of racial unity. *Bahá'í News* reported that they travelled

> by motor busses, eating together and most of the time sharing the same room, in their social relations thus running counter to all the traditions of their environment, yet without a single unpleasant

incident to mar the harmony and usefulness of their trip, at each stage of their journey feeling under divine guidance and protection.³

Now however, the few months of shared domesticity came to an end and the Gregorys soon went their separate ways again, Louis to the southern states and Louise to Europe. Despite the Great Depression which had struck in October 1929, Louise was able to find the money to head off for Europe again on another teaching tour. She and Louis had decided in the autumn of 1930 that she would go to Europe again that winter. Following the advice of the Guardian, she now considered the Balkans to be her main goal and intended to work in Romania and Bulgaria as these were the two countries mentioned by Shoghi Effendi as her priorities.⁴

As she sailed on the *SS Sinaia* of the Fabre Line from Providence in November 1930 she wrote on board to the Guardian and elaborated on her travel plans, mentioning that she would visit Bucharest in Romania and possibly Poland before heading for Sofia again. The *Sinaia* carried her on a leisurely journey via the Azores, Algiers and Istanbul before she disembarked at Constanta in Romania.

By January she was back in Sofia where she could continue her study classes with the group of interested friends, could pick up her contacts with the local newspaper and advertise her series of public talks. She carried on her teaching work despite the political unrest in Bulgaria which she had also experienced in Romania on this trip, making teaching the Faith publicly very difficult.⁵

The severity of the Bulgarian winter made living conditions hard once again and she struggled with the difficulty of encouraging people to come out to talks and classes which took place in cold, uncomfortable rooms. During the course of the winter she began to feel that she needed some support. Not surprisingly, her good friend Marion Jack came to mind. The two women had met in Paris back in the heady days of the early 20th century when Louise had first encountered the Bahá'í Movement, and Marion always claimed that she 'was a sort of nurse maid to [Louise] when she was struggling to get into the Cause years ago in Paris'.⁶ After Louise married and settled in the United States the two friends kept in touch and met from time to time. Marion (known as Jacky to her friends) had bought a cottage with a studio in Green Acre in 1923 and in 1925 was elected to the Local Spiritual Assembly of Eliot, Maine, so their paths would have undoubtedly crossed again in New England at that time.

In January 1931 Louise wrote to Marion inviting her to come to Bulgaria to help with her teaching efforts. She reminded Marion that the two of them had spread the Baha'i teachings in North America a few years before.[7] Shortly after this, in March 1931, Marion travelled to Haifa for pilgrimage, her second visit there and her first since Shoghi Effendi became Guardian. It seems that Shoghi Effendi also felt that Marion's presence in Bulgaria would be beneficial because towards the end of her pilgrimage he suggested this to her and she looked into the cost of a ticket from the Holy Land to Bulgaria.[8]

Marion's pilgrimage covered the period of Naw-Rúz, the Bahá'í New Year, which was celebrated on Mount Carmel attended by the Guardian and a large party of American visitors and pilgrims. Marion, a talented professional artist, took the opportunity to paint several scenes of Haifa and Akka while she was there. During her pilgrimage she was present when Shoghi Effendi spoke on the necessity for people of different races to mix in society and she later recorded that he

> spoke quite at length on the question of mixing with the Colored friends socially and even of intermarrying with them. He feels that we in America are not without prejudice and that we have carried on that inclination from our early days. He says we are very little different in our attitude from the non-Bahá'ís in our conduct towards that race. He says it is not enough to meet them formally, but we must go out of our way to have them in our homes. He said there was no difference whatever between the black & white race and we must realize that, but must if there is a choice give them the preference. He said that Green Acre was an excellent place to demonstrate this, that the Amity Conferences were good, but they were a little formal too . . . He spoke of the Gregorys' marriage and said that Abdul Baha [sic] must have had great wisdom in joining these two, and that it would have been an excellent thing if more people would follow suit . . .[9]

Shoghi Effendi clearly appreciated the significance of Louise and Louis's marriage and commented on it in his history of the Bahá'í Faith *God Passes By*: 'and, last but not least, the exemplary act He ['Abdu'l-Bahá] performed by uniting in wedlock two of His followers of different nationalities, one of the white, the other of the Negro race – these must rank among the outstanding functions associated with His visit to the community of the American believers . . .'[10]

Marion left Haifa towards the end of March together with some other pilgrims and stopped briefly in Cyprus for some sightseeing before sailing on through the Greek islands and into the Adriatic to Brindisi, Italy and north to Trieste where she disembarked and, after spending one night there, travelled south to Sofia. Unfortunately, what she did not know was that Louise's stay in Sofia had been abruptly interrupted and curtailed. As Louise wrote:

> On April 1 [1931] I was sent for by the American Legation & informed that the police said through my work on behalf of a religious movement [which] they considered non-Christian they object to it & this came through the Foreign Affairs who asked them to let me know that if I asked for an extension of my 3 months' permit to stay which expires April 7, it would not be granted.[11]

Louise wrote to Shoghi Effendi about her distress at having to leave Sofia just when Marion Jack was coming to join her. She identified three seekers whom she believed would carry on the Bahá'í activities without her, one of them being the young university student who was receptive to the teachings and who had been helping her to find other waiting souls among the student population. But on the whole she was pessimistic at this time about the possibility of doing future work in Bulgaria because of the unstable conditions there.[12]

So, with her permit expired and no chance of an extension, Louise left Sofia by train on 8 April going north and presumably crossing with Marion who was travelling south, although both of them were unaware of this irony at the time. Louise took her time to travel through Europe, stopping for a while in Geneva, Switzerland where she took the opportunity to visit her friends at the International Bahá'í Bureau. She wrote from Geneva of the arrangements she had made for Marion to be received by friends in Sofia. As she would be returning to the United States from England she looked forward to visiting her brothers and sisters there before returning home. Louis would be arriving back home in Portsmouth, New Hampshire from one of his trips in May so she felt happy that she would be back there in time to prepare the house and make it comfortable for his return. She finally sailed back to the United States on 24 April from Liverpool, arriving in Boston on 2 May on *SS Britannic*.[13]

Meanwhile Marion arrived in Sofia on 9 April, unaware that her friend Louise, the only person she knew in Bulgaria, was no longer there. She had had doubts about going to Bulgaria at all as she later confided:

> It was to aid Louise in her difficult task, that the Beloved Guardian afforded me the bounty of joining her in the spring of 1931. I regret to say that I was rather averse to such a move, at the time. The wonderful & awful language of Bulgaria seemed an insurmountable obstacle. The Guardian however, would not take no for an answer. He assured me of the receptive nature of the Bulgarian people, and said many kind things about that nation. Seeing that I looked doubtful, he said two or three times 'Just try it and see.'

She described the shock of her arrival:

> You may imagine my positive dismay, when I reached Sofia, a few weeks later, to find that Louise had been forced to leave and I seemed to be a lost Robinson Crusoe without his man Friday on a desert island. I really had serious thoughts about taking a ticket back, somewhere. Strange to say the fanatic landlady, who had been the cause of, we believe, Louise's departure, & who met me at the platform gave me the same advice as the beloved Shoghi Effendi; for she said, 'Just wait a few days & see how things go.' She came the next day at Louise's request, and took me to a noted Vegetarian Restaurant, where I met a charming German lady & her son. They have been my best friends from that day to this and both of them are now on our Spiritual Assembly.[14]

From this inauspicious start Marion was to go on and make Bulgaria her home for the rest of her life, bravely enduring many hardships and passing away there at the age of 88.

Louise had written to Shoghi Effendi and enquired whether she and Marion might work together the following winter. At that time she was doubtful of the possibility of teaching the Cause again in Bulgaria because of the difficulties there, so she envisaged that they might choose another European country. Her heart was still yearning to continue her work in Europe and she asked the Guardian if he would encourage her husband so that he 'might be willing for [her] to come again'.[15]

As it turned out, there was no problem in convincing Louis that she should make another trip and in October 1931 she did return to Bulgaria, but this time she went to the city of Varna, a resort on the Black Sea. She may have felt that the authorities would not welcome her back to Sofia and that it would be easier to obtain a permit to stay for a while in Varna. She later wrote:

> At Varna where I went in the late autumn of 1931 to meet Miss Jack I was able to teach two students [of] whom the first believer, a poor Armenian youth taught by Miss Jack through her smiles & Bahai literature in Bulgarian, [was] sent to me after Miss Jack left Varna. Later an elderly Armenian who translated some of the teachings into Armenian became a believer, unfortunately he died later . . .[16]

In January 1932 she received a letter from Shoghi Effendi's secretary with advice on her current trip. This letter was full of praise both for Marion Jack and for Louise's work of the previous year. The secretary reported that Marion 'has accomplished much success. Not only is there a group of strong and firm believers in Sofia but she has started another one in Turnova.' However, although Marion had worked hard and been assisted by 'the guiding hands of the Master', it was Louise who had sown the seeds of success, aided by a devoted German pioneer, George Adam Benke.

Marion had learnt to be prudent as a result of Louise's experiences. The Guardian's secretary wrote to Louise:

> The opposition you received made her be more careful and work her way quietly rather than attempt any propaganda of a public nature. The Balkans is a much disturbed country [sic], and being neighbours of the Bolshevists is in constant fear of communistic uprising. They are therefore suspicious of any new movement that seeks publicity or attempts to spread ideas contrary to those that already exist. This suspicion is rendered even more acute by the priesthood who still wield a great power over the mind and life of the public.

This situation in Bulgaria made any more public meetings out of the question: 'Any teacher who desires to serve the Cause there, should therefore, work in a quiet way and try to convert individuals in a private way rather than deliver public lectures and appeal to groups at large.' So it seems that Louise, although naturally a rather quiet and retiring person, had through her love for the Baháʼí teachings been too outgoing in contacting local newspapers and advertising public meetings. In a way she had been the victim of her own selfless devotion and enthusiasm. The resulting banishment must have been disappointing for her, as she had put so much effort into her teaching work, and putting herself in the limelight to become such a prominent teacher was not second nature to her.

However, any doubts that Louise may have had regarding whether she should have continued her work in Europe were quickly dispelled by this letter of January 1932, which continued:

> Shoghi Effendi fully endorses your going to Europe. He has no preference for any special country. You could choose the place that will suit you best, but he much prefers that it should be one of the central and Eastern states where the Cause has not yet reached. Central and Eastern Europe are much more receptive than any of the western countries. They have felt the evils of war and therefore are more receptive to spiritual matters.

Shoghi Effendi himself added his own note to the letter, encouraging her, writing that the seeds she had sown were fast germinating: 'Sofia is ablaze with holy fire! You should feel proud and elated with your magnificent work.' He advised her to retrace her steps to Europe and devote special attention to the central and south eastern parts of that continent, adding,

> I would leave the choice to yourself. May the Beloved guide and bless your glorious work for His Cause. Your name will be gratefully remembered by the rising generation of Baháʼí workers in Europe. Your true and grateful brother, Shoghi.[17]

Small wonder that Louise was encouraged by such words, and she was also inspired to investigate other countries in central and Eastern

Europe bearing in mind the Guardian's recommendation that she should choose the place that suited her best as long as it was a country where the Cause had not yet reached. She set off on her central European travels that spring and spent some time in Czechoslovakia. In May she sent a hasty postcard with a picture of Prague to Louis announcing that she was about to leave the city of Brno by catching a train to Budapest within the hour. She expected to arrive in Budapest shortly before midnight and assured him she would go straight to the Hotel Hungaria (5 minutes by taxi) and not stay near the station. The Hotel Hungaria was one of the best hotels, but cheap for her at the present rate of exchange especially if she took one of the rooms on the lowest floor. Unfortunately Budapest could be very noisy with so much music late at night and boisterous night life. However, her friend from previous visits, Mrs Szirmai, had invited her to dinner on the day after her arrival.[18]

Louise continued her exploratory tour of central Europe and by July she was in Salzburg, Austria, a city that delighted her so much that she returned to it time and time again and where she was happy to find at least one person receptive to the message. This person would later become a steadfast and devoted believer until her untimely death.

The hot summer weather of central Europe did not agree with Louise, who found it incapacitating and sought the coolness of the mountains and lakes of Germany and Austria. In August she wrote to Louis, sending him a postcard of Berchtesgaden and Lake Königsee. She reported that she was travelling with Franz Pöllinger of Vienna, meeting people and enjoying the beautiful lake.[19]

Although she was reconnecting with friends she had made in previous years and meeting new people, she was obviously missing her husband and wrote to him around this time encouraging him to join her in Europe so that they could travel together. Sadly it was not to be and Louis replied to her in February that he regretted he could not 'think seriously now or perhaps for some time to come, of a trip to Europe'. He wrote that he had received new instructions from Shoghi Effendi and added, 'You may recall that we discussed some of these possibilities before you left and you felt called away by duty.' Although they had been apart during the summer of 1932, however, they had the prospect of a summer spent together to look forward to: 'I appreciate you wish to come home and wish that we might be there together next summer; and it may be that things will turn out that way.' At this time Louis was in business with Australian Bahá'í Charles Wragg with whom he made an extensive teaching tour in 1933. He was finding it hard to make ends meet during the Great Depression and he wrote: 'We may even lose all [our] present possessions.'[20] Clearly it was hard for both of them, each one feeling that their duty lay in working for the Cause in different continents and with limited financial means. Louise had now been away from home for nearly a year and was pining for a spell of peaceful home life with Louis.

But by autumn 1932 she was back in Bulgaria and had settled once again in Varna on the Black Sea where the winter climate might suit her better and where she could assist Marion who was now based there. In Sofia the two stalwart Bahá'ís from Germany, Lina and George Adam Benke, were doing their utmost to spread the Bahá'í message, working mainly with Esperantists. George Benke had been born in Russia and he and his wife Lina had become Bahá'ís in Leipzig after hearing the Bahá'í message from Harlan and Grace Ober and Alma Knobloch. First in June 1931 and later in May 1932 the couple travelled to Sofia to spread the Bahá'í teachings and settled there as Bahá'í pioneers.

Marion wrote about the Benkes' contribution to the teaching work in Bulgaria:

> At last the dear Benkes have come and I feel all is well. Although Mr Benke was exhausted after forty-eight hours ride on hard seats in the third class carriage, he courageously faced the meeting the day of his arrival, and everyone listened breathlessly, while he spoke fervently, & reverently, first in German, which was translated in Bulgarian by Olga Srebova, then by the request of a new enquirer in Russian . . . I was thankful that our meeting was well attended the night the Benkes came, we were sixteen.'[21]

In the few months that they were in Bulgaria George Benke travelled to Stara Zagora, Varna and Plovdiv, all towns some distance from their base in Sofia and tragically, always frail in health, he passed away in November 1932 at his pioneering post in Sofia.[22] A telegram arrived in Varna announcing the news of his death and Marion was able to travel hurriedly to Sofia, arriving just after his funeral, but Louise was unable to travel, sick at that time with an inflamed throat. Shoghi Effendi bestowed upon George Benke the status of 'the first European martyr for the Faith'.

Louise remained in Varna where there was now a small group studying the Bahá'í teachings. She and Marion had avoided holding public meetings in Varna and had concentrated on forming new friendships with people they met in restaurants and hotel lounges, and this strategy was proving successful. Marion appreciated Louise's persistence and steadfastness and wrote of her pioneering efforts: 'Louise, a noble pioneer of great devotion . . .'[23]

By April Louise had begun to wonder whether she should spend another summer in Europe or whether she should return home to a cooler climate and the company of her husband Louis. She wrote to Shoghi Effendi towards the end of the month giving a report of her activities in Bulgaria and asking for advice. The Guardian's secretary replied with praise for her achievements and commented that Dr Howard Carpenter and his wife, Marzieh Gail Carpenter, were currently visiting Haifa and 'give a glowing report of what is being accomplished in Bulgaria and the other countries of Eastern Europe. Shoghi Effendi hopes that these seeds which these few American ladies are sowing so lovingly, will receive showers of divine blessings and gradually start to germinate.'[24]

The Guardian wrote to the American and Canadian Bahá'ís at this time:

> In the northernmost capitals of Europe, in most of its central states, throughout the Balkan Peninsula, along the shores of the African, the Asiatic and South American continents are to be found this day a small band of women pioneers who, single-handed and with scanty resources, are toiling for the advent of the Day 'Abdu'l-Bahá has foretold.[25]

It seems likely that Louise was included in this 'small band of women pioneers' so commended by Shoghi Effendi.

The Guardian's secretary conveyed to Louise Shoghi Effendi's concern for her health, writing: 'Shoghi Effendi wishes me especially to emphasise the importance of taking care of your health, for without that you will not be able to achieve much in these foreign countries and away from your home.' Shoghi Effendi himself added a note in the same vein with advice for her: 'If it is convenient and feasible, and Louis does not feel in the least inconvenienced and your own health permits, I advise you to stay in Europe, but spend the summer in a country where the heat is not oppressive and where you can continue your pioneer and highly meritorious services to the Cause.'[26]

Apparently Louise was not convinced that Louis would 'not feel in the least inconvenienced', or perhaps her longing to see him again and to be home for a summer spent in the cooler climate of New England won the day because shortly after receiving this letter she left Varna and set off for northern Europe on her way home. By May she was in Stuttgart, Germany from where she wrote to Louis that she was coming home – but would return to Europe in the autumn. Financial considerations were uppermost in her mind and she commented that it would be cheaper to live at home in summer. Varna was cheap but 'too hot in summer weather' and it was difficult to obtain good healthy food there in summer. In addition there would not be many chances for teaching in Varna in the summer and she would probably be able to tell more people about the Bahá'í teachings on the journey home. The delights of Salzburg had called her back and she had spent four days there before moving north to Germany. She added that she had recently met one lady there who was a receptive soul. She still had the journey from Stuttgart to Hamburg to endure and was not relishing the idea of travelling third class by train for 14 hours to get there. Her travel plans were now confirmed and her transatlantic ship would arrive in New York on the morning of 26 May. That being the case, she hoped that Louis might not leave for Chicago until the 28th or 29th of May.[27]

A few days later she wrote to Louis again. She had received a letter from her brother Vincent with good and bad news. The good news was that he had sent a large sum of money – £400. The sad news was that this was because Louise's younger sister, Edith, the photographer, had passed away. Each of the surviving siblings was to receive £400 from her will. Vincent, employed in the family firm, had sent the money to Louise suggesting it would be more useful for her to have the money than for him to invest it for her in England. He suggested moreover that she could use it against the debt that she and Louis owed on their house.

It is clear that Louise kept in constant touch with her siblings or Vincent would not have been able to forward the money to her while she was in Germany, but her relationship with her brothers and sisters was somewhat ambiguous. In her letter to Louis she reminded him that her investments in England already brought her a useful $50 a month. Using the extra money to pay off the debt on the house 'would appeal to them [her siblings] as very wise' but not a priority for a Baháʼí pioneer, it seems, and she added, 'So much for my family... They don't need to know our affairs – it is no business of theirs.'[28] And she suggested to Louis that they need only put £100 into the house mortgage. No doubt the rest would be spent on their pioneering activities and travel teaching. One wonders what her family thought of her marriage and lifestyle. Once she had embarked on her life as a Baháʼí she had presumably departed from any accepted norms that her siblings would recognize.

That summer Marion Jack travelled to Germany for the second Baháʼí summer school (known as Baháʼí Week) held in Esslingen in June. Meanwhile Louise was on her way home for a well-deserved rest. On 26 May she arrived back in New York on *SS Hamburg* of the Hamburg-American Line in time to snatch a couple of days with Louis before he left for Chicago.

16

A CHANGE OF PLAN

'Dear Roy, I am sailing from Boston for Europe on 13 Sept. & should be very grateful if I could have some copies of "The Goal of a New World Order" for distribution on the boat, train etc. & in the countries I stay.'

Having spent three months back in the United States during the summer of 1933, Louise was preparing for another extended trip to Europe when she wrote these words on a postcard to Roy Wilhelm, a devoted American Bahá'í. Her request for literature entirely filled one side of the postcard, written in haste a week before her departure. 'Also, the pamphlet on the Temple (the small one long & narrow) with the 2 pictures "As it will be" and "As it is now" with reproduction of the article from the Technology Review is most valuable for travelling & attracting people if I could have a few copies.' She apologized to Roy in case he was not responsible for sending literature: 'I do not know to whom I should apply for free literature for teaching purposes & the time is short so please pardon me for bothering you', and added a note, 'I regret to leave Louis but I believe he will be leaving to go to teach soon after I leave. He sends his greetings.'[1]

At this time there were very few of the Bahá'í writings translated into English, although Shoghi Effendi, assisted by various Bahá'ís, was working consistently at addressing this problem. Dr Esslemont's book *Bahá'u'lláh and the New Era* was already translated into languages such as German, Bulgarian and Hungarian and was being translated into Serbian. It was of supreme usefulness to travelling teachers like Louise but in addition she found that selected pamphlets and magazine articles were of interest to people she met and she wasted no opportunity in bringing the Bahá'í teachings to fellow passengers' attention, making friends with other passengers on ships and trains and offering them such literature.

A CHANGE OF PLAN

By October Louise was settled again in Varna, Bulgaria from where she wrote once more to Roy Wilhelm, sending him a cheque for three pounds twelve shillings and sixpence. She asked him to send a receipt for the equivalent of one pound two shillings and sixpence to Miss S. Fürth at the Hotel Elisabeth, Salzburg, while the remaining amount of two pounds and ten shillings was from Louise herself for the Chicago Temple Fund. Louise's address in Varna was 28 Boulevard Slivnitza and 'likely to be for a month or two or more'.

It turned out that Miss Steffi Fürth was the receptive soul that Louise had met in Salzburg in July 1932 and who was now 'a new believer since about a year ago or so that I had the happiness of giving the Message to the summer of last year and as far as we know the only believer at Salzburg as yet'. Louise was thrilled with her new friend and described her as 'a very firm and enthusiastic believer of very reliable character. She gave me 30 Austrian schillings for the Temple though very poor now (formerly rich) and obliged with her invalid mother to live on the charity of their relations.' Miss Fürth's donation was the result of a gift of 20 schillings from a friend or relative so that she could attend 'the famous Salzburg [August] Musical Festival concerts but she preferred to offer it to the Temple and add 10 [schillings] she made (part of money she earned by painting a miniature). She used to paint these often but now it is seldom she can get an order on account of financial conditions in Austria as elsewhere.' It seems that Miss Fürth was a victim of the Great Depression which had hit Europe in the 1930s and she now found herself in reduced circumstances. She was to be a firm supporter of the Bahá'í Cause despite her limited means.

Turning to her teaching activities in Varna, Louise reported that a small group of believers was now active there: 'I think we have now 4 believers at Varna, two have declared themselves believers for some time and I think the other two are also now convinced. They are all four anxious to spread the Cause anyway and giving the Message where possible.' She was hoping to start regular weekly meetings soon and went on to describe the members of the group: 'There are youths of 20, 21 and 28 years and the fourth an elderly man of near 70 I think but maybe younger only looking older because of suffering through the war from rheumatism.' It is interesting to note that Louise was now not far from the age of 70 herself, being 67 years old at this time.

She went on to give more details of the youths: 'Two are Commercial

College students and come to me very often to study the Teachings in French and German. The youth of 20 is an Armenian' (as was the elderly man). 'So I am very happy about them especially. They promise to do all they can with the other students this year.' Louise closed her letter by requesting that the *Bahá'í News Letter* should be sent to her current address in Varna and also a copy to Miss Fürth direct.[2]

With such good news to report, Louise had written to the Guardian on 22 October and received a reply written on his behalf by his secretary at the beginning of November. He reported that Shoghi Effendi was delighted to hear from her after such a long time. The Guardian had not received a letter from Louise since the spring and it seemed that he had missed her frequent reports of her teaching. In her October letter she had included a message to Shoghi Effendi from the new believers in Varna and the Guardian was happy that her efforts were bearing 'golden fruits' and encouraged her to persevere. He had received many reports of her visits to new Bahá'ís, including Miss Fürth in Salzburg, and they had been greatly stimulated by her visits which brought them 'into close harmony with the spirit as well as the outer organization of the Cause'.

Louise had informed the Guardian of her wish for Louis to come to Varna to be with her next spring or summer but Shoghi Effendi felt that Louis should remain in America and not 'dissipate his energies', because teaching in the United States was of vital importance. He would not object if she decided to return to America during the summer of 1934 'in case you feel that joining Mr Gregory is necessary' but he would prefer her to spend the summer in a 'cool region' or perhaps in Salzburg with Miss Fürth. Shoghi Effendi's handwritten note on the letter expressed his gladness that she was 'back to the field of your labours – a field wherein you have worked so splendidly and devotedly in recent years'.[3]

Shortly after receiving this letter Louise sent a postcard making maximum use of both sides of the card to Horace Holley, thanking him for sending her three parcels of books and filling him in with news of the teaching work in Bulgaria. She wrote that Martha Root and Jacky (Marion Jack) were in Sofia and she would send some of the books to them as English was understood more in Sofia: 'Several friends there know English while here [in Varna] very few and we mostly have to use French or German.' She added, 'The Temple pamphlet will be specially

useful with its pictures which give me an opportunity to say much.'
She reported that a student was lately 'bringing me nearly every day
a new student to talk to'. She was holding regular meetings with the
three youths mentioned in her letter to Roy Wilhelm plus two girls
who were 'very interested and reading diligently' so she hoped 'we may
before long get 9 declared believers between them all'. Louise would
also be grateful for the *Bahá'í News Letter*, which she would share 'with
the believers who are very enthusiastic youths and I see every few days
and in fact often almost every day'.[4]

Although Louise was glad to receive these parcels of books from
Horace she became alarmed when, soon afterwards, the flow of parcels
became a torrent. She wrote to Horace again a week later: 'Since I wrote
thanking you for 3 parcels that came through the P.O. [post office] a
fourth one came the next day through the P.O. Since then I received a
notice to go to the Customs for parcels and found 5 parcels of books.'
This deluge of parcels became problematic, as she described:

> The official opened one and enquired for what purpose these books
> were . . . I told the official I was connected with a peace movement
> in the USA that was trying to create friendship between our nations
> – it is much needed I said and the only way to prevent war. He
> agreed it was much needed so I hope he was satisfied.

But she must have been reminded of her permit difficulties in Sofia and
was anxious to avoid a similar situation in Varna. She continued:

> . . . the Cause is not known or understood in this country and we
> are not working officially or publicly and asked by our Guardian to
> act with caution at this stage till we know how it would be taken
> at head quarters so besides being much easier for us and causing no
> expense to us it is also wiser when sending to Europe to send only a
> small parcel [at a] time so please do not send any more until we ask
> again as I fear it may seem to require explanation and we are only
> working quietly and individually by [Shoghi Effendi's] request as
> yet – otherwise we might not be able to work at all.

Martha Root was in Sofia at that time and was using her diplomatic
skills to try to improve the situation regarding the official view of the

Bahá'í Cause, as Louise described: 'Martha is seeing important people at Sofia, maybe she will be able to put things on another basis soon.' The fact that the books were in English and therefore most likely incomprehensible to the Customs official seemed to work in Louise's favour, but 'I had not in mind more than one or two small parcels by Book Post when I asked for Lit. as here [in Varna] very few know English but I will send several of each to Jacky in Sofia by Book Post as many more know [English] there.' The pamphlets in English would not be wasted because 'I want to send some to England to my family and friends.'[5]

January 1934 brought an unexpected windfall when Louise's brothers Ralph and Percy credited twenty pounds twelve shillings and twopence to her bank in London. When she had received the £400 as a result of her sister Edith's will a small amount was left undivided among the surviving siblings and held in case of death duties. She wrote joyfully to Louis that this sum had now been released and reminded Louis that he had been anxious to make a payment on their house and now they could put the new amount towards the $100 for the house. However, she was also considering other uses for the money, such as using it to pay for translations of booklets and prayers in Bulgarian. Yet another possibility was that Louis might be short of funds and might need the money himself, so she added: 'Should however you be in need of this £20 now for yourself I can easily send it if you ask me to do so', adding the endearment 'my sweet boy', a term of affection she frequently used in her letters to Louis.[6]

Although everything seemed to be going swimmingly for Louise in Varna there were clouds on the horizon. At the beginning of February she wrote a letter to Louis which stretched to 16 pages and was written over a period of several days. She was clearly worried about Louis's health while he was travelling in the southern states and wrote that she considered the food in the south too starchy to be healthy. She thought that he would not be eating enough vegetables while travelling so she wrote giving him advice on making salads with good fresh ingredients.

However, a misunderstanding had arisen between the three fervent teachers of the Cause concerning the location of Louise's future Bahá'í work. Not surprisingly, since the three women were working in different parts of the Balkans and communication was so difficult in those days, there had been letters back and forth and crossing each other, and confusion had arisen. Louise wrote to her husband with some anguish:

'Martha is trying to get me to Belgrade and has written to Shoghi Effendi.' Somehow Louise had seen a letter from Shoghi Effendi to Marion Jack concerning herself and the possibility of moving to Belgrade in Yugoslavia, 'so a letter of his to Jacky informs me and suggesting March 1 for my visit'. She continued:

> I was quite astonished when I read what she [Martha] had written to Jacky making plans for me and writing [to Shoghi Effendi that] <u>I could go there</u> without consulting me even about going at all . . . I told her Sh. Eff. [Shoghi Effendi] wrote me to stay here as long as possible as if I left the interest would . . . die and my work be in ruin and I should follow his instructions until I received further orders.

The Guardian had been persuaded that Louise should follow up Martha's work in Belgrade and Louise was now anxiously awaiting a letter from him to explain the change of plan. Martha had suggested that she and Louise could work together in Belgrade for three weeks in March but Louise felt she could not leave Varna until April because her 'boys' Nicola and Ivan had exams at the beginning of March and she felt she should be there to offer support. Meanwhile there was a new believer in Varna, a boy named Jotü, and Mr Minersian, the Armenian, had given Dr Esslemont's book in Bulgarian to a very interested youth. She also commented on the sad news that her good friend Agnes Parsons had suffered an accident. Tragically she had been hit by a car in Washington and had passed away four days later.

To add to Louise's confusion, Marion Jack wanted Louise to go to Plovdiv, Bulgaria's second biggest city. This would involve a 13-hour journey by train which would be very expensive so that it seemed the $100 for reducing their mortgage would be eaten away. Louise commented that Martha would travel third class with a wooden board for a seat on such a journey, but she (Louise) would prefer to take a second class sleeper. In the course of writing the long letter to Louis she remembered that she knew a French teacher in Turnova who was interested in the Faith, so perhaps she should go there. By now she was thoroughly confused about where she should go and what she should do and was only waiting for a letter with instructions from Shoghi Effendi.[7]

The anxiously awaited letter duly arrived from the Guardian and Louise fell in with his instructions immediately. By means of a postcard she wrote to Louis briefly that Shoghi Effendi approved the suggestion and she was going to Belgrade, Yugoslavia.[8]

Her last letter to Louis from Varna was written at the beginning of March and she wrote that she was going to Belgrade that Friday because Shoghi Effendi wanted her there. She felt that there was not much more to do in Varna where people seemed more interested in her French lessons than in learning about the Bahá'í Cause. However, although Louise had become fully reconciled to changing her base of activities from Varna to Belgrade, there had still been worries and anxieties. Martha's energy and resilience were legendary. Louise wrote to Louis that she had felt 'working with Martha 2 or 3 weeks [in Belgrade] would give me nervous prostration and I felt I could not go. Finally after I candidly told Martha she was too strenuous for me to work with[,] Martha promises to leave me quite free to come to her only when I feel like it and to expect me to rest for the first 2 days.' Louise, always fragile in health, wrote that she had explained to Martha that 'when I was tired I had pains in my head'.

Martha had willingly accepted that Louise would need to rest and nurse her delicate health and so their difficulties had been resolved in the best spirit of friendship and mutual appreciation. Louise wrote: 'Really Martha has been most sweet about it. Jacky and I agree she is a saint but we also agree she is too strenuous for the comfort of either [of us].' Although now happy with her change of plan, Louise was still unsure whether she would return to the United States during the autumn or winter but she closed her letter to her husband with the greatest affection: 'So good night - my sweet boy. Take care of yourself and with lots of hugs and kisses. Ever your loving wife Louise.[9]

A month later she wrote to Horace Holley updating him on her new location and the progress of her work in Belgrade. She had arrived in Belgrade on 14 March

> at Martha's desire and with Shoghi Effendi's approval to try to carry on the work she (Martha) had begun here where up till lately nothing had been done except one or two talks given by Martha in the University a few years ago and a little said by Martha to members of the royal family when Martha visited Queen Marie at her daughter's home here.[10]

Martha had arranged for some translations to be made into Serbian 'by a very clever, sweet and spiritual woman'. This was Mrs Draga Ilić, who 'has become a believer though she is so ill that I fear she may not be with us more than a year or two at most'. These turned out to be prophetic words because although Draga Ilić served the Cause faithfully for the rest of her life, not least through her achievement of translating *Bahá'u'lláh and the New Era* and the *Hidden Words* into Serbian, sadly her life had not many years left to run.

Louise also recorded that a very clever university professor 'also declares himself a believer . . . through translating a tiny pamphlet into Serbian'. But during the three weeks that she had been in Belgrade it had been difficult to know whether the people she had met would be seriously interested, 'especially as out of that three weeks or so it has been impossible to see people for the last 10 days or rather over 2 weeks on account of what I call the Easter obsession in these countries there being two Holy Weeks and two Easters, Catholic first and a week later then Orthodox (Greek) Church, the latter being the official and most important and of which we are now in the midst as today is their Good Friday.' Martha had done her best to introduce Louise to people in Belgrade and 'had just time before she left for Athens on 25 March to introduce me to a number of people, a few separately and the rest at a tea Mrs. Draga Ilitch (the Serbian new Bahá'í) and Martha gave so that I might meet them, before the Easter preparations began and I am still waiting for these festivities to finish before being able to take advantage of those introductions.'

In Belgrade Louise was living with Mrs Kossikowsky and her husband, a Russian general. The lady was the daughter of a famous Russian general,

> yet now they are living in a small 2 room apt. [apartment] on the ground floor of one room and a kitchen and have given up their one bed sitting room to me and are living for a few months altogether in their kitchen to save money as Madame has lost her position at the American Consulate on account of the reduction of the staff. The general was wounded and is more or less a nervous wreck, but his wife has courage enough for two and is very clever. I hope she will become a believer. She is helping me to find people to teach.[11]

Louise had been delighted to receive visitors from America passing through Belgrade and reported that 'We had the great and unexpected pleasure of a day's visit from our Bahá'í friends from Portland, Oregon, Mr and Mrs Bishop [Charles and Helen Bishop] on their way to Geneva from Haifa two days ago.' The couple had been on pilgrimage and were now heading for Geneva where they would serve at the International Bahá'í Bureau. Louise wrote that they 'spent two nights here and I saw a good deal of them during the day they stayed and also we went to see Mrs Draga Ilitch . . . and stayed there to tea and spent 3 hours with her and her sister . . .'[12]

A few years later Helen Bishop would record for volume VI of *The Bahá'í World*:

> Mrs. Louise Gregory has been working in Belgrade courageously; and, at this writing, her return is immediate. Before her departure at the end of April in 1935, new Bahá'ís were declared; and a study class of six Russian students was formed.
>
> Madame Draga Ilić became a Bahá'í when she translated *Bahá'u'lláh and the New Era* into Serbian. A manuscript translation of *Some Answered Questions* into Croatian was made at the Bureau in Geneva, and sent to Belgrade for circulation. The outlook is more than hopeful: Mrs. Gregory finds the Jugoslavs to be '. . . the most responsive I have found in any of the countries of Europe.'[13]

It had been a wrench for Louise to leave Varna after her months there but she had been persuaded that she could be of better service in Belgrade and she wrote as much to Horace Holley:

> I was sorry to have to leave the few believers of Varna alone but it seemed important to come [here] as so little has been done previously in this country and Yugoslavia is a large and important centre which is liable to be a great danger spot for the peace of Europe.[14]

The college students back in Varna had promised to continue studying the Bahá'í literature she left with them and possibly do some translation, 'but so far I have only received one p.c. [postcard] from them so do not know how far they are keeping their promise'. The students were all studying in Varna and lived elsewhere but 'one of the two who live at Burges [Burgas] is very active when home in teaching the Faith to his family and friends so maybe if the two who live at Varna do nothing and lose interest, the interest will be transferred to Burges which I am told is a much better field for work of this kind.'

Meanwhile poor Miss Fürth in Salzburg had still not received any copies of the *Bahá'í News Letter* despite Louise's request, so she renewed her entreaties on her friend's behalf:

> Miss S. Fürth of Elisabeth Hotel, Salzburg who . . . is sending a miniature of Abdu'l Baha she has painted to be sold for the Temple, was promised in the letter enclosing her receipt, the News Letter every month. She has however not received any copies I believe . . . Would you be so kind as to enquire into this and see she has it. She is the only Bahá'í in Salzburg though she tries very very hard to teach others and having an invalid mother she is unable to go even to Vienna even if she had the money to do so to see other Bahá'ís.

Louise herself had also barely seen a copy of *Bahá'í News Letter*, as she explained: 'I also would appreciate it if I could have it sent as I only see it now and then if some Bahá'í happens to think of it and send me one.' Marion Jack, staying in the Union Palace Hotel in Sofia, was also in need of the *Bahá'í News Letter*:

> She has been now 3 years there at great self sacrifice but her name was somehow missed from the list some time ago put in the News Letter of those Bahá'ís living in Europe to teach. She often has over 20 persons in her hotel room for a meeting and as we have to work quietly in Bulgaria it is only in a hotel that she can receive all these people. Miss Jack's devotion and self sacrifice with those people to whom she is a real mother are really wonderful.[15]

Louise's affection and admiration for her friend Marion are apparent and Marion returned these sentiments in equal measure to her friend, writing:

> See how you inspired me! If you had not come to Europe, maybe I never should either. I read with awe of Martha's achievements in meeting this & that great one, & in doing all sorts of stunts. I used to wish I had her capacity of journalism & so on, but it was <u>your</u>

<u>firm determination to stick to your work in a modest way</u> which carried the day with me, so I thank God for my dear Louise.[16]

In addition, many years later Marion credited her friend Louise with the ground-breaking work of opening Bulgaria to the Faith with the words: 'It was through her [Louise Gregory] that I came here and she is the Mother of Bulgaria. She and sweet Martha – twin mothers – a new species.'[17]

Louise's plans for summer 1934 had now taken shape and Salzburg was to be her summer location. 'Shoghi Effendi has asked me not to go back to America this summer as he is very anxious about the work in Europe', but it seemed that Louis would not be coming to join her as she had hoped. He was no longer a full-time travelling teacher but, as the Guardian had written to her:

> neither does he wish Louis to come to me for the summer (even if he could afford to do so which he cannot) as he says his work in America is too valuable and too much needed for him to leave. So evidently I shall be obliged to stay here at least another year much as Louis and I long to be together. Shoghi Effendi has suggested I go to Salzburg this summer and cheer Miss Fürth by my company when too warm here.[18]

By late April Louise had established herself in Belgrade as a language teacher, giving private lessons. She wrote to Louis that in response to her advertisement she now had five lessons a week arranged and had given her first conversation lesson to a local doctor. There seemed to be a great demand for lessons and she was now making sufficient money for her expenses.[19]

The professor who had become a Bahá'í visited Louise and brought various dignitaries one Sunday morning and stayed for two hours, and she described a new acquaintance, a Councillor, who visited with his wife as 'a fine man'. She reported in her last letter to Louis before leaving for cooler climes that they had had 'a lovely time'. They were very interested in the Faith and would come to meet Martha Root the following Wednesday when she arrived in Belgrade from Sofia on her way to Vienna.

Louise's travel plans for the summer were now confirmed and on

Friday she would move to a larger house in the mountains near the Austrian border. She assured Louis that it would be very cheap. Then after a week or two she would go to Salzburg to be with Miss Fürth until the end of July when she would travel to Esslingen for the German Bahá'í summer school, as Shoghi Effendi had requested. Meanwhile she wrote to Louis that she was glad he would have company in their house in Portsmouth, New Hampshire, over the summer with someone cooking his meals for him (although later there was a change of plan and he lived alone that summer, a cause of worry to her) and she ended her postcard sadly by expressing how sorry she was not to be able to join him.[20]

17

A SUMMER IN SALZBURG

July 1934 found Louise cosily ensconced in the Hotel Elisabeth in Salzburg. From here she wrote to Louis in a long letter addressing him as 'My precious darling' and describing her peaceful life in the small hotel. The mornings were spent lazily: she described how the hotel's waitress brought her hot milk and a Brötchen (a bread roll) at 7.45. Louise would make Kaffee Haag on a little stove and take her breakfast in bed using her own sugar, honey, butter and some fruit. Later she would have lunch in the Garden Restaurant and take supper in her room, occasionally ordering soup to be brought up from the hotel's kitchen. She realized she had written to him only a week before but she wanted to cheer up 'my poor boy' alone in the house without any electric light and 'your little wife' not there 'to see to things'. She regretted there was 'No one to prepare your food and kiss you good morning and cuddle you etc. etc.' As usual she was worrying about Louis's diet and whether he was eating properly for his health and recommended he should eat cheese sometimes with 'plenty of cabbage salad and tomatoes', adding 'I hate for you to have no one to look after you my darling.' As it was summer time and there was a small garden at their house in Portsmouth she suggested he should grow fresh vegetables for himself, giving him some gardening tips and recommending he grow dwarf string beans (not the climbing kind).[1]

Her worries about Louis's health predominated in the many letters she wrote home to him that summer and she wrote that she hoped he was resting and not getting sick. She was so reluctant to leave him on his own during the summer that twice she had nearly booked her passage home instead of coming to Salzburg. She described how she had been very tempted to go home, look after him and live 'on my money', but his next letter said that he was only needing rest after his travels. She was longing to hear news about the North American Convention that

Louis had attended and glad to get a copy of his letter he had received from Shoghi Effendi which spoke of the Guardian's appreciation for Louis's sacrifices including having no wife for the summer. In New England Louis was 'low on funds' but Louise wrote that possibly her decision to stay abroad was the cheaper option, cheaper than paying for her passage to America and back to Europe.

After going to Esslingen in Germany for the Bahá'í summer school she hoped to go straight back to Yugoslavia – possibly to a cheap place near the border with Jacky. Salzburg would be too dear during August because of the music festival. However, it might be difficult to persuade Marion Jack to move because 'Though so sweet and smiling Jacky has a decided will of her own and until she chooses one cannot get her to move unless a "marching order" as she calls it from Sh. Eff. [Shoghi Effendi] comes.'[2]

In one of her many letters to Louis that summer she expressed her worries about his health and finished with a comical verse to cheer him up, styling herself as 'Dr Gregory':

> So goodbye and much love
> as well as a hug
> good wishes,
> and kisses,
> be a good boy,
> you have no one to annoy,
> take care of yourself
> as well as your health,
> eat food that you need
> or you'll soon run to seed
> and your doctor you'll need
> to look after your feed
> then what will become of the Cause?
> for I'll quickly take rail
> and to America sail
> if my boy cannot look after himself
> but pines and loses his health!
>
> Ever your loving wife
> Louise (Advice from Dr Gregory)[3]

The political situation in Europe was another worry during the summer of 1934. Hitler had come to power, becoming Chancellor of Germany in 1933 and Führer (Leader) in August 1934. The Federal Chancellor of Austria, Engelbert Dollfuss, was assassinated in July 1934 and later that year, in October, King Alexander of Yugoslavia would be assassinated. Louise had heard Shoghi Effendi warn of the danger of war in Europe during her pilgrimage in 1929. She wrote to Louis that she feared it might not be possible to work again in Europe the following year, there was so much 'war talk' and preparation for war. 'People in Europe' had told her they expected war by 1936. It was no wonder Shoghi Effendi wanted them to work as much as possible this year. She wrote that she expected the communists were at the bottom of it as they seemed to be the greatest danger. She seldom mentioned the National Socialists or Nazis in her letters of this period but most probably she was fully aware of the evils of their regime.

Later that summer after her visit to Esslingen and Munich she appeared more anxious than ever about the future. She was now convinced that war was coming and wrote to Louis: 'None of us know what is going to happen to us financially after the war, even the richest, if the world financial situation is going to be all upset, and banks should be unable to function but Bahá'u'lláh will look after us.'[4]

Money was another worry for the Gregorys that summer. Staying even in inexpensive family hotels in Austria and Germany was proving too dear and Louise considered returning to Belgrade earlier than planned because life was cheaper there and there was the possibility of earning money through language lessons. They were both worried about their house in Portsmouth and whether it should be let to tenants, which would provide them with a source of income. Louis had written that he would leave to her the decision about letting the house and she greatly appreciated this, writing back to him: 'But first my darling I want to say I am touched with your care for me and your confidence in me and wanting to leave the decision about the house to me.'[5] She suggested perhaps rather forlornly that Louis could come to Europe with her the next year and they could stay for two years. Her suggestion that Louis should join her in Europe so that they could teach together was repeated frequently in her letters to him but it never proved feasible. It is interesting to speculate how their interracial marriage would have been viewed by the Nazi authorities in Germany and

Austria, committed as they were to their ideology on racial purity.

Around this time Mr Abbott, the editor of the *Chicago Defender* newspaper, became a Bahá'í and Louise wrote to him congratulating him on his declaration of faith. She took the opportunity to send him the verses she had written in the form of a Bahá'í hymn entitled 'A Message to Christians', suggesting he might like to publish the verses in his newspaper. Miss Fürth had seemed 'rather charmed with what she calls my poem and I think she has a rather good understanding of such things so I feel encouraged to send it to meet your literary criticism'. She must have felt she needed to give him some explanation for being in Europe while Louis was in the United States because she wrote, 'I am in Europe because of my knowledge of French and German and there was no one else to do the work I have to do in the Balkans and Central Europe.' She explained that she and Louis were in fact united in spirit because they were working for the same Cause although on different continents. They had responded to the call to teach the Cause because 'we could not refuse to answer the pleading of our Guardian who has the future of Europe at heart and sees the danger of the world conflict coming'. And she observed: 'the war clouds are growing so dark and threatening.'[6]

Louise waited in Salzburg for Marion Jack to arrive so that they could travel together to the summer school, but Marion was delayed, possibly because she was so busy in Sofia where she reportedly now had 25 declared Bahá'ís and expected to form a Local Assembly soon. There was no news from Louise's 'boys' in Varna who had finished their exams by now and she thought they were probably 'relaxing'. Finally however Marion arrived and they travelled together to Munich and Göppingen and then to Esslingen for the summer school from 5 to 12 August. Here she met Dr Grossmann, Mrs Schwarz, widow of Consul Schwarz, and also 'a very clever man, Doctor of Science. I think he is called Dr. Muhlshlegel [sic].' (Dr Grossmann and Dr Mühlschlegel were both later appointed Hands of the Cause.) Helen Bishop also attended the school and gave a talk on Bahá'í administration following the guidelines that Shoghi Effendi had taught her in Haifa, and Louise gave a talk in German which she felt was well received. She also praised Jacky's splendid work in Bulgaria.[7]

After the summer school Louise went with Marion to Stuttgart where they stayed in the Frauenklub (women's club), but they were looking at renting rooms in a house higher in the mountains because 'I do not feel well here, Stuttgart never suits me and I will get higher as soon as possible.' Louise had had to apply for a new passport in Stuttgart and reminded Louis how much she hated having her photograph taken. This was part of the nuisance of getting a passport as well as having to pay an increased price for it. She wrote: 'Now I have my new passport for which I had to pay $10 instead of $5. It seems they put the price up last year to $10 again also it can only last 4 years now instead of 6 as mine was.'[8]

The house higher in the mountains had beautiful grounds, woods and clear air but there was a snag because, with her heart condition, Marion could not 'do hills' and was reluctant to leave Stuttgart.[9]

Louise arrived back in Salzburg on 3 September and found a letter from Louis waiting for her. A decision had finally been made regarding their house and it was decided it would be best for Louis to stay there and rest. Regardless of their rocky financial situation, Louise advised her husband not to worry about earning money but to concentrate on teaching the Cause, writing to him: 'As you say when one stops teaching the confirmations cease.' She put an extra slip of notepaper into her letter as a postscript to Louis telling him not to be anxious and get 'the proper kind of nourishment to keep you in health'. He should not worry because 'Bahá'u'lláh will show us what to do my sweet boy . . . Concentrate on teaching now and have faith.'[10]

However, in the event, it was Louise who had cause to worry because she found she had problems obtaining a visa (she writes 'a visa for Austria' but most likely meant 'a visa for Yugoslavia'). She had been forced to travel again to Munich to try to get it. Munich, she reported, was very noisy and full of people and she had not had much sleep for two days and nights. Finally, the visa had not been forthcoming. Nevertheless she had travelled to Salzburg in the hope that the Tourist Office there would be able to facilitate the visa for her. Then there would just be the long journey back to Yugoslavia. She planned to leave for Belgrade in two days' time doing the 20-hour journey in easy stages. She wrote that she could not go third class on hard seats all the way like Martha Root but instead would travel third class with two night stops, pausing in Bled, a city now in present-day Slovenia, for three nights 'in good air'. Then she would take the express train to Zagreb for one night and on to Belgrade. She planned to take a cushion for use on the hard seats and would spend two hours in the restaurant car which was known to have more comfortable seats! This solution to the problem of the long journey would be less hard on her fragile health and might have another advantage, as she wrote: 'I shall be better off in health as well as pocket. I think I may meet people to whom I can give the Message.'

But all her planning came to nothing when she learnt that the Tourist Office could not get her visa for her and she must go to Vienna in person. She wrote to Louis that she would leave for Vienna the next day, obtain her visa there and take the Sunday boat down the Danube to Belgrade. This would be more expensive but 'I am beginning to wonder if there is some Wisdom in this and I am to meet and give the Message to some soul or souls on the boat'. With this philosophical and spiritual thought she closed her letter: 'With much love and a good hug and kisses, ever your loving wife Louise.'[11]

Being back in Vienna turned out to have its advantages after all because, in addition to finally obtaining her visa, she also was able to meet up again and have dinner with her good friend Franz Pöllinger. From Vienna she sent a postcard to Louis informing him she was having dinner there with Mrs Wittmann and Franz, who both wrote a message to Louis on the postcard. Franz's message ran: 'I also am always very grateful to see Mrs Gregory as she is a living symbol of the pure Baha'i Spirit. With loving greeting sincerely yours F. Pöllinger.'[12]

18

RETURN TO BELGRADE

Back in Belgrade, Louise was living in the Jewish quarter in the Hotel Royal, a hotel under Jewish ownership. Her life there was busy, mainly because she found people there were very keen to take English lessons.

A group of Russian students came frequently for lessons, and among them was a young man who had been in Shanghai, China. Aside from practising his English, he was also learning about the Bahá'í Faith. 'He seemed very interested in all I told him', she wrote to Louis. But she was not so naïve as to think that her students might not have an ulterior motive in hearing about the new religion: 'It is true they all probably are also interested in improving their English and I do not know if they would be so anxious to come if I could speak in Serbian or Russian and told them the same things in either of those languages which I think they know about equally well.' She used articles in Bahá'í magazines for English reading practice with her students and considered them the 'Best teaching means we have . . . People who would not read such a book as Dr. E's [Esslemont's] will gladly read the magazine.'[1]

She had become friends with Mrs Popović, the English wife of a Serbian professor. He had met Martha Root, had written an introduction in Serbian to Dr Esslemont's book and had been interested in Martha's magazine article on the recent Esperanto Congress. By going every day to eat at the same restaurant Louise had met a number of people interested in English lessons. Situated as it was in the Jewish quarter, the restaurant was frequented mostly by Jewish people. Amongst those she had met at the restaurant were Miss Carrido, a teacher of English who habitually ate at the restaurant and who was helping her to find pupils for English lessons; a Jewish woman who was planning to go to Palestine and needed English tuition before she went; and a man who frequented the restaurant, a friend of Miss Carrido's. There were also a clerk at the bank she was using and his wife who were interested in

3. Dec. 1933

Dear Mr. Holley,

The Esperanto pamphlets will be useful even when the reading matter cannot be understood on account of the pictures.

Thank you very much for the list you so kindly sent. Since I wrote thanking you for 3 parcels that came through the P.O. a fourth one came the next day through the P.O. Since then I received a notice to go to the Customs for parcels & found 5 parcels of books. The official opened one & enquired for what purpose these books were, also charged a small duty on them about 40¢ in all. I told the official I was connected with a peace movement in U.S.A. that was trying to create friendship between all nations — it is much needed I said & the only way to prevent war. He agreed it was much needed so I hope he was satisfied. But the Cause is not known or understood in this country & we are not working officially or publicly & asked by our Guardian to act with caution at this stage till we know how it would be taken at headquarters so besides being much easier for us & causing no expense to us it is also wiser when sending to Europe to send only a small parcel

A postcard from Louise to Horace Holley, 1933

Marion Jack in the kitchen at Esslingen

Louise with Helen Bishop, Marion Jack and fellow Bahá'ís at Esslingen 'Bahá'í Week' summer school 1934

Louise with Marion Jack and fellow Bahá'ís at Esslingen 'Bahá'í Week' summer school 1934

Photo of Louise taken in Varna, Bulgaria with note of place and date in her own handwriting

*Louise with her group of students in Varna in 1933.
The older gentleman on the right is probably Mr Minersian, an Armenian*

Draga Ilić, a Bahá'í in Belgrade who translated The Hidden Words and Bahá'u'lláh and the New Era into Serbian. She was a journalist and professor of poetry

Martha Root, named by Shoghi Effendi as 'peerless herald of the Cause'

Draga Ilić with Martha Root. The two women met whilst Draga was working as a journalist in Paris

A Message to Christians

1. Simple His garb & lowly His mien
   (or when)
   As the Christ walked the earth, His Glory unseen
   By earth's flesh-bound children in days long of yore
   Veiled from them the Logos that gave Life Evermore.

2. Why think ye, ye'd have known Him, had ye lived here before
   Have ye learned the first lesson that opens the door
   To the World of the Placeless that Heaven above
   Within & around us, that Kingdom of Love?

3. Are ye less blind & deaf to spiritual law
   Than those of past ages who saw Him before?
   To the letter & creed, to the outer form wed
   That killeth the spirit —! Will He come to the <u>dead</u>?

4. Did He not tell you He'd come as of yore
   Veiled in the clouds as He left earth before?
   As a thief in the night He would come & be gone
   Ere the orrow would know it, know it only at morn

5. Could ye pierce those clouds, the inner Light win
   To see in the <u>new</u> form the Logos within?
   And hear in the <u>new name</u> the song Heralds did sing
   Resounding on all sides to Heaven's great King?

6. He has come in His Glory, veiled in flesh as of yore
   And lived on this earth the life Christ lived before
   To unite the whole world, bring Peace to the earth
   To establish His Kingdom, that Heaven on earth

7. But the children of men, save only the few,
   Saw not His Reality, the outer but knew;
   When He came & walked with them in the land of the Sun
   Conquering death as the Christ did & victory won

8. For the children of men, save only a few,
   Saw Him scorned & ill-treated, defeat only knew,
   Nor guessed not He'd conquered death just as of yore
   But soon all will know it, as He told us before.

9. For out of the prison He has come forth to reign
   Light conquering darkness, joy conquering pain,
   The Lord of the Vineyard has come as Christ said
   Turning earth into Paradise, giving Life to the dead

Louise's poem A Message to Christians written here in her original handwriting

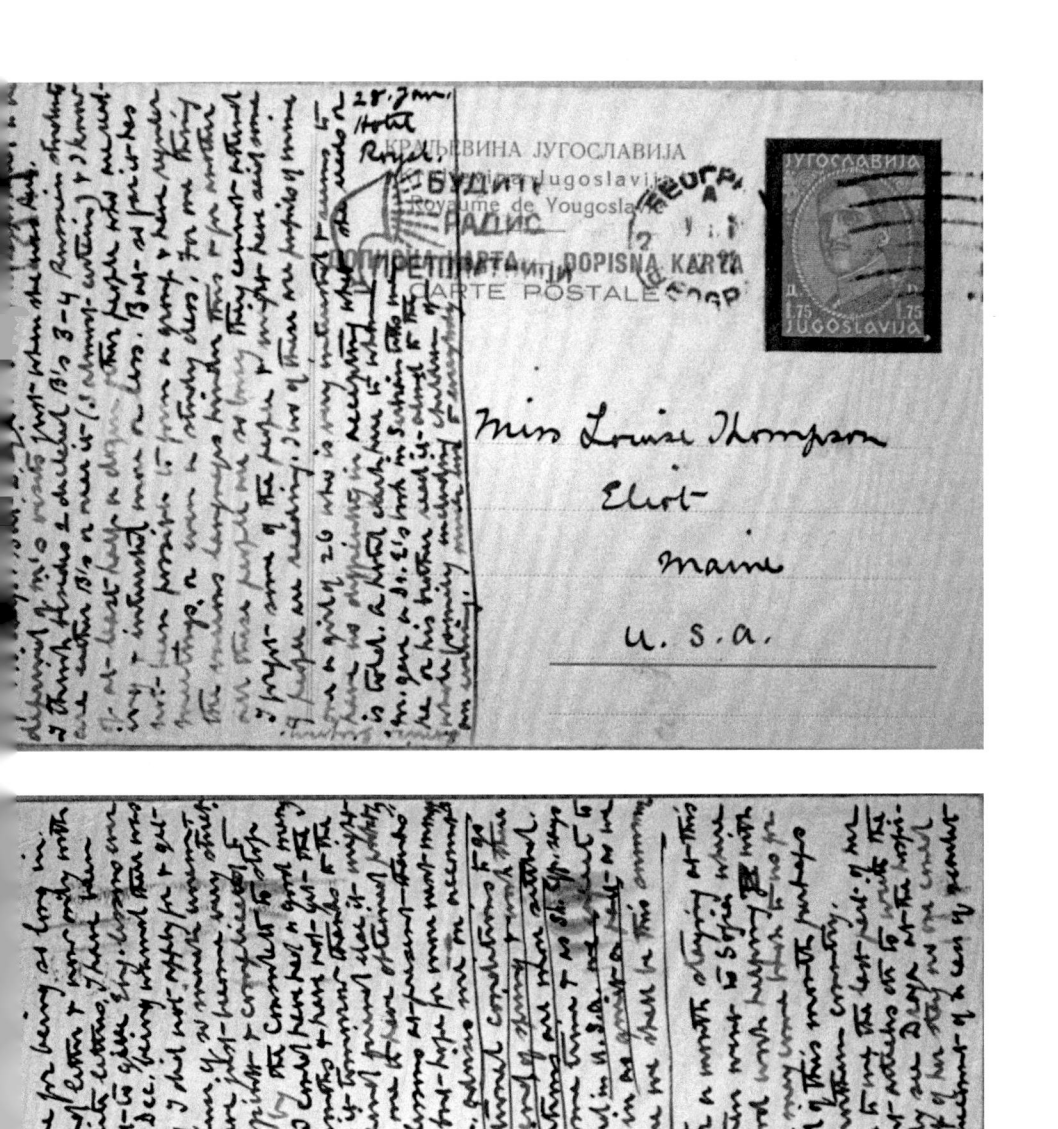

Louise's postcard to Louise Thompson written in 1936

© Andrew Rose

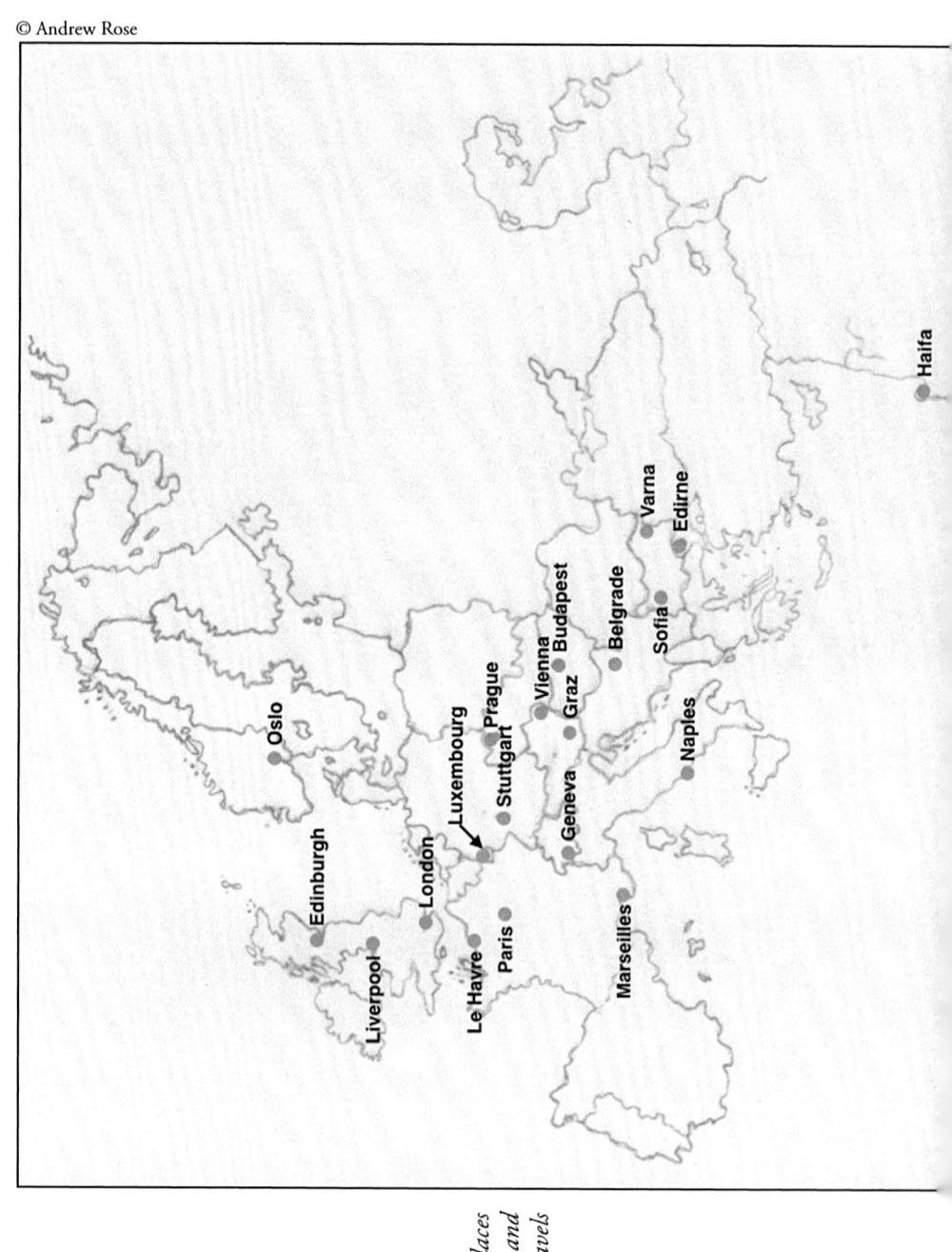

Map showing places where Louise lived and visited on her travels

lessons. Louise commented sadly that lots of people wanted English lessons but they did not pay much.²

At the Hotel Royal she had become friendly with several of the staff and had given Bahá'í literature to the desk clerk, who was especially interested in Horace Holley's pamphlet *The World Economy of Bahá'u'lláh* which had been translated into German.³

For some time Louise had been expecting Marion Jack to visit Belgrade and she reported in a letter to Louis that she had heard from Marion who had arrived in Leipzig where she was attempting to unify the Bahá'í community. She would be coming on to Belgrade.⁴

In a letter written to Louis in the spring Louise told him that Marion had subsequently arrived and was still in Belgrade after some months 'though leaving I <u>believe</u> tomorrow morning (unless she should feel too tired after packing or her heart is bad or something)'. Marion had been present when two newspapermen from the English paper in Belgrade came to interview Louise about the Bahá'í Faith. The interview had not been entirely to their liking because they felt the men 'asked too many questions'. They had wanted a photograph of Louise but because of her dislike of having her photo taken she had refused and instead gave them a photo of Martha Root and told them about Martha's lectures. The editor, who was English, had put an article about the Faith in the paper together with the photo. She felt that there were some mistakes in the article but on the whole the publicity had been good. This article had brought the Faith to the attention of English speakers in Belgrade and Louise wondered whether she should stay longer there, although this would be a problem because she needed a permit to 'do propaganda' in Yugoslavia and she only had a permit for another month, until 3 May.⁵

Another exciting development for Louise was the arrival on the scene of a 'Russian lady' who had been given Bahá'í literature by one of the group of Russian students who were coming for English lessons. She came to visit Louise who described that she was 'already almost a Bahá'í'. It seems that the Russian lady knew the student well, 'because she knew him when she and he lived at some other smaller city and she provided a room and food for some Russian students to meet in to save them going to bad cafés for their social contact. She also helped this youth to go to the University to study engineering and I think also found him occupation to earn part of his expenses.' She was very helpful to Louise in her teaching and 'Her husband was in a very high position as engineer in Russia so he has a good position here though their means are only very moderate. They have a daughter studying at the University to be an architect.'[6]

Louise was trying to estimate how many of the Russian students really could be counted as Bahá'ís and how many were only coming to her classes to practise their English. The Russian lady told Louise she felt the student in question was 'a believer in the Bahá'í Teaching' and Louise was naturally very glad to hear this. However in a letter to Louis she debated the beliefs of the other students, and sent a photograph to Louis of several of them, saying,

> The enclosed snap shot shows you three of these Russian youths [.] I teach the one in the middle and the one to our right but on his left is the one who gave this lady the Message. I am not quite sure of the belief or not of the third one on the left. He like the others has read Dr. E's book and is quite interested but I am not sure how much he has grasped. The one who took the photo talks more and better than the others in English but I feel more uncertain of his spiritual interest than the others.

But this student had brought others to the class:

> He however had given the Lit. to two friends whom he brought to me. One of these comes to our classes and is very interested and has read quite a bit[,] the other had to leave after I had once seen him for work outside Belgrade a good way off. He said he was more interested than he had thought possible the one time he came and he took away a Baha'i magazine.[7]

So she decided that, out of the group of Russian students, there were four who could be called believers: 'There seems therefore . . . a good possibility that there may be 4 believers without counting the one I feel rather doubtful about.' This latter student 'likes to come to the class but it is possible his interest is more to get on with his English' whereas there was real spiritual response from other students, because she noted that 'those other two boys have shining eyes when I tell about Bahá'u'lláh, Abdu'l Baha etc.' She felt she needed to know exactly where the students stood on their belief or not in the Bahá'í teachings: 'I think if I can get them alone or those 3 alone I could find out better where they stand. I don't want to press them unduly but should like to be able to know whether they are really believers.'[8]

Louise was aware that she would have to leave Belgrade when her permit ran out and was anxious that her work with the students and others should not be in vain. On this subject she was prepared to take advice: 'This Russian lady says we really ought to have some one here to teach the Cause and give talks in groups at least if not in open lectures and she would be I am sure a great help in finding interested listeners.' And she would not mind if other Bahá'í teachers followed in her steps and made even greater progress. She wrote to Louis: 'If you see May Maxwell do tell her if she and Mary would come here they could soon get a centre started and as they speak French and most of those I know speak it and others could translate a very great work could be done.'[9]

May Maxwell and her daughter Mary, the future wife of the Guardian, were at that time busy teaching the Faith in Europe: May in France and Belgium and Mary in Germany. Shoghi Effendi suggested to May in January 1936 that on their way to pilgrimage in the Holy Land, as well as visiting cities where there were Bahá'ís in Germany, they could extend their trip to Austria and the Balkans 'where we have now a chain of active and prosperous communities that link the Western with the Eastern part of Europe'.[10] But by the end of 1936 the situation in Germany and Austria had escalated and travel through Austria and the Balkans was considered unsafe, so that the Guardian urged them to come to Haifa directly from Germany.[11]

Louise had written to Horace Holley twice since she returned to Belgrade and he included an entire column about her activities there in the March 1935 *Bahá'í News*. Her plea for other individuals to come and help in the Balkans was sent out via this newsletter:

> If some capable and devoted workers could come over and help us our Guardian would be very happy. Both Marion Jack and I would be too delighted to give all necessary information to any Bahá'í teacher who finds it possible to come and stay some time either in this country [Yugoslavia] or in Bulgaria. The living costs are very low. Teachers who work well with student and youth groups would be particularly helpful.

The newsletter quoted extensively from Louise's letter to Horace and gave a picture of her life and teaching experiences in the Balkans:

> I am writing a few lines just to tell you that I am very hopeful now about the work at Belgrade since recently meeting two very receptive souls who seem ready to become believers. One is a spiritually minded educator, the other a musician. The professor says that he will translate 'The Goal of a New World Order' into Serbian as a service to the Cause.

Her previous activities in Bulgaria were also mentioned: 'I have good news from Varna . . . that the students are continuing to meet and one of them teaches the Cause during vacation in his home town of Burges [Burgas].'

But Yugoslavia had stolen Louise's heart by now and she continued:

> There is much more that I can do here than at Varna, and up to recently this large country has scarcely had the Message, though Martha Root has for some years when passing through given a few talks. This last year she stayed more than once for over a month, and besides lecturing and meeting individuals she arranged for the translation and publication of Esslemont's 'Bahá'u'lláh and the New Era'. Besides this we have a tiny pamphlet in Serbian which is a great help. The translator of the 'New Era' (Mme. Draga Ilié [sic]), has become a devoted believer. Unfortunately she is in the hospital and must have a serious operation. I should be so glad if the friends will pray for her. The work here depends so much on this dear and gifted spiritual sister.
>
> Things are progressing slowly but surely! Two people have declared themselves believers, both well educated and ardent to pass on to others what they know about the Cause . . . Besides these, a number of poor Russian University students are getting interested in the Teachings by attending a free class I give them in the English language.[12]

The musician mentioned in Louise's letter who had become a Bahá'í was 'Mme. Desanka Forgovice-Tokin, a Bahá'í who teaches music in Vrsac, Jugoslavia.' Some years later she communicated with the newsletter and expressed 'deep gratitude for all that Mrs. Louise Gregory did for her in confirming her in the Faith'.[13]

If no other teachers came forward to assist in the Balkans, Louise wrote, she would be happy to return to Belgrade at a later date: 'If I can come back I have no doubt things will move rapidly in the autumn with this [Russian] lady's help.'[14]

The Russian students continued to come for their free English lessons and Louise recorded that they 'are happy to get the English free and now are extremely interested in the Teachings'. They were also very interested in prayer and had offered to translate Bahá'í prayers into Serbian. Things were going so well that she estimated she could form a Local Assembly of nine believers before long. A lady had read Dr Esslemont's book and came to Louise to ask questions on the Faith and had been 'entirely satisfied'. She wrote to Louis: 'I really think we shall have enough for an Assembly before I leave.'[15] There was also the chance of putting an article on the Faith in a prominent Belgrade newspaper whose name meant 'The Times' and this could be excellent publicity.

All of these developments were very positive but, Louise considered, perhaps it would be better to wait until the autumn to form the Assembly when the new believers would be more deepened. One problem, and a great worry, was Draga Ilić's health as the poor woman was still in hospital. Also the political situation was worsening and Louise began to think that if she returned in the autumn that would be the last winter she could work in Europe before war broke out.[16]

However, time was running out and Louise was making her plans to return to the United States and Louis. Originally she had planned to sail to America from Le Havre, France but later she decided to travel to England instead and take the boat from Liverpool to Boston, leaving on 11 May. This meant that she would leave Belgrade on 28 or 29 April. However, she realized she might find it difficult to cross London as her visit there would coincide with the Silver Jubilee celebrations of King George V and Queen Mary, commemorating 25 years of their reign. She pondered whether to stay a few days with her sister Ethel or her brother Ralph while she was in England: 'maybe I could leave London on Friday and stay at Ethel's in that case or not go to Ralph's at all if Ethel is home'.[17]

Although Louise was now busily planning her return to America, she was well aware that she had been away for 18 months and she was naturally anxious about how she and Louis would get used to living together again after such a long time apart. She wrote to Louis: 'I think we need to get to know each other again after such a long separation and to be alone for a time together as much as possible. You have been thinking of me as an angel so long that I fear you are expecting too much of me and I shan't be able to rise to your expectations!'[18]

While she had been away Louis had been at home in Portsmouth and had made new friends in the neighbourhood and was especially friendly with a group of young people who frequently came to visit him. She wrote to Louis: 'My darling I am very glad you have the love of these young people as your adopted spiritual children, especially I feel grateful to them for their love when you were so lonely . . .' But understandably, she would have preferred to have Louis to herself for a while and dreaded meeting new acquaintances who would come in and out of the house. Children visiting might be even more of a problem because 'children always made me nervous even when I was young'.[19]

She expressed her anxiety in her letters to Louis: 'I shall arrive home tired from my long journey and you know I am not far off 70' – in fact she was over 69 at this time and it seems she was aware of the difference in their ages – 'even if I have still no grey hairs, so you must not expect me to have all the energy and strength of your comparatively youthful age you know, which in reality I have never had . . .' 'I don't want to go home with fears that there will be troubles ahead when I get there through these new young friends!' 'So don't expect too much from me my darling and remember we shall both need to adapt ourselves again to one another after such a long absence. Don't let us complicate things by making these young people a source of difference between us, unity does not mean thinking alike on every subject you know or even loving all the same people personally[;] we cannot be a copy of each other, it must be unity in diversity!'[20]

She had had a letter from Horace Holley in which he mentioned plans to find a government job for Louis. She wrote to Louis that she hoped it would not be in Washington 'because of several reasons and especially because when I am away in Europe I know your colored acquaintances who are not Bahá'ís make you unhappy by their hints I go to Europe because of race conditions . . . I do hope my darling if you have to go and work at Washington you will not let the opinions of such people make you unhappy as they did before.'[21] Sadly it is clear that the rumours that their marriage was unhappy because of the difficulties faced by an interracial couple had not diminished with the passage of time.

On her way to England when she was returning to America Louise hoped to consult Dr Goehring, a homeopath in Salzburg. She had greater confidence in him than in the homeopath they had previously consulted: 'Dr Clark (was that his name?) used to look in our eyes to find out what we needed. I think Dr Goehring's remedies are much better and he has a much surer way of knowing by his instrument by which he diagnoses the cases.'[22]

After wending her way across Europe once more and arriving in England from Antwerp, Louise planned to catch the *Laconia* in Liverpool and wrote to Louis, 'I suppose my boat will arrive 18 or 19 May. You can find this out.'[23] And also, 'You will probably get home first and can meet me at Boston when I land.'[24]

Helen Bishop wrote to Louise in June from the International Bahá'í Bureau in Geneva but she sent her letter to Belgrade and it needed to be forwarded to Portsmouth, New Hampshire because Louise had arrived home by then. She wrote that when Louise went to Stuttgart on her journey home she had just missed Helen and that Helen would be sorry not to see her at the German summer school that year. She reported that Draga Ilić, now out of hospital but unfortunately 'penniless' had received a copy of the *Kitáb-i-Íqán* and nine copies of the *Hidden Words* in Russian and was distributing them.[25] In a previous letter Helen had complained that rented rooms in Europe had no baths. Louise, the experienced European traveller, had written to Louis jokingly that Helen should 'do as Europeans do' and be thankful if she could at least get hot water![26]

19

THE LAST TRIP TO EUROPE

After Louise returned home to Portsmouth, New Hampshire in May 1935 and was reunited with Louis after their long separation, for whatever reason, the couple did not stay in Portsmouth long but moved to Eliot, Maine in August of that year. In Eliot they would be close to Green Acre Bahá'í school and would be able to participate freely in the summer activities at the school.

It was necessary for the Gregorys to complete registration cards when they moved into the Bahá'í community of Eliot and the information they provided on the cards offers insights into their early association with the Faith as well as their marriage. Louis writes that he became a Bahá'í 'On or about June 1909' in Washington DC, while his wife writes that she embraced the Bahá'í Faith in December 1909 in Paris, France.

Significantly, they both write about their marriage on these cards. Louis wrote about his pilgrimage 'to Akka and Haifa, 1911, meeting 'Abdu'l Baha and Shoghi Effendi, the latter a youth of fifteen at Ramleh, Egypt. Here also met Louise A. M. Mathew of England, whom I married a year later by advice and instructions of 'Abdul Baha.'[1] Louise confirmed this, writing:

> First came to this country with Abdu'l Baha in 1912, having previously met Him in Egypt, London and Paris and having been directed by Him to go to America with Him. Met Louis G. Gregory in Egypt at Abdu'l Baha's Home. Our marriage made by Abdu'l Baha at Chicago. 'I made that marriage' Abdu'l Baha declared to Mrs. Parsons. 'I wish the white and colored races to marry['] Abdu'l Bahá declared to me.[2]

Louise's insistence on the fact that 'Abdu'l-Bahá had made their marriage – and made it clear to them in Chicago that He desired it – implies that they had frequently suffered masked criticism and false rumours about the wisdom of their marriage over the years. Tellingly, she includes the words of 'Abdu'l-Bahá on His desire to see interracial marriages as an irrefutable statement of His intent. Although the couple had now been married for 23 years, they still found it necessary to quote 'Abdu'l-Bahá's 'advice and instructions' on the desirability of their marriage.

On his registration card Louis briefly outlines his Bahá'í service, mentioning his membership of the Bahá'í Temple Unity from 1912 to 1913, his membership of the National Spiritual Assembly – 'seven years in all' – , his service on the National Race Amity Committee from 1927 to 1935, his work with Race Amity Conferences and his time as a 'travelling worker' when he 'helped to spread the Message in Canada and through nearly all of the United States, especially the Southern states'.

Louise writes of her own service: 'Have done teaching work in Luxemburg [sic], Hungary and Czechoslovakia since 1923 but chiefly in Bulgaria and Jugoslavia as follow up work in co-operation with Martha Root.'

Theirs was a life of constant mobility and changes and in October of the following year they moved again, this time to live in Boston.

But meanwhile in the autumn of 1935, Louise, having realized that no other souls were going to arise to answer her plea to assist in teaching the Faith in eastern Europe, went back one last time to Europe.

She wrote to Shoghi Effendi on arriving back in the Balkans and in the New Year she received a reply from the Guardian's secretary written on his behalf. In this letter the secretary expressed Shoghi Effendi's 'abiding appreciation and gratitude' for the sacrifices Louise had made in returning to the Balkans and resuming her teaching of the Faith. He greatly admired her 'devotion and complete dedication to the service of the Cause' and also very much appreciated 'the assistance extended to you by dear Miss Jack who . . . has made it possible for you to return to Europe once more.'

However, Shoghi Effendi was well aware of the political situation in Europe and now felt 'the urge to advise you to return to the States at the end of next spring, in view of the growing unrest and uncertainties in the present international situation'. There would be an additional benefit in Louise returning to the United States because 'Not only it would be safer for you to teach in America, but also more helpful and pleasant, as you will be no longer separated from Mr. Gregory whose inspiration, support and guidance are such valuable assets to you and to all our American friends.'

In addition Shoghi Effendi had written to Louis 'advising him to give up for the present any plans he may have conceived for teaching the Cause in Europe'. So Louise's dream of teaching the Faith in Europe together with her husband was destined never to come true and Louis's 'presence in America is very much needed now, in view of the new teaching campaign which the American believers have just started to launch'.

Although Louise must have been downhearted to read Shoghi Effendi's advice to leave the Balkans, there was good news regarding Mrs Draga Ilić's translation of the *Hidden Words* into Serbian. The Guardian was 'delighted to learn that the manuscript is ready for publication, and is sending enclosed a cheque for six pounds for the printing of the book'. Louise was to give this sum to Mrs Ilić and ask her to have the work completed as soon as possible with the request that she should send 50 copies of the book to Shoghi Effendi when it was ready for distribution.

Sadly, Louise had had to inform the Guardian of the passing of her dear friend, Miss Fürth, which was a great personal sadness to her as well as a loss to the Faith in Salzburg. The Guardian's secretary informed Louise of Shoghi Effendi's prayers for her and all the friends in Belgrade and especially for the soul of 'Fräulein Fürth and her mother whose tragic death has filled his heart with an overwhelming grief'.

Shoghi Effendi left Louise in no doubt regarding his advice to her, writing in a handwritten note at the end of the letter:

> Dearly beloved co-worker, What you have accomplished in the Balkans, and now recently in Yugoslavia, is highly meritorious in the sight of God. I am deeply indebted to you. I would advise you, in view of the complications in the European situation, to join Mr. Gregory in the States and to remain there until the situation improves. I will continue to pray for you from the depths of my heart.[3]

Since Adolf Hitler had become Chancellor of Germany in 1933 and subsequently assumed full power in the country, the Bahá'í teachings were considered 'international and pacifist' there and in 1936 the Nazis closed the Bahá'í summer school in Esslingen. In May 1937 all Bahá'í activities and institutions were banned in Germany, Bahá'í books and records were confiscated and Bahá'ís were arrested and imprisoned. A year later the Bahá'í Faith was also banned in Austria.[4]

The Balkans were also becoming more and more troubled. After the assassination of King Alexander in 1934, Prince Paul, son-in-law of Queen Marie of Romania, became regent for the young Crown Prince Peter. Rumours of communist activities were widespread. However, Louise was loath to leave Belgrade before she could establish an Assembly there, which required nine Bahá'ís, and while there were people still keen to take English lessons from her. She wrote a postcard to Louise Thompson in Eliot, filling every conceivable space on the card with news of her difficulties and successes. She wrote that she had been trying to obtain a permit to give English lessons for the past two months. There was so much unemployment in Yugoslavia now that she had been informed she would be given a large fine if she taught without a permit and the American Consulate had advised her to stop her lessons just when demand was high.

Martha Root had visited Belgrade for a month over the Christmas period, staying in the Hotel Royal with Louise, and then had returned to Sofia where she was doing good work 'helping with Jacky's crowd', meaning Marion Jack's large number of interested enquirers. There was a chance Martha might come back to Belgrade soon on her way to northern Europe. She had been a great help to Louise in Belgrade, had written important articles for the newspaper and visited the royal family. She went once to see Draga Ilić who was in hospital, but unfortunately, later in her stay she was not able to visit because of an outbreak of scarlet fever and, naturally, Draga had been very disappointed.

So far Louise had not found it possible to form a Bahá'í group or to have regular meetings or a study class. There were so many different languages involved and people had been so busy. However, she could say that in Belgrade there were two declared Bahá'ís and three to four of the Russian students were either Bahá'ís or nearly so and about nine people were reading Bahá'í literature and interested. Two of these were pupils of Louise: one was a young woman of 26 who was very interested and the other the hotel clerk to whom Martha had given Dr Esslemont's book in Serbian; this man said that either he or his brother was reading it aloud to the whole family including the children of an evening.[5]

Louise wrote to Shoghi Effendi in February and again in March bewailing the difficulties she and Louis were experiencing in finding somewhere suitable to live in the United States, especially now that they had sold their house in Portsmouth, New Hampshire. She had taken on board the Guardian's urging for her to leave Europe and particularly the Balkans without delay and she had suggested to him that Norway would be an ideal place for her to spend the summer, so that she could assist with the teaching there. Martha had been in Norway the previous year and, despite illness, had overseen the translation of Dr Esslemont's book into Norwegian and had met King Haakon of Norway who had greatly impressed her with his spirituality.

Shoghi Effendi's secretary replied on his behalf: 'As far as this summer is concerned, however, he fully approves of your stay in one of the Northern countries, preferrably [sic] Norway as you suggest.' Louise's difficulty with hot summer weather was fully understood and he wrote: 'You need, therefore, not hurry going back to the States until the great heat is over. Oslo, aside from the fact that it has a very cool and pleasant climate in summer, has many possibilities for teaching. So with the help of Miss Schubarth you can no doubt be of some real assistance to the friends there.' Johanna Schubarth, a trained nurse and pioneer to Norway, had become firm friends with Martha, had nursed her through her extreme weakness following influenza and had accompanied her to Copenhagen and Iceland. Louise planned at this time to stay in Norway for most of the summer so 'The approximate date you have fixed for your return to the States (August 20th) meets, therefore, with the full approval of the Guardian.'

Draga Ilić was now out of hospital and her health was improving. Shoghi Effendi's secretary wrote: 'Regarding Mrs. Ilitch [sic]; Shoghi Effendi is very happy to learn of her good news. He hopes that although not yet fully recovered she can nevertheless proceed with her work for the Cause, specially in connection with the publication of the Serbian "Hidden Words". Please assure her again of the Guardian's deepfelt gratitude, as well as of his best wishes and prayers for her health.'

In a handwritten note Shoghi Effendi wrote:

> Dear co-worker: I fully approve of your plan, and wish to assure you again of my deepest and loving appreciation of your efforts, your constancy and accomplishments. You have rendered services which future generations will remember and extol. Persevere, and convey

to your very dear and distinguished husband my affectionate greetings and the expression of my profound gratitude.[6]

However, Louise's plan to spend the summer in Norway was short-lived. She wrote again to Shoghi Effendi on 16 May informing him that she and Louis had now found somewhere to live in Eliot. The Guardian's secretary replied to her on 29 May that her letters of 'April first & May 16th have duly arrived and were read with greatest pleasure and satisfaction by our beloved Guardian. He is indeed happy that you have found a suitable place where you can spend the summer together with Mr. Gregory. Being in Eliot you can both attend the Green Acre Summer School, & contribute all the help you can to the further upbuilding & success of that institution.'

The fledgling Bahá'í community in Belgrade was maturing under Louise's care and no doubt this made it less hard for her to leave it and return to the States. The Bahá'ís in Belgrade had written twice to the Guardian, once following their own initiative and again in a message that Louise had enclosed with her letter to him. His secretary wrote to Louise:

> The Guardian has also received and read with deepest interest the enclosed message addressed to him by the friends in Belgrade. He has recently written them, in answer to a letter they had jointly addressed to him; but wishes you also to convey to them once more his heartfelt greetings, as well as his appreciation of the wonderful work they are accomplishing for the Faith in Belgrade.

The letter ended with 'his renewed greetings and best wishes to you, and also to dear Mr. Gregory', and a handwritten note from Shoghi Effendi which prayed: 'May the Beloved guide and reward you, sustain you in your devoted, patient and unsparing efforts for the diffusion of His Cause and fulfil your heart's desire in His service. Shoghi.'[7]

The fact that Louise's spiritual children in Belgrade were themselves now able to communicate by letter with the Guardian and that they were pursuing 'wonderful work . . . for the Faith' must have brought great satisfaction to her and may have seemed like a sign to her that it was now time for her to leave them to work on their own.

Shortly after writing her letter to the Guardian on 16 May, Louise left Belgrade and the Balkans for the last time and travelled to Norway where she only tarried a few days before sailing from Oslo to New York on 26 May, arriving in America on 4 June to be reunited with her beloved Louis and to enjoy the quiet calm of Eliot, Maine together for the summer. Green Acre held its summer school in August that year and both Louise and Louis will have been delighted that Martha Root was able to attend the school, having spent time again in Scandinavia and sailed from Bergen to New York in July.

20

A TRIP TOGETHER – HAITI

Although Louise had returned home to the United States, this did not mean that her efforts to teach the Bahá'í Faith had ended. On the contrary, she was shortly to embark on a fresh travelling tour, to a non-European destination. And she would finally achieve her dream of travelling and teaching together with her husband, Louis.

At the National Convention of the Bahá'ís of the United States and Canada in 1936 a cabled message from Shoghi Effendi was read in which he referred to the 'historic appeal' of 'Abdu'l-Bahá's Tablets of the Divine Plan, urging them to consult on how to achieve the 'complete fulfilment' of the Divine Plan at the time when humanity was 'entering outer fringes most perilous stage its existence'. Furthermore, he gave them goals that would later evolve into the first Seven Year Plan, exhorting them: 'Would to God every State within American Republic and every Republic in American continent might ere termination of this glorious century embrace the light of the Faith of Bahá'u'lláh and establish structural basis of His World Order.' The 'glorious century' referred to was the first century of the Bahá'í Faith which would achieve its centenary in 1944.[1]

Shortly after this the Guardian cabled again with a call for international teachers and pioneers to travel to lands where the Faith was not yet established. The National Spiritual Assembly promptly set up an Inter-America Committee to advise it on activities 'related to the promotion of the Faith in Mexico, Central America, South America and the Islands of the Caribbean area'[2] together with ten Regional Teaching Committees to create a systematic plan for the expansion of the Faith in accordance with the wishes of 'Abdu'l-Bahá and the Guardian. The words of Shoghi Effendi in another message later that year appeared in *Bahá'í News* that autumn and served to inspire the hearts:

The present opportunity is unutterably precious. It may not recur again. Undaunted by the perils and the uncertainties of the present hour, the American believers must press on and prosecute in its entirety the task which now confronts them. I pray for their success from the depths of my heart.[3]

Louis and Louise Gregory once again arose, despite their advancing years, and chose to travel to the Caribbean republic of Haiti in order to help fulfil the goals. Their aims were to teach the Faith there, to bring it to the attention of people of prominence and, once there were sufficient declared Bahá'ís, to establish a centre there. They must have seemed like 'the dream couple' for this endeavour: he was tall, black and dignified, she was a petite, earnest white woman, they were a living example of a loving interracial marriage, an embodiment of the Bahá'í principle of the unity of mankind. And in addition, she spoke fluent French which was widely understood in Haiti as one of the official languages together with Haitian Creole.

A largely mountainous tropical country in the central Caribbean, Haiti occupies the western third of the island of Hispaniola and was formerly a French colony where large numbers of African slaves were brought to work on the prosperous sugar plantations in the 17th and 18th centuries. During the French Revolution the slaves revolted against their masters and later achieved the defeat of Napoleon's army and the abolition of slavery, proclaiming the sovereign nation of Haiti in 1804, the first independent nation in the Caribbean and Latin America.

'Abdu'l-Bahá had mentioned Haiti in His Tablets of the Divine Plan, linking it with other Caribbean islands and Panama in importance as 'a center for travel and passage from America to other continents of the world' and stating that:

> Likewise the islands of the West Indies, such as Cuba, Haiti, Puerto Rico, Jamaica, the islands of the Lesser Antilles, Bahama Islands, even the small Watling Island, have great importance; especially the two black republics, Haiti and Santo Domingo, situated in the cluster of the Greater Antilles.[4]

He exhorted the Bahá'ís:

O ye believers of God in the United States and Canada! Select ye important personages, or else they by themselves, becoming severed from rest and composure of the world, may arise and travel ... also in the group of the West Indies islands, such as Cuba, Haiti, Puerto Rico, Jamaica and Santo Domingo ... Consequently, the believers of God must display the utmost effort, upraise the divine melody throughout those regions, promulgate the heavenly teachings and waft over all the spirit of eternal life, so that those republics may become so illumined with the splendors and the effulgences of the Sun of Reality that they may become the objects of the praise and commendation of all other countries.[5]

Louis and Louise were delighted that they were finally able to travel and teach together. Louis wrote to the National Assembly shortly before they left: 'May I add that Mrs. Gregory and I are happy that thru this opportunity we can continue to be together in service.'[6] They left in January 1937, sailing to Haiti with letters of introduction to prominent Haitians. As they arrived in Haiti it was recorded in the official arrival records that they had such letters and customs officials there asked for copies of each Bahá'í publication intended for circulation.

Louis recorded his first impressions of Haiti in a letter to the National Assembly:

After a month here we have some perspective of possibilities for service and think them excellent . . . suffice it to state that we are almost continuously contacting people of high culture and capacity and rarely receive any rebuffs, but on the contrary, a courteous and inquiring attitude. We are also well advertized and our purpose here is well known. A few of the most influential people show a disposition to study deeply into the teachings. Also the young intelligentsia seem interested . . . We hold our meetings twice weekly whether or not anyone comes. That attitude will in time prove effective. We know that a great many seeds must be sown before anything in the way of organization can be attempted.[7]

The contrast between rich and poor was very pronounced. They found the living conditions of the poor people shocking and wished to contact them with the Bahá'í message, as Louis wrote: 'We are also taking some steps toward contacting the most primitive people, the burden-bearers, the poor whom Bahá'u'lláh especially wishes to help and bless in His day.'⁸ Despite the difficulty of lack of education among the poor and their use of Haitian Creole rather than French, it was eventually possible to start a study class.

Louis later recorded that the couple were treated courteously, but appearances were deceptive. A fellow visitor from the United States soon alerted them to the fact that their every movement was being watched by the authorities. They were informed that a 'high ecclesiastical authority' had warned Haitians that strangers would come to the country ostensibly to teach religion but really to spread sedition and revolution. Becoming aware of this, the Gregorys resolved to put their time in Haiti to the best possible use.⁹

On a more positive note, they knew that two eminent Haitians had contacted Bahá'ís in Washington enquiring about the Faith. One was a former minister of Haiti who had been in Berlin and Paris, and the other was a former delegate to the League of Nations. They had had friendly relations with the Bahá'ís in Washington and had read several Bahá'í books, stating enthusiastically 'This is the truth!'

With this successful outcome in mind Louis and Louise sent Bahá'í literature to the President's Secretary, the ex-President and members of the Haitian parliament. They included the Secretary of State for Foreign Affairs, the staff of the American Legation in Haiti and the Prefect of Police in their literature donation and contacted doctors, lawyers, dentists, businessmen, educators and visiting Americans. The sons of the first Episcopal bishop of Haiti and two Protestant clergymen were not forgotten.

However, they began to realize that establishing the Faith in Haiti would be slow work and would take longer than the three months they had originally planned for their campaign. They debated whether to return to the United States after three months and to come back to Haiti and resume their work there in the months of the northern winter, or whether to attempt to stay for at least a year, possibly moving up to the cooler mountain region of the country for a while to escape the intense heat.

They made the decision when they had been in Haiti for over a month to increase their activities to include a series of publicly advertised meetings in the capital, Port-au-Prince. Their plan met with approval from the friends they had made there who offered advice for the meetings during which Louise was to act as translator.

But the meetings could not go ahead because a government official told them meetings would be impossible without the approval of the police. Not to be put off, the couple did their best to overcome the setback and sought permission from the Prefect of Police who appeared at first to agree to the idea but referred them to the Secretary of the Interior for final permission. This set them on a trail of a dozen unsuccessful visits to police headquarters and the Department of the Interior until they finally received a letter stating that such meetings were forbidden. The frustration of this embargo must have reminded Louise of her difficulties in Bulgaria when she was unable to obtain a permit and, without it, was forced to leave the country.

It was in March that they received a letter from the Department of the Interior acknowledging Louis's letters of 5 and 9 March requesting permission for the meetings. The language of the letter was very emphatic and stated that the Department formally opposed the 'vulgarisation' in Haiti of what it called the 'mystique nouvelle' known as 'the Bahá'í religion', so it could not authorize any meetings on 'Bahaisme'. Louis wrote a polite and friendly letter in reply assuring the writer that the Bahá'í Faith was 'on a spiritual basis' and had 'no connection with politics'. But he wrote that they respected the decision and would not be holding any meetings. He ended his letter by offering: 'Within a few weeks I shall return to my country. If either before or after my departure it will be possible to aid you it will be a privilege.'[10]

The couple were advised that they could initiate a court action or diplomatic procedure to achieve their aim but they decided to accept the decision. They later learnt that the official who had made the prohibition held a high position in the country at that time, but a few months later he fell from power. They felt that he had not looked deeply into the Bahá'í teachings but had been influenced by prejudiced colleagues.

The months she spent in Haiti must have been a chequered experience for Louise. She would have recognized similar attitudes from officialdom in Haiti to the ones she had encountered from time to time in the Balkans when she had had difficulty obtaining permits. But at least in Haiti she had the satisfaction of knowing that at last she was travelling on behalf of the Faith with her beloved husband and in this way her dream of many years for them to travel together had finally come true. She had had long experience in conducting study classes and giving talks while she was in Europe so she would have had much to offer, apart from merely translating, if they had been able to go ahead with their planned meetings.

On another level, it is difficult to imagine how she coped with the humid tropical climate of Haiti. When she lived in Washington Louise found the hot summer weather there unbearable. She wrote to Agnes Parsons in 1921: ' I cannot stay in Washington . . . after about April on account of the heat and have to go north.'[11] In her European travels she had always tried to avoid the hot summers of Central Europe and had invariably managed to spend the summer months in the mountains or in cooler regions because she found her health was worse in the hot weather. How much more so must she have suffered during her three months in the tropics, unaccustomed to the unrelenting heat.

The couple made one final attempt to sway the opinion of the government in power and on 10 April Louis wrote to the President and sent him three Bahá'í pamphlets on the subject of a future world commonwealth, the destiny of the human race and Bahá'í economic teachings, requesting an interview. However, the interview was not forthcoming and on 21 April the couple left Haiti, returning to the United States via Kingston, Jamaica.

Although the Gregorys had not achieved their goal of holding a series of meetings or establishing a centre, they had certainly brought the Faith to the attention of a varied cross-section of Haitian society and distributed Bahá'í literature. They had sown seeds and, even though the government of the time appeared hostile to the teachings, they had made a number of friends including 'one teacher of rare ability' and at least three others who could form the nucleus of a small group.[12]

A few years later there was a new government in Haiti which was more friendly to the Faith and Bahá'í pioneers Ruth and Ellsworth Blackwell, another interracial couple, were able to establish themselves there. In April 1942 the first Local Spiritual Assembly was established in Haiti in Port-au-Prince and in 1961 Haiti formed its first National Spiritual Assembly.

21

'YOUR MANIFOLD AND TRULY HISTORIC SERVICES'[1]

Louis and Louise missed the National Convention of April 1937 because they returned too late to the United States from their time in Haiti. So they were not present when Shoghi Effendi gave the Bahá'ís of North America a Seven Year Plan which he launched in his cabled message to their National Convention that year. The goals of the Plan were: to complete the exterior ornamentation of the Bahá'í Temple in Wilmette, to establish a Local Spiritual Assembly in each state and province of the United States and Canada and to establish a centre in each of the republics of Latin America. This was the first of a series of plans overseen by the Guardian for the expansion and consolidation of the Faith throughout the world in accordance with the Divine Plan of 'Abdu'l-Bahá. It marked a transition from the former approach to spreading the Cause, which had been by sending teachers whenever they arose to serve in various destinations, to a new method introduced by the Guardian of systematic, planned endeavours with clear goals and predetermined time frames. The Seven Year Plan which began in 1937 would be completed to coincide with the centenary of the birth of the Faith in 1944.

Louis immediately took up the challenge and set off in order to help fulfil one of the goals of the Plan, namely ensuring that there was a Bahá'í community in every state and eventually, when there were sufficient numbers of Bahá'ís, a Local Spiritual Assembly in every state. For him it was natural to turn his attention once again to the southern states of America and he spent seven months travelling and teaching the Faith, principally in Atlanta, Georgia and Tuskegee, Alabama.

Louise, therefore, found herself in much the same position as she had been in the first decade of their marriage when Louis was travelling for the Faith and she was unable to accompany him because of the anti-miscegenation laws of the time. The couple were living in Cambridge, Massachusetts on their return from Haiti, although they soon moved to a little cottage at Green Acre.² Louise was now restricted to serving the Faith in America, having been strongly advised by the Guardian not to embark on any more teaching trips to Europe while the political situation there was so troubled.

There was a possibility she might go to Wilmington, Delaware in the winter of 1937, as she remarked in a letter to Horace Holley: 'Louis thinks I might go to Wilmington, Delaware this winter where there is one believer though maybe not very confirmed, a niece of Mrs. C. Cash of Washington.'³ However, the Balkans where she had laboured through so many difficulties were still constantly on her mind, as were the friends she had made there, especially those she had successfully been enabled to lead to the Cause, and she endeavoured to keep in touch with them by correspondence. Knowing the Guardian's interest in Yugoslavia and Bulgaria, she kept him informed of the progress of the Cause in those countries and the situation of the believers there.

She wrote to Shoghi Effendi on 9 February 1938 and received a reply from his secretary on his behalf dated a few weeks later. Together with her letter to the Guardian she had enclosed a postcard sent to her by Draga Ilić from Belgrade. Draga reported to Louise on 'the conditions of the Cause in Belgrade' and informed her of her brother's severe illness. But tragically events had moved on and the letter from Haifa informed her that 'Since Draga wrote you, however, the Guardian received a letter from her telling him of the sad news of the passing away of this good and devoted brother of hers.' This development left poor Draga emotionally and materially bereft, as was well appreciated by the Guardian: 'He can well imagine in what a desperate condition Mrs. Ilić must now be, having lost so unexpectedly such a dear and faithful brother, who had been helping her financially, and in so many other ways, and who had been drawn so closely to the Cause and was promising to become an able and devoted Bahá'í worker.'

Shoghi Effendi had himself written to Draga 'conveying to her his profound sympathy, and assuring her of his prayers for the soul of her departed brother, that in the Realms Beyond he may receive such measure of Divine Blessings as would compensate for his lost opportunities of service in this world.' Without her brother's support, Draga, still an invalid, would find life very hard, especially during the coming years of war.

Louise still maintained a keen interest in another of her friends in Yugoslavia, Mrs Desanka Forgovice-Tokin, the music teacher from Vrsac, with whom she had so much in common through their mutual love of music and singing. Louise had written to Shoghi Effendi suggesting it might be possible to ask the American National Bahá'í Teaching Committee 'to extend financial help to Mrs. Tokin to enable her to travel to Northern Yugoslavia this summer for teaching purposes'. But the reply came that

> much as the Guardian is anxious that the Cause in that country may make a speedy headway [sic], he nevertheless feels that in view of the paramount importance of the teaching work in America it would be inadvisable for the American believers to dissipate their energies and resources in such distant fields as Yugoslavia . . . The friends in America should now first concentrate on the teaching program of the Seven-Year Plan, and cannot therefore undertake any financial responsibility in connection with any teaching work outside America.

This must have been disappointing news for Louise but it underlined the importance of the goals set for America in the Seven Year Plan. The Guardian included a handwritten note to this letter addressed to his 'Dear & valued co-worker', informing her that 'The card you have sent me, addressed to you from Belgrade, has also reached me, & I have already assured [Draga Ilić] of my sympathy and special prayers.' To Louise and her 'beloved and distinguished husband' he expressed his 'abiding love and gratitude for your manifold and truly historic services', adding 'I will continue to pray for you both from all my heart. Be happy. Shoghi.'4

In her desire to serve the Faith Louise turned once again to putting her writing skills to work and wrote an article about the Faith for *World Order* magazine. She sent a copy of this article to the Guardian and his secretary replied that it was interesting and hoped that 'after having introduced in the text the alterations suggested by the editors' it would be published and 'serve to stimulate widespread and genuine interest in the Faith'. A handwritten note by Shoghi Effendi recommended she should 'seek the advice of the Publishing and Reviewing Committee and act in accordance with any suggestions they may give you'. Her suggestion that she could send the manuscript of the article to Draga Ilić so that she might 'use it for writing a scenario' was also approved and the Guardian 'hopes she will have the time and the strength to undertake such a work, which evidently requires much time and considerable effort'.

The continuing services that the Gregorys offered to the Faith were undiminished and unabated. The Guardian himself wrote, 'I deeply appreciate your constant endeavours and wish you to assure dearly-beloved Louis of my ever-abiding gratitude for all that he is achieving in the service of the Cause of God.'[5]

All the predictions of a period of intense turbulence and bloodshed proved fatally true when World War II erupted later that year. Britain declared war on Germany on 6 September 1939 and Louise once again had cause to worry about her English relatives who might be serving in the forces overseas, as well as those living on English soil who would be in danger from bombing raids and missile attacks. Most of Louise's surviving siblings lived in the south of England, in Kent, Surrey, Sussex or London itself and would have experienced at first hand the German bombing raids and the London blitz. Her youngest brother Harold lived in the industrial Midlands, working as a civil engineer, and would have also been subject to terrifying bombing raids in that area. Louise, far away in America, must have prayed daily for their safety.

It was not until after World War II ended that she found out how her eldest brother, Ernest, who lived in France, had fared during the war. She learnt that sadly her brother had passed away under very difficult circumstances during the Nazi occupation of France. In 1946 she wrote about his passing:

> my eldest brother who had a business in Deux Sèvres[,] France for some 60 years or so and died there at the age of 82 in 1942 – narrowly escaping being carried off to a concentration camp by the Nazis who found him dying when they came to his house so they took what money they could get hold of and left with the intention of coming back later and selling up his quite considerable property.'[6]

Almost simultaneously with the outbreak of war came another piece of tragic news: the stoic and courageous Martha Root, Louise's friend and her inspiration in so many audacious teaching campaigns, had passed away in Hawaii on 28 September. Valiant and steadfast to the last, Martha had travelled to the Pacific islands to deliver the message of Bahá'u'lláh to the peoples of Hawaii but her ill health had finally overcome her and her radiant soul had ascended to the Abhá Kingdom. Shoghi Effendi conferred upon her the honour of the rank of Hand of the Cause of God and in a cable to the American believers he announced that 'Posterity will establish her as foremost Hand which 'Abdu'l-Bahá's will has raised up first Bahá'í century.'[7]

The news of Martha's passing spread quickly and Louise must have learnt of Martha's death with enormous sorrow and lamented that her dear friend was no longer on this earthly plane to inspire, direct and advise her.

In December 1941 the United States entered World War II. Unfortunately, this was a time of racial discontent when many black people had moved to the cities to find work in industries, and tensions there flared into conflict, such as the Detroit race riot of 1943 which resulted in a number of deaths and the destruction of buildings. There were reports of black soldiers, fighting for their country, receiving abuse and discrimination.[8]

Inspired by Shoghi Effendi's *The Advent of Divine Justice*, and aware of this climate of renewed racial tension, the National Assembly decided in 1939 to form a Race Unity Committee with a view to putting into action the Bahá'í teaching of the oneness of humankind. Louis was heavily involved in the Committee, which from 1940 embarked on a lecturing project in the south, and he spoke at black colleges, schools and clubs throughout the south, work in which Dorothy Baker, later a Hand of the Cause, also took a prominent part.

Louis served on the National Assembly continuously from 1939 to 1946, so was frequently away from home on Assembly business. He was also on the Committee on Assembly Development, work which involved travelling to visit and advise Assemblies. In addition he was a member of the Green Acre school committee for several years in the 1940s. He served as race unity activity editor on the editorial committee for *The Bahá'í World*. He also wrote for the *Bahá'í World* volumes and *World Order* magazine and was on the editorial committee of *Bahá'í News*. For many years he was convention reporter for National

Convention and his reports appeared in *Bahá'í News*. It is to be expected that Louise travelled with him to National Convention from time to time – she certainly knew Horace and Doris Holley personally and would have had the opportunity to get to know them and other Bahá'í friends at conventions. However, it was still out of the question for her to accompany Louis on his visits to the southern states because of the prejudice against their interracial marriage. When Louis was able to be at home Louise showered him with her love and support, offering him a haven of rest and a beneficial diet.

When he was at home the couple took part in Bahá'í community activities in Eliot together, such as the celebration of the Birth of the Báb in May 1941.[9] At these gatherings in Eliot Louise tended to stay in the background and preferred to allow Louis to be in the limelight. He was often invited to address the Eliot believers, who greatly appreciated his inspiring talks.

From 1941 to 1946 a series of Race Unity Conferences was held in the summer at Green Acre which Louise and Louis could attend together. A letter to Louise from Horace Holley notes that the Gregorys would spend the summer of 1943 at Green Acre,[10] and in August of that year a Race Unity Conference was organized to take place there and both Louise and Louis took part in the programme. The conference was divided into four sessions over three days and speakers included Harlan Ober, Horace Holley, Mme Ali-Kuli Khan, Dr Glenn A. Shook, Doris Holley and Louis himself who chaired the final session.

During the third session, it is recorded, 'Mrs. Louise A. M. Gregory sang Negro spirituals'. There are few records of Louise singing in public but she had studied voice culture during her teacher's training and music in Paris in her 30s and it is heartening to learn that her talent for singing was appreciated and she was still singing in her late 70s.

The conference was of such interest locally that it was reported extensively in the Portsmouth, New Hampshire *Herald* newspaper of 17 August 1943.[11]

During 1944 Louise was inspired to travel to Brattleboro, Vermont from where she wrote to Louis in April 1944. Although she was by now nearly 80 years old, she had embarked on a 'residence project' or short-term pioneering project in Brattleboro. The *Bahá'í News* of spring 1945 reported: 'we mention with pride the pioneers of the Second Century who by responding to new calls during this year have contributed a notable share to the safeguarding of the spiritual prizes'. Although not qualifying as a full-time pioneer in this enterprise, Louise was amongst three believers who completed 'residence projects' in answer to the Guardian's call: 'Urge utmost vigilance for preservation at whatever cost of the newly constituted Assemblies throughout the Americas.'[12]

By May 1945 Louise was back in Eliot, trying to cope on her own while Louis was away. She replied to a letter from Horace Holley, apologizing for her delay in writing to him. There were complications with her brother Ernest's will because he had passed away in France in wartime, so it was not until after the war ended that his will could be granted probate. He had left a considerable sum of money and Louise was one of the beneficiaries together with her surviving siblings. She wrote to Horace: 'I have been so busy of late with some business from France requiring me to answer at once as the rest of the family in England were anxiously waiting for my signature to something they have all signed and I must get my signature witnessed before a Notary Public.'

Looking after their cottage and attending to the everyday tasks made difficult by living in a country recently at war were proving onerous to Louise, who was elderly and in poor health: 'besides digging my garden and planting seeds and tomato plants in addition fetching pails of water as up to the present Mrs [_____] who lets us use [water] from their outside faucett [sic], has not been able to find anyone to turn her water on and Mr Remick, who used to do it has been drafted. Our cottage also demands cleaning . . .' At least the arrival of spring meant the end of some back-breaking domestic tasks: 'The warmer weather saves me keeping two fires going as I had a long time and almost no fire is now required. Carrying up coal did not suit my back at 79, nor the oil can either.'

Apart from her weak back which had troubled her throughout her life, she had now to worry about finding sufficient nourishing food: 'I have often to go to Portsmouth to a restaurant to keep myself in good health as Abdu'l Bahá [sic] was very insistent I should eat meat or chicken which cannot be bought now for love or money at Portsmouth.' Louise worried about the state of their cottage and the garden: 'if Louis could see our grass growing as it is and already as high as it is, from constant recent rains – which by the way rained also on my bed (as our roof leaks and I do not know where to find a man to repair it) – I fear Louis would be so unhappy at seeing it he would worry himself sick . . .' Her many chores took up most of her time and exhausted her: 'my strength also is very limited and after any activity I have to sleep to recuperate and rest my back that also takes up my time.'[13]

When Louis was not away lecturing or on National Assembly business, life for them in Eliot was more restful and tranquil. They were later remembered walking through Eliot town, an elderly couple, greeting friends and acquaintances on the main street, fully accepted as residents there, their interracial marriage causing no comment or problems.[14]

The Seven Year Plan given to the Bahá'ís of North America was triumphantly completed in 1944 and the centenary in May 1944 was celebrated around the world, including at the House of Worship in Wilmette. Shoghi Effendi commended the believers in a later message the following year:

> The first Seven Year Plan, ushered in on the eve of the greatest conflict that has ever shaken the human race, has, despite six years of chaos and tribulation, been crowned with a success far exceeding the most sanguine hopes of its ardent promoters.[15]

Close on the heels of the first Seven Year Plan the Guardian announced to the American Bahá'ís the inauguration of the second Seven Year Plan for North America, at Riḍván 1946. The goals of this plan were: to consolidate and expand the Faith throughout North and South America, to complete the House of Worship in Chicago and landscape its grounds, to form National Spiritual Assemblies in Canada, Central America and South America and, most importantly, to spread the Bahá'í teachings in the 'war-torn, spiritually famished European continent'.[16]

The goal of teaching the Faith in Europe sounded like a clarion call to Louise despite the fact that she was now 80 years old and in poor health. The news that the National Spiritual Assembly of Germany and Austria had been re-established was greatly encouraging. Already in March 1946 she had written to Horace Holley: 'I have wondered if in the autumn conditions in Europe will be such that I (or Louis and I) could go over there.' She had received news at last from Mme Tokin in Yugoslavia, although most of the news was sad, especially concerning Draga Ilić: 'Mme Draga Ilić of Belgrade died during the war in 1942[,] so Mme Tokin wrote me[,] owing largely she thinks for want of proper nursing and proper food.' It seems Mme Tokin was now the only Bahá'í in Yugoslavia: 'As far as I know there is only one Bahá'í alive in Jugoslavia, Mme Tokin who was my spiritual child and lives now at a suburb of Belgrade where she teaches music.' Communication with Europe had been next to impossible:

> Her letter took 5 months to reach me. She was not well herself she said for want of proper food – says meat, tea, coffee and cocoa and such things were unobtainable. I sent a parcel and a letter but do not know if she ever got them. Shoghi Effendi to whom I sent a message from Mme Tokin has asked me to keep in touch with Mme Tokin if it is possible. Maybe it may become possible for me to go to see her. She says she is still devoted to the Cause – I fear poor dear she has been nearly starved. She says her nerves are all to pieces. She was already a very nervous person. Shoghi Effendi regrets very much the loss of Draga to the work of the Cause in Jugoslavia.

Louise had clearly been worried throughout the war years about her friends in the Balkans and remembered particularly the students she had taught:

> There were two declared students who were Russian refugees whom I taught who disappeared Draga said the last time I heard from her. One of them had gone to work in the country but no one knew what became of the other . . . He gave coaching lessons to help in his expenses and was in some kind of refugee home supported from England when I knew him, a very sweet youth but very delicate . . . They were the sons of Russian officers killed in the first war and I gave them English lessons in a class to help them and we used Bahá'í Literature. It was very sad.

Naturally she was also very concerned about her friends in Bulgaria: 'There were also two students in Bulgaria who came to me and were declared believers. I could get no news from them when I wrote.'[17]

Louise was still writing stories with a Bahá'í theme and, on Horace's advice, she had sent a short summary of her story *Am I my Brother's Keeper* to the Guardian for his approval. He had replied with comments and she wrote to Horace: 'So glad our Guardian approves of the story being published with changes.'[18]

She did not give up on her plan to visit Europe and was inspired to write to Shoghi Effendi in June 1946 enclosing Mme Tokin's letter and outlining her plans for a travel teaching trip – preferably with Louis – to England and various other European countries. She had written about Louis's recovery from a spell of ill health and the reply from Rúhíyyih Khánum, who was serving as the Guardian's secretary at that time, began by expressing Shoghi Effendi's pleasure in learning that Louis's health had improved and went on to say: 'As to your going to England, and perhaps the Continent: he feels this is a matter you should consult about together and decide if it is feasible for you to go.' They could undoubtedly help in the teaching work: 'No doubt if the way should open, you could be of assistance to the friends in the British Isles very much, but you should consider your mutual well being and future plans.'

The note written by the Guardian assured Louise of his 'heartfelt and abiding appreciation of the spirit that animates you in the service of our beloved Faith, and of my constant prayers for your welfare and success, as well as for your dearly-beloved and distinguished husband. Your true brother Shoghi.'[19]

Louise made a copy of the letter from Shoghi Effendi and enclosed it with her letter to Horace Holley of 24 July 1946. It appears that questions had been raised about the suitability of the elderly couple undertaking a rigorous trip to Europe because she remarks to Horace: 'You will see our Guardian makes no mention of our ages.' Louise had written to the Committee for Europe and there had been misunderstandings which she felt needed explanation: 'I think I should explain to you as I did to Mrs. Sprague that I was not asking to be sent to Europe as a pioneer and that if I went I would pay my own expenses.' Her enquiry had been motivated simply by a need for information: 'The reason I asked the Committee for Europe about the matter was that I thought the Committee would know something about prices of hotels etc. in various countries (if I went to Paris for a short time etc.) and they would no doubt be glad to pass on any such information.'

It must have seemed to her that her plan to visit Europe was made feasible by the inheritance she expected to soon receive from her brother Ernest's will. She wrote: 'What I had in mind as a possibility was that quite a large sum of money left by my eldest brother . . . a considerable sum to be divided amongst our family equally after the Government expenses and the legacies in France have been paid as we are to have the residue.' The situation, however, was far from straightforward: 'The Estate however was not settled owing to war conditions and is only now being done' and was very complicated: 'However the Government insists that our part shall be paid into a blocked account till they choose to release it as they will not at present at least let the money go out of the country [France].'

Louise was still in touch with Laura Dreyfus-Barney and she quotes her: 'Mme Dreyfus-Barney says if I were in France the Government would allow me a monthly sum sufficient for my expenses out of it.' She had also been in touch with her brother Percy who was executor of Ernest's will and he had written that 'it may take some time before our residue is in the Bank owing to these delays otherwise the Estate would have been settled and the money in the Bank'. In the event Ernest's will was not granted probate until 1948. Percy also had reservations on the feasibility of Louise going to Europe: 'My brother in England who is 85 says I should have to get permission from this country [United States] to go to Europe and I could not get it except necessary for business.' But Louise's optimism caused her to think otherwise: 'I think to visit my family etc. might get the permission, don't you?'

In fact there was another inheritance which Louise was expecting at this time following the death of her sister Florence: 'However there are two amounts coming to me soon owing to the death of a sister which will amount to over $2000 and this will take care of my travelling expenses and Louis' needs and much more for this winter.' She added: '(I said Louis could have half of it.)'

Louise's plans for this projected trip were extensive and included visiting the south of France in the winter and possibly helping with teaching work near Toulon; also staying with her college friend 'who lived with me years ago at Luxemburg [sic] and is married since many years to a Belgian at Spa, Belgium' and who 'has just written me that if I could come over in the early autumn she would find me a room somewhere (she has no maid now and is not well herself and in the seventies so could not put me up herself.) She would be so happy to have me and has a nice home. She wants to go to Switzerland to see her only remaining brother who lives there with his wife, but she does not like to go alone and would be so happy if I could go with her.' The friend's husband had 'for many years kept a summer hotel at Spa, but now it is occupied else I could stay there as I have before'.

The trip would include a visit to England 'to pay short visits to my brothers and sisters in England'. The sad news was that her youngest sister Ethel was dying: 'a sister is very seriously ill and not expected to recover and if permitted I should very much like to see her once again – she had invited me to stay a week with her before she was so ill but now her husband says I must not come, she is so ill.'

Louise's first preference was for Louis to accompany her on this planned trip to Europe but she notes early in the letter, 'Louis so far has not expressed any opinions', and towards the end of the letter when the consultation between them that the Guardian recommended had presumably taken place she writes: 'he probably would be willing to stay [in the United States] with friends and do Bahá'í work and let me go to my college friend if your N.S.A. Committee were satisfied it was safe for me to go.'[20]

Here finally at the end of this long letter she had arrived at the crux of the issue, which was not money or whom she could visit but the appalling state of Europe at this time when the Second World War had finally ended and many European cities were in ruins, the whole infrastructure of roads and railways was damaged and displaced persons or refugees were flooding across the continent in search of safety and new futures. It seems unlikely that Louise was unaware of the situation in war-torn Europe at the time, but her fervent desire to revisit family and friends there, to try to find her spiritual children again and to assist in spreading the much needed teachings of the Faith overrode any practical reservations for her.

Nevertheless, at the end of August she wrote a postcard to Horace Holley informing him that she had given up on the idea of going to England or to Europe. For some time the Gregorys had been struggling with their perennial problem of not having a permanent home. This may have been influencing her in her desire to travel to Europe while they were in effect homeless. But a solution had now presented itself and she wrote to Horace: 'I have given up the idea of going to England or Europe and we have suddenly been able to rent a cottage here at Eliot for the winter which Bahá'ís have just bought and wanted to rent for the winter.' She saw this as a sign that she and Louis should stay in Eliot as they now had somewhere to live and assured Horace: 'I feel there is only one way such a thing could have happened', and added: 'The house was only bought yesterday.'[21]

BAHÁ'Í HISTORICAL RECORD

1. Name of individual believer: Louise A. M. Gregory (née Mathew)
2. Reported through Spiritual Assembly: Eliot, me. (City)
3. Address: 47 (Number) South Street (Street), Portsmouth (City), N.H. (State)
4. Birthplace: London, England.   Birthdate: 1866
5. Naturalization (if foreign born): By marriage at New York (City and State) 27. Sept. 1912 (Date)
6. National origin (Whether of English or other stock): English   7. Race: Aryan
8. Color: White   9. Sex: Feminine   10. Married? Yes, 27. Sept. 1912 (Date)
11. Children or dependents: ——— Minor   ——— Adult   ——— Adopted
12. Religious origin (religion before becoming a Bahá'í): Church of England.
13. Date of acceptance of the Bahá'í Faith: Dec. 1909
    A. As isolated believer ___   B. As member of Bahá'í group: Yes.   C. As member of Bahá'í Community ___
14. Place of acceptance of Bahá'í Faith: Paris, France

[SEE OVER]

15. Date of enrollment in present Bahá'í community (No. 2): 4. Aug. 1935
    A. By transfer from previous community: Yes, Portsmouth, N.H.   B. By enrollment as Bahá'í for first time ___
    C. Subsequent transfers (leave blank): to Boston community Oct. 7, '36
16. General information you would like to have preserved in this historical record (about Bahá'í services, connection with the Cause in early days, special talents, etc.)

    ...ave done teaching work in Luxemburg, Hungary, Czecho-
    ...since 1928
    ...worker, but chiefly in Bulgaria & Jugoslavia as follow-up
    ...ith in co-operation with Martha Root.
    ...first came to this country with Abdu'l Bahá in 1912 having pre-
    ...viously met Him in Egypt, London & Paris & having been directed
    ...by Him to go to America with Him. Met Louis G. Gregory in
    ...Egypt at Abdu'l Bahá's Home. Our marriage was by Abdu'l Bahá
    ...at Chicago. "I made that marriage" Abdu'l Bahá declared to
    ...Mrs. Parsons. "I wish the white & colored races to marry" Abdu'l Bahá
    ...declared to me. (Additional notes may be attached to this card)

18. Photograph
    (If possible, please attach photograph to this record. Write name and date the picture was taken on back of photograph.)

17. Additional information (do not fill in)
    Transferred to Boston Community Oct. 7, 1936   Signature: L. A. M. Gregory.

Louise's record card completed on her transfer to Eliot, Maine Bahá'í community in 1935. It includes biographical details and information on her Bahá'í teaching work and her marriage to Louis

Louise with an unknown lady

The modern building at Green Acre named for Louis and Louise Gregory

Louise and Louis in their later years

The final resting places of Louise and Louis Gregory in Mount Pleasant cemetery, Eliot, Maine.

22

'YOUR HEARTS ARE YOUNG'[1]

Although now advanced in years, Louise did not relinquish her correspondence with her remaining contact in Yugoslavia, Mrs [Mme] Tokin, nor her duty of keeping the Guardian informed about the situation of the Faith in that country. She wrote to Shoghi Effendi three times in the spring of 1947 and forwarded Mrs Tokin's latest letter to him. The Guardian sent his reply to Mrs Tokin via Louise so that she could forward it to Mrs Tokin as he felt this way it would be more certain to reach her.

It seems that Louise had not altogether given up the idea of pioneering to Europe again. Rúḥíyyih Khánum, writing in her capacity as the Guardian's secretary, wrote to her: 'He fully realizes that your heart's greatest desire is to be out in the pioneer field, but with Mr. Gregory so frail and in need of care he considers your first duty is to be with him at the present time.' Louis's health was now failing, but Shoghi Effendi advised that there was still much that Louis could contribute to teaching the Faith: 'His spirit is so devoted, however, and he has so much stored-up wisdom that the Guardian feels he should, as much as possible, teach and associate with the believers in order to deepen their faith.' Rúḥíyyih Khánum assured Louise that Shoghi Effendi would pray for them both in the Holy Shrines, adding 'You are both very dear to him.'[2]

It was almost miraculous that Louise was able still to be in contact with her spiritual daughter, Mrs Tokin, who had lived through World War II in Yugoslavia, a period of intense conflict with heavy bombing and violent factional fighting. Somehow she had survived and lived to see the Communist Partisans under Marshal Tito conquer the royalist Chetniks and the Socialist Federal Republic of Yugoslavia come into existence in January 1946. The extracts of Mrs Tokin's letter published in *Baháʼí News* in September 1946 speak of the 'awful strain of these days' which has 'injured her health', and mention that 'She has been obliged to move to very poor quarters because her former lodgings were confiscated by the state.' Her letter went on: 'We spent the days of May 23 and 29 in ardent prayers for the realization of the religious brotherhood in the whole world. May the Abater of all troubles grant us our prayers. I deeply regret that I cannot write to Palestine, and thank you for having sent my respects there.'[3]

Eastern Europe was now disappearing behind the so-called Iron Curtain of the Cold War, a term used by Winston Churchill in his speech in Fulton, Missouri in March 1946:

> From Stettin in the Baltic to Trieste in the Adriatic, an iron curtain has descended across the continent. Behind that line lie all the capitals of the ancient states of Central and Eastern Europe. Warsaw, Berlin, Prague, Vienna, Budapest, Belgrade, Bucharest and Sofia, all these famous cities and the populations around them lie in what I must call the Soviet sphere, and all are subject in one form or another, not only to Soviet influence but to a very high and, in some cases, increasing measure of control from Moscow.[4]

Even more miraculous than Mrs Tokin's survival in war-torn Yugoslavia was the news Louise received from that country in 1948 that the Faith was actually growing there despite the Communist regime. Louise had the joy of writing to Shoghi Effendi in March 1948 and enclosing letters from Mrs Tokin and her friend Mrs Milutinović with the heartening news of 'the addition of two new believers in Jugoslavia'. The news made Shoghi Effendi very happy and Rúḥíyyih Khánum wrote that 'It is the first really big step forward in the Cause there since dear Draga Ilić and her group disappeared!' Louise's services in Yugoslavia had not been forgotten by the Guardian and the new declarations 'must also be a great source of joy to you, after all you did to establish the Cause there'. Shoghi Effendi enclosed replies to Mrs Tokin and Mrs Milutinović for her to forward to them and in his handwritten note at the end of this letter he assured her 'of my abiding appreciation of the indefatigable efforts you are exerting for the promotion of our beloved Faith'.[5]

Late the following year when the Gregorys heard again from Shoghi Effendi, there had not been any news for some time from Mrs Tokin and the Guardian recommended caution. Rúḥíyyih Khánum wrote on his behalf: 'He hopes you will eventually receive good news from dear Mrs Tokin. It seems wise not to press her now with letters that might get her into trouble with the system she lives under.' The Iron Curtain had truly descended by this time and communication with countries in Eastern Europe was next to impossible and likely to put the person who received letters from America into extreme danger. The fate of Mrs Tokin and the small group of believers in Yugoslavia can only be guessed at and Louise must have prayed constantly for their safety.[6]

Louis's health was a frequent source of worry to Louise in the late 1940s and he suffered several bouts of illness. In October 1948, however, he flew to Kansas City for the funeral of Dr Thomas C. Chapman. He enjoyed the trip despite the sadness of the occasion and on his return he wrote, 'Louise, my dear wife, is glad that I took the trip.'[7]

However, two months later in December she wrote to Horace Holley and his wife from their home in Eliot that they had named 'Little Akka'. Louis had suffered a stroke and was ill in hospital. He had been taken there by ambulance because the doctor felt his situation was serious. Louise had visited him with her neighbour Polly Marlowe and they 'prayed quietly standing up in his room and though he did not seem to notice it or see us, he breathed more peacefully . . .' She added that 'A number of Bahá'ís are praying constantly for Louis and I expect Louis is the most prayed for person in this country now.' She enquired whether Horace would be writing to Shoghi Effendi about Louis's illness because 'if not I should like to do so and get his very valuable prayers in his behalf'. Alarmingly, the doctor treating Louis 'says Louis can only live a few days'. But Louise was optimistic, writing to Horace: 'Of course he [the doctor] is not a Bahá'í and many miracles happen to Bahá'ís and remarkable recoveries when so many are concentrating on Healing in prayer.[8]

Three days later Louise had much better news to relay to them. The Holleys had cabled to the Guardian about Louis's illness and Louise wrote to them: 'We have now since yesterday good news of Louis.' Louise attributed her husband's improvement to the many fervent prayers and also to goat's milk. She wrote that 'the idea came to me that Louis always found goat's milk do him [sic] so much good and [I] asked John Marlowe, who has goats, to bring him some milk which he did after I had obtained permission over the phone to take him some'.

The remedy was quickly adopted by Louis himself and Louise 'heard from the nurse that he drank <u>1 & a half</u> glasses and also ate a good dish of cereal <u>for which he had asked</u> and he has spoken normally to some of our friends'. A friend who visited Louis frequently was Polly Marlowe, the daughter of Nancy Bowditch who ran the Arts and Crafts building at Green Acre. She had known the Gregorys for many years. Louise visited her husband 'most days twice a day with Polly and John Marlowe to the hospital, but he was almost always asleep so we did not waken him, but prayed silently. We knew how good sleep was for him.'

Louise had been an advocate for good nutrition and natural remedies for most of her life and the goat's milk remedy was enthusiastically continued: 'Polly Marlow [sic] took Louis another quart of milk (goat's) today and will see he is kept supplied. So with a lot of sound sleep (in a room to himself) and the right food he is getting, he ought to make rapid progress.' John Marlowe had had a dream in which he saw Louis 'all dressed up and coming gaily out of the hospital saying "Well I got over that!" Polly says many of John's dreams come true.' A day later she continued the letter: 'Phil Sprague just called me up and said he had been to see Louis and had been able to talk to him a little.' Polly had 'been most successful with him in getting him to talk yesterday and today . . . and reading prayers to him.' The weather had been so cold that Louise was not able to go out: 'I did not go today because of the extreme cold. He told her [Polly] to tell me not to come if so cold.'

Louis was obviously making progress and Louise wrote with great delight: 'So you can see he is much more normal and that he will[,] we feel sure[,] fool the doctors and John's dream will come true . . . The goat's milk we feel sure is doing him a lot of good and John and Polly say they will see he has all he needs . . . I must write an air mail letter to the Guardian soon telling the good news and please tell any one you see the good news.' She closed the letter 'With love and many many thanks and love to Doris also', adding that 'Miss Haber [Roy Wilhelm's former secretary] is with me and is a great help to me.'[9]

Louis was soon back home and writing letters. He wrote to Edith Chapman informing her of his experience: 'Quite worth while was it to be ill, with so many prayers ascending from many friends and the very best service, both hospital and now at home with my devoted wife and a Bahá'í friend who shares our home.'[10]

Louis made such good progress that Louise was able to write to

Shoghi Effendi in January 1949 telling him of her husband's recovery. In March she received from Rúḥíyyih Khánum a 'little line of acknowledgement on [the Guardian's] behalf of your letter of Jan. 15, just received'. She reported that Shoghi Effendi 'was delighted to hear dear Mr. Gregory is so very much better' and Shoghi Effendi himself added a note assuring her of his 'constant, loving and ardent prayers for your dear self and for your precious, well-beloved and distinguished husband, the news of whose recovery has truly rejoiced my heart.'[11]

All throughout the year of 1949 Louis's health was stable and Louise mentioned this in her letter to Shoghi Effendi in December of that year so that in her reply on behalf of the Guardian Rúḥíyyih Khánum reported: 'He was so pleased to hear you are both in good health and able to serve the Cause inspite [sic] of "old age"! He feels sure your hearts are young and as full of enthusiasm as if you were a good 20 years younger. It is the heart that counts!' In this, one of the last letters the couple received from the Guardian, he wrote commending their devoted service: 'May the Almighty, Whose Cause you have served with such zeal, devotion, constancy, ability and loyalty, bountifully reward you for your labours . . .'[12]

Louise and Louis, now an elderly couple, were still active in their Faith, contented with their life together. Louis wrote again to Edith Chapman: 'Louise and I are happy and grateful for countless favors, both material and spiritual. Not only are we free from debt, but the long years of privation to serve the Cause have now brought to us increasing prosperity and new capacities to serve the beloved Faith.'[13] Their relative prosperity was due in large measure to the terms of Louise's father's will which ensured that each surviving sibling would receive a share of their estate whenever a sister or brother died. Several of her siblings passed away during the 1940s so, however sad these events were for Louise, she would nevertheless have benefited financially from their wills.

Louis wrote as if surprised at their sudden increase in means: 'Louise and I now have a large and growing income in an incredibly short time. It is now our effort to teach as long as we can and to aid others in the most confirmed of activities, especially those who have struggled and sacrificed so long for the Faith.' Green Acre, so beloved to their hearts, would also be a recipient of their beneficence: 'Now that wealth is needed for the upbuilding of Green Acre, Bahá'u'lláh has given me a Midas touch.'[14]

But Louis had another plan for some of the newly acquired wealth. In his 70s, Louis passed both his written and practical driving tests and obtained a driving licence, whereupon he bought a second-hand car. All went well until one day, driving home from Green Acre, he ran off the road and hit a maple tree. Although he was not badly hurt, this marked the end of his driving escapades and no doubt it was a great relief to Louise who had always been anxious about his driving.[15]

In the summers of 1949 and 1950 Green Acre was closed as an austerity measure so that funds could be directed to the completion of the Wilmette Temple. This was a blow to the Gregorys, who looked forward so much to the influx of summer school participants numbering many of their old friends as well as new acquaintances, and to studying the Bahá'í writings with them. Many of the domestic chores such as gardening, cooking and cleaning now fell to Louis to carry out because Louise, although willing, was increasingly frail. He wrote: 'Louise, my good wife, of course shares my efforts, with a strong will and an unusual range of accomplishment, but quite noticeably lessening strength,[16] and later: 'My devoted wife is strong in will and spirit, but now quite frail in body, and so a great variety of tasks devolve upon me.'[17]

Despite Louise's frailty the couple continued holding firesides and study classes in their home and delighted in any visitors who crossed their threshold. Green Acre reopened for summer 1951 and the Gregorys were looking forward to its excitement, but suddenly and unexpectedly, while the school was in progress, Louis passed away on 30 July 1951, having held a study class in their home just a week before.

A memorial service was held for him at Green Acre two days later on 1 August, and on 6 August a cable was received from Shoghi Effendi in which he deplored the 'grievous loss of dearly beloved, noble-minded, golden-hearted Louis Gregory' and bestowed upon him the station of Hand of the Cause of God, the 'first Hand of the Cause of his race'.[18]

The Guardian's cable advised that a memorial meeting should be held at the Wilmette Temple in Chicago. A national memorial service was duly held on 24 November 1951 in Wilmette and Louise, an elderly woman in her mid-80s, travelled the many hundreds of miles to Chicago to attend. Tributes to Louis were received and read from Britain, India, Egypt, Tanganyika and Ethiopia. Harlan Ober, Joy Hill Earl and Dorothy Baker spoke their own tributes and Louise read a prayer for the departed.

After Louis's passing it seemed the light went out of Louise's life. He had been her 'precious darling', her 'sweet boy', the husband ordained for her by 'Abdu'l-Bahá. Her friend Marion Jack, who was the same age as Louise, passed away in Bulgaria in 1954 after suffering extreme hardships living in Bulgaria during the Second World War and remaining there afterwards in the Communist era. Shoghi Effendi had strongly advised her to leave the country and move to Switzerland on the outbreak of war, but she had begged him to be allowed to remain at her pioneering post, a request to which he had acquiesced.

Louise had lost touch with her former students in Bulgaria and Yugoslavia when the Iron Curtain separated eastern Europe from the West and she must have worried constantly about them, having no news of their situation. What became of the helpful Dr Binder of Sofia, Louise's 'boys' in Varna or the Russian students in Belgrade during the Second World War and the Communist era? One can only hope that they survived, in eastern Europe or elsewhere. The fact that the Balkan countries that she loved and knew so well were now Communist states where religion was discouraged and the followers were persecuted must have been sad and even depressing for her, but it is to be expected that, like Louis, she believed in the eventual victory of the Cause of God. How vindicated she would have felt when 'the doors opened' in eastern Europe 40 years later, when religion could be taught again and hundreds embraced the Bahá'í Faith!

During her long life Louise achieved much: she attended university and qualified as a teacher, a remarkably modern achievement for a Victorian woman; in the early days of the 20th century she travelled to European countries and established herself there as a single woman working and studying in Luxembourg and in Paris; as a new Bahá'í she travelled alone to Egypt and attained the presence of 'Abdu'l-Bahá, later witnessing His talks in London and Paris and even accompanying Him, as one of a select group of westerners, when He sailed from Naples to America.

After her marriage she was the first Bahá'í to teach the Faith in Luxembourg. On her own initiative and with the blessing of Shoghi Effendi she was the first Bahá'í, after 'Abdu'l-Bahá's visit, to teach the Faith in Hungary. When she settled for months on end in Bulgaria and Yugoslavia she acquired the distinction of being the first pioneer to those countries, accorded the status of 'pioneer' by Shoghi Effendi.

She excelled, in her quiet way, at seeking out waiting souls and encouraging them in their spiritual quest by holding informal group meetings and study classes. Although reserved and self-effacing by nature, she was not afraid to address audiences when called upon to do so and her mastery of French, German and Esperanto aided her in her endeavours. In effect, her teaching work spanned the two continents of Europe and North America. Sometimes she was in the vanguard and led the way in finding receptive souls, such as in Budapest in 1925 when she opened the way and established friendships that were later of assistance to Martha Root, and at other times she was happy to follow up on the teaching initiatives of Martha and others. Her efforts to give the message of Bahá'u'lláh to the peoples of the Balkans earned her the praise of the Guardian and she only reluctantly suspended her teaching work there because of his insistent advice that Europe was becoming too dangerous.

But surely her greatest achievement was her marriage to Louis, which she embarked upon when no longer in her youth, in accordance with the wishes of 'Abdu'l-Bahá, taking up her residence in an unfamiliar country and in the face of extreme prejudice from current society regarding her marriage. She succeeded in being an independent woman, travelling for the most part alone in foreign lands and pursuing the teaching goals that her heart dictated, always following the guidance of the Guardian. But at the same time as being independent she achieved a happy and loving marriage to Louis. For nearly 40 years the couple were united by their love of their Faith and an enduring love for each other. This was despite enforced separations when they were unable to travel together to states where the law prevented them from being together as a married couple. Their interracial marriage was, at that time, considered eccentric at best and downright illegal at worst, but as a united couple, they presented an example of a happy marriage and a role model for future unions of black and white. Truly they nourished the 'seed' that 'Abdul-Bahá had planted in their hearts and overcame the many difficulties that He had foretold she would encounter.

Increasingly frail, in June 1954 Louise went to live in a 'convalescent home', which was probably what would be known now as a care home. When Horace Holley was informed by the Eliot community of her move to the home, he replied on behalf of the National Spiritual Assembly: 'How sad that dear Louise Gregory must be treated in a convalescent home! But as she dies in this world she acquires life in the next.'[19] On 20 May 1956 she passed away at the age of 90. Informed of her passing, Horace Holley on behalf of the National Spiritual Assembly wrote: 'The passing of dear Louise Gregory takes from us one of the early pioneers and one of the firm souls remaining who had direct association with 'Abdu'l-Bahá. We can realize something of her joy at rejoining Louis in the Kingdom.'[20]

A cable from Shoghi Effendi was received by the National Spiritual Assembly in which the Guardian expressed himself: 'Grieved news passing faithful, consecrated handmaid (of) 'Abdu'l-Bahá. Confident rich reward Kingdom. Pioneer services highly meritorious.'[21] In a simple ceremony she was laid to rest in Mount Pleasant cemetery, Eliot, alongside her beloved husband Louis.

THE END

APPENDIX
LOUISE'S TRAVELS

Date left United States	Date returned United States	Places visited
30 October 1922 from New York to Liverpool on board RMS *Ausonia* of the Cunard Steamship Line (RMS = Royal Mail Ship)	16 August 1923 from Southampton to New York on board SS *Volendam* of the Holland America Line	Leeds, England Les Ambiers, Deux Sèvres, France Spa, Belgium Luxembourg Wiesbaden, Germany Ferndown Lodge, England
3 July 1924 from Boston on SS *Winifredian* of the Leyland Line. Arrived Liverpool 8 July	17 June 1925 from Antwerp to New York on SS *Zeeland*	Liverpool, England Luxembourg Vienna & Graz, Austria Budapest, Hungary Zuffenhausen near Stuttgart, Esslingen, Frankfurt, Wiesbaden, Nuremberg, Germany Spa & Brussels, Belgium
28 October 1926 from Boston to Liverpool on SS *Winifredian*. Arrived Liverpool 28 October	20 June 1927 from Boulogne-sur-Mer, France to New York	Liverpool, York, London, England Brussels, Belgium Graz & Vienna, Austria Budapest, Hungary Sofia, Bulgaria

LOUISE'S TRAVELS

Date left United States	Date returned United States	Places visited
March or April 1928, probably to Bremen in Germany	May 1929 Haifa to Providence, RI on SS *Asia*. Arrived Providence 13 May 1929	Dresden, Germany Prague, Czechoslovakia (with Martha Root) March–May 1928 Sofia, Bulgaria (she spent summer 1928 in Teplice, Czechoslovakia). At the end of August back to Sofia until March 1929 Then overland to Haifa for pilgrimage
At April 1930 she is in the United States for the 1930 census. Mid-November 1930 she sails on SS *Sinai* from Providence heading for Romania and Bulgaria and possibly Poland	24 April 1931 from Liverpool to Boston on SS *Britannic*. Arrived Boston 2 May 1931	Arrives in Sofia, Bulgaria 8 January 1931 (probably after being in Romania during December) She is in Sofia March 1931. Marion Jack leaves Haifa early April 1931 hoping to join her although Louise left Sofia early in April. 11 April 1931 Louise is in Switzerland and 13 April 1931 she is in Geneva, Switzerland
October 1931. This date seems likely because her report says she went to Varna, Bulgaria in late autumn 1931	26 May 1933 arrived New York from Hamburg on SS *Hamburg* of the Hamburg-American Line	Varna, Bulgaria late autumn 1931 In spring 1932 she visited Brno in Czechoslovakia, Budapest (Hungary), Salzburg (Austria) and Berchtesgaden & Stuttgart in Germany in the summer. She was in Varna again in November 1932 and from 27 February–9 April 1933

Date left United States	Date returned United States	Places visited
13 September 1933 from Boston to Europe	4 May 1935 from Le Havre, France to New York on SS *Georgic*. Arrived New York 13 May 1935	Varna, Bulgaria Salzburg, Austria Belgrade, Yugoslavia (from April 1934) Esslingen, Germany (end of July for summer school), Munich and Göppingen, Stuttgart, Germany (August 1934) Salzburg & Vienna, Austria Back to Belgrade September 1934
September or October 1935 to Europe	26 May 1936 from Oslo, Norway to New York on SS *Bergensfjord*. Arrived New York 4 June 1936	Belgrade, Yugoslavia Oslo, Norway
14 January 1937	April 1937	Haiti with Louis

BIBLIOGRAPHY

'Abdu'l-Bahá. *'Abdu'l-Bahá in London: Addresses and Notes of Conversations.* London: Bahá'í Publishing Trust, 1987.

— *Paris Talks: Talks Given by 'Abdu'l-Bahá in 1911–12.* (1912). London: Bahá'í Publishing Trust, 12th ed. 1995.

— *The Promulgation of Universal Peace: Talks Delivered by 'Abdu'l-Bahá During His Visit to the United States and Canada in 1912.* Comp. H. MacNutt. Wilmette, IL: Bahá'í Publishing Trust, 2nd ed. 1982.

— *Tablets of 'Abdu'l-Bahá* (etext in the Ocean search engine; originally published as *Tablets of Abdul-Baha Abbas.* 3 vols. Chicago: Bahá'í Publishing Society, 1909–1916). Wilmette, IL: National Spiritual Assembly of the Bahá'ís of the United States, 1980.

— *Tablets of the Divine Plan.* Wilmette, IL: Bahá'í Publishing Trust, 1993.

Asdaq, Rúhá. *One Life, One Memory.* Oxford: George Ronald, 1999.

Atkinson, Anne Gordon et al. *Green Acre on the Piscataqua: A Centennial Celebration.* Eliot, Maine: Green Acre Bahá'í School Council, 1991.

Bahá'í Holy Places in Haifa and the Western Galilee: Historical Description and Documentation. Haifa: Bahá'í World Centre, 2005.

Bahá'í News. National Spiritual Assembly of the Bahá'ís of the United States and Canada, 1924–. Dec. 1925–Jan. 1926, Feb. 1926, Aug. 1927, July 1928, April 1929, March 1935, June 1938, Nov. 1943, April–May 1945, Sept. 1946.

Bahá'í Prayers: A Selection of Prayers Revealed by Bahá'u'lláh, The Báb, and 'Abdu'l-Bahá. Wilmette, IL: Bahá'í Publishing Trust, rev. ed. 2002.

The Bahá'í World: An International Record. Vol. V (1932-1934), Wilmette, IL: Bahá'í Publishing Trust, 1936; vol. VI (1934–1936), Wilmette, IL: Bahá'í Publishing Trust, 1937; vol. VII (1936–1938), Wilmette IL.; Bahá'í Publishing Trust, 1939; vol. IX (1940–1944), Wilmette, IL:; Bahá'í Publishing Trust, 1945; vol. X (1944–1946), Wilmette, IL: Bahá'í Publishing Trust, 1949; vol. XII (1950-1954), Wilmette, IL: Bahá'í Publishing Trust, 1956; vol. XIII (1954-1963), Haifa, The Universal House of Justice, 1970; vol. XVI (1973–1976), Haifa: Bahá'í World Centre, 1978; vol. XX (1986–1992), Haifa: Bahá'í World Centre, 1998.

Bahá'í World Centre. *Century of Light.* New Delhi: Bahá'í Publishing Trust, 2001.

Bahá'u'lláh. *The Kitáb-i-Aqdas: The Most Holy Book*. Haifa: Bahá'í World Centre, 1992.

Balyuzi, H. M. *'Abdu'l-Bahá: The Centre of the Covenant*. Oxford: George Ronald, 1971.

Beavan, Arthur Henry. *Imperial London*. London: J. M. Dent, 1901.

Behman, Natalia. *L'implantation de la foi bahá'ie en France et impact de la venue de Abdu'l Baha à Paris au début du XXème siècle*. Mémoire D.E.S. Available at www.bahai-biblio.org.

Blomfield, Lady. *The Chosen Highway*. London: Bahá'í Publishing Trust, 1940. RP Oxford: George Ronald, 2007.

Cameron, Glenn; Momen, Wendi. *A Basic Bahá'í Chronology*. Oxford: George Ronald, 1996.

Thomas Cook & Son. *Cook's Tourists' Handbook for Palestine and Syria 1911*. London: Thomas Cook & Son, 1911.

— *The Traveller's Handbook for Belgium and the Ardennes with Maps and Plan*. London: Thomas Cook & Son, 1921.

Crawford, Elizabeth. *The Women's Suffrage Movement: A Reference Guide 1866–1928*. London: UCL Press, 1999.

— *The Women's Suffrage Movement in Britain and Ireland*. London: Routledge, 2006.

Dichter, Bernard. *Akko: Sites from the Turkish Period*. Ed. Alex Carmel and Zalman Baumwoll. Haifa: Gottlieb Schumacher Institute for Research of the Christian Activities in 19th Century Palestine, University of Haifa, 2000.

Dreyfus-Barney, Laura C.; Shoghi Effendi. 'Biography of Hippolyte Dreyfus Barney' (1928). Ed. Thomas Linard. Available at: https://bahai-library-online.

Ecclesia, Mariana *Life for the Faith: Key Moments in the Life of Annemarie Krueger and Her Path into the Bahá'í Faith*. Sofia: Sonm Publishers, 2004.

Egea, Amín. *Apostle of Peace: A Survey of References to 'Abdu'l-Bahá in the Western Press 1871–1921. Vol. 1, 1871–1912. Vol. 2, 1912–1921*. Oxford: George Ronald, 2016.

Gail, M. *Arches of the Years*. Oxford: George Ronald, 1991.

— *Summon up Remembrance*. Oxford: George Ronald, 1987.

Garis, M. R. *Martha Root: Lioness at the Threshold*. Wilmette, IL: Bahá'í Publishing Trust, 1983.

Gregory, Louis. *A Heavenly Vista*. Available at: https://bahai-library.com.

Guéry, Annaïck. *May Bolles-Maxwell: La 'Servante bien-aimée'*. Paris: Association Baha'ie de Femme, 1998.

Hall, Richard C. *The Balkan Wars, 1912–1913: Prelude to the First World War*. London: Routledge, 2000.

Harper, Barron Deems. *Lights of Fortitude*. Oxford: George Ronald, 1997.

Hart, Peter. *The Great War 1914–1918*. London: Profile Books, 2014.

Hogenson, Kathryn Jewett. *Lighting the Western Sky*. Oxford: George Ronald, 2010.

Jasion, Jan Teofil. *Never Be Afraid to Dare*. Oxford: George Ronald, 2001.

Ma'ani, Baharieh Rouhani. *Leaves of the Twin Divine Trees*. Oxford: George Ronald, 2008.

McKay, Doris with Paul Vreeland. *Fires in Many Hearts*. Manotick, ON: Nine Pines Publishing, 1991.

Maude, R.; Maude, D. *The Servant, the General and Armageddon*. Oxford: George Ronald, 1998.

Momen, Moojan (ed.). *The Bábí and Bahá'í Religions, 1844–1944: Some Contemporary Western Accounts*. Oxford: George Ronald, 1981.

— *John Ebenezer Esslemont* (1995). Available at: https://bahai-library.com.

Morrison, Gayle. *To Move the World: Louis G. Gregory and the Advancement of Racial Unity in America*. Wilmette, IL: Bahá'í Publishing Trust, 1982.

Nakhjavani, Violette. *A Tribute to Amatu'l-Bahá Rúḥíyyih Khánum*. Available at: www.bahai.org.

— *The Maxwells of Montreal*. Vol. 1: *Early Years 1870–1922*. Oxford: George Ronald, 2011.

— ; Nakhjavani, Bahiyyih. *The Maxwells of Montreal*. Vol. 2: *Middle and Late Years*. Oxford: George Ronald, 2012.

Old Ordnance Survey Maps: Anerley & Penge 1868 (Kent sheet 7.14); Beckenham & Penge 1894 (London sheet 146)

Osborn, Lil. *Religion and Relevance: The Bahá'ís in Britain, 1899–1930*. Los Angeles, Kalimát Press, 2014.

Parsons, Agnes. *'Abdu'l-Bahá in America: Agnes Parsons' Diary April 11, 1912–November 11, 1912*. Annotated and ed. Richard Hollinger. Foreword by Sandra Hutchison. Los Angeles: Kalimát Press, 1996.

The Passing of 'Abdu'l-Bahá: A Compilation. Los Angeles: Kalimát Press, 1991.

Perkins, Mary. *Servant of the Glory: The Life of 'Abdu'l-Bahá*. Oxford: George Ronald, 1999.

Rabbani, Rúḥíyyih. *The Priceless Pearl*. London: Bahá'í Publishing Trust, 2000.

Redman, Earl. *'Abdu'l-Bahá in Their Midst*. Oxford: George Ronald, 2011.

— *Shoghi Effendi Through the Pilgrim's Eye*. Vol. 1: *Building the Administrative Order, 1922–1952*. Oxford: George Ronald, 2015; vol. 2: *The Ten Year Crusade, 1953–1953*. Oxford: George Ronald, 2016.

Ruhe, David S. *Door of Hope: The Bahá'í Faith in the Holy Land*. Oxford: George Ronald, 2nd rev. ed. 2001.

Ruhe-Schoen, Janet. *Champions of Oneness: Louis Gregory and his Shining Circle*. Wilmette, IL: Bahá'í Publishing, 2015.

Rutstein, Nathan *Corinne True: Faithful handmaid of 'Abdu'l-Bahá*. Oxford: George Ronald, 1987.

Shoghi Effendi *Citadel of Faith: Messages to America, 1947–1957*. Wilmette, IL: Bahá'í Publishing Trust, 1965. Available at: www.bahai.org (Baha'i Reference Library).

— *God Passes By* (1944). Wilmette, IL: Bahá'í Publishing Trust, rev. ed. 1974. Available at: www.bahai.org (Baha'i Reference Library).

— *Messages to America 1932-1946*. Wilmette, IL: Bahá'í Publishing Trust, 1947. Published online by the Project Gutenberg, also available at: www.bahai.org (Baha'i Reference Library).

— *The World Order of Bahá'u'lláh: Selected Letters by Shoghi Effendi* (1938). Wilmette, IL : Bahá'í Publishing Trust, 2nd rev. ed. 1974.

Sohrab, Ahmad. *'Abdu'l-Bahá in Egypt*. New York: New History Foundation, 1929. Available at: irfancolloquia.org; also at http//bahai-library.com.

Sollors, Werner (ed.). *Interracialism: Black-White Intermarriage in American History, Literature, and Law*. Oxford: Oxford University Press, 2000.

Sparey Fox, Carolyn. *Seeking a State of Heaven*. Oxford: George Ronald, 2018.

Spence, Martin. *The Making of a London Suburb: Capital Comes to Penge*. Monmouth: Merlin Press, 2007.

Star of the West: The Bahai Magazine. Periodical, 25 vols. 1910–1935. Vols. 1–14 RP Oxford: George Ronald, 1978. Complete CD-ROM version: Talisman Educational Software/Special Ideas, 2001. Available at: https://bahai-library.com

Szanto-Felbermann, Renée. *Rebirth: The Memoirs of Renée Szanto-Felbermann*. Oakham: Bahá'í Publishing Trust, 1980.

Thompson, Juliet. *The Diary of Juliet Thompson*. Los Angeles: Kalimát Press, 1995.

Tudor Pole, Wellesley. *Writing on the Ground*. London: Neville Spearman, 1968.

Ward, A. L. *239 Days: 'Abdu'l-Bahá's Journey in America*. Wilmette, IL: Bahá'í Publishing Trust, 1979.

Weinberg, Robert. *Ethel Jenner Rosenberg: England's Outstanding Bahá'í Pioneer*. Oxford: George Ronald, 1995.

— *Lady Blomfield: Her Life and Times*. Oxford: George Ronald, 2012.

Whitmore, Bruce W. *The Dawning Place: The Building of a Temple, the Forging of the North American Bahá'í Community*. Wilmette, IL: Bahá'í Publishing Trust, 1984.

Zarqání, Mírzá Maḥmúd. *Maḥmúd's Diary: The Diary of Mírzá Maḥmúd-i-Zarqání Chronicling 'Abdu'l-Bahá's Journey to America.* Trans. Mohi Sobhani with the assistance of Shirley Macias. Oxford: George Ronald, 1998.

Archival collections

United States Bahá'í National Archives (USBNA)
Louise M. Gregory Papers

Louis G. Gregory Papers

Agnes Parsons Papers

Hannen-Knobloch Papers

Martha Root Papers

Office of the Secretary of the NSA Files on Individuals 1925–1929

Office of the Secretary of the NSA Files on Individuals 1930–1939

Office of the Secretary of the NSA Files on Individuals 1940–1949

Original Shoghi Effendi Letters Collection

Translations of Tablets of 'Abdu'l-Bahá Collection

Gregory, L. G. & Gregory, L. A. M. *A Teaching Campaign in Haiti*

Spiritual Assembly of the Bahá'ís of Eliot, Maine Archives
Louis G. Gregory Papers

Louise Gregory Papers

Thomas Cook Archives
Guidebooks, timetables etc. including:

The Overland Desert Mail: The Direct Road to the East, Nairn Transport Company brochure, 1925

Summer in Czechoslovakia, Thomas Cook brochure, 1931

The Traveller's Handbook for Belgium and the Ardennes with Maps and Plan, Thomas Cook & Son, 1921

Frequently used websites
www.ancestry.co.uk and www.ancestry.com (for UK and US censuses, ship passenger logs, US passport applications, military records and death records)

www.bahai-library.com

NOTES AND REFERENCES

1. The First Pilgrimage
1. Morrison, *To Move the World*, pp. 16–17.
2. 'Abdu'l-Bahá, *Tablets of 'Abdu'l-Bahá*, p. 430.
3. Morrison, *To Move the World*, p. 42.
4. Osborn, *Religion and Relevance*, p. 105.
5. Gregory, *A Heavenly Vista*.
6. ibid.
7. ibid.
8. ibid.
9. ibid.
10. ibid.
11. ibid.
12. Sohrab, *'Abdu'l-Bahá in Egypt*, pp. 109–10.
13. Gregory, *A Heavenly Vista*.
14. For further information about the Templers, see Sparey Fox, *Seeking a State of Heaven*.
15. *Cook's Tourists' Handbook for Palestine and Syria 1911*, p. 197.
16. Ethel S. Stevens, 'Abbas Effendi: His Personality, Work and Followers', in *The Fortnightly Review* (June 1911), quoted in Egea, *Apostle of Peace*, vol. 1, p. 46.
17. Gregory, *A Heavenly Vista*.
18. ibid.
19. Munavvar Khánum, letter to Louise, 28 January 1922, USBNA, Louise M. Gregory Papers.
20. Gregory, *A Heavenly Vista*.
21. ibid.
22. 'Abdu'l-Bahá, Tablet to Döring, translated 15 August 1911, quoted in Morrison, *To Move the World*, p. 47.
23. 'Abdu'l-Bahá, Tablet to Mary Ellen Hooper, translated 15 August 1911, quoted ibid. pp. 47–8.
24. 'In Memoriam' article on Alma Knobloch, in *The Bahá'í World*, vol. IX, p. 642; quoted in Redman, *'Abdu'l-Bahá in Their Midst*, p. 312.
25. *Star of the West*, vol. II, no. 17 (19 January 1912), p. 8.
26. ibid. no. 5 (5 June 1911), p. 7.
27. Louise Gregory, letter to Agnes Parsons, 18 January 1921, USBNA, Agnes Parsons Papers.

2. The Egg Merchant and His Brood
1. Obituary of Michael Mathew, *Beckenham Journal*, 20 March 1909.
2. *London Gazette*, Issue no. 19826 (14 February 1840), p. 320; and *London Gazette*, Issue no. 20485 (4 July 1845), p. 2018.
3. Spence, *The Making of a London Suburb: Capital Comes to Penge*.

4   Obituary of Michael Mathew, *Beckenham Journal*, 20 March 1909.
5   United Kingdom census 1861.
6   Obituary of Michael Mathew, *Beckenham Journal*, 20 March 1909.
7   Beavan, *Imperial London*, p. 277.
8   United Kingdom census 1891.
9   Obituary of Michael Mathew, *Beckenham Journal*, 20 March 1909.
10 United Kingdom census 1911.
11 United Kingdom census 1881.
12 Information from Crawford, *The Women's Suffrage Movement in Britain and Ireland*, p. 548.

3. Louise Spreads Her Wings

1   Obituary of Louise Gregory, in *The Bahá'í World*, vol. XIII, p. 876.
2   Will of Emma Mathew dated 11 November 1910, HM Probate Records.
3   Letter from Louise Gregory to Pauline Hannen, 15 October 1912, USBNA, Hannen-Knobloch Papers, Pauline Hannen correspondence.
4   1870 Education Act, available at: www.parliament.uk.
5   See the Royal Holloway website at www.royalholloway.ac.uk.
6   Archives of Royal Holloway College.
7   University of Edinburgh Archives.
8   'Pupils honour teacher who blazed a trail for women', in *The Scotsman*, 10 November 2008. Available at: http://www.scotsman.com/news/pupils-honour-teacher-who-blazed-a-trail-for-women-1-1278743.
9   University of Cambridge Archives.
10 Letter from Louise to Horace Holley, 24 July 1946, USBNA, Office of the Secretary of the NSA Files on Individuals 1940–1949.
11 Letter from Louise to Agnes Parsons, 5 February 1925, USBNA, Agnes Parsons Papers.
12 ibid.
13 Laura C. Dreyfus-Barney and Shoghi Effendi, 'Biography of Hippolyte Dreyfus-Barney' (ed. Thomas Linard).
14 Hogenson, *Lighting the Western Sky*, p. 190, and note 74 to Chapter 11.
15 Nakhjavani, *The Maxwells of Montreal*, vol. 1, p. 106.
16 Shoghi Effendi, *God Passes By*, p. 259.
17 Nakhjavani, *The Maxwells of Montreal*, vol. 1, p. 145.
18 Jasion, *Never Be Afraid to Dare*, p. 22.
19 *Beckenham Journal*, 13 March 1909.
20 ibid. 20 March 1909.
21 Tablet of 'Abdu'l-Bahá directed to Louise Mathew in Paris via Marion Jack and Mr Dreyfus before her declaration, USBNA, Louise M. Gregory Papers.
22 Tablet of 'Abdu'l-Bahá to Louise Mathew before her declaration acknowledging her letter of 14 November 1909, ibid.
23 Tablet of 'Abdu'l-Bahá to Louise Mathew received after her declaration, December 1909, ibid.
24 Tablet of 'Abdu'l-Bahá to Louise Mathew received c. 1910, USBNA, Translations of Tablets of 'Abdu'l-Bahá. Translated for Louise into French, paraphrased here by the author from the French.

4. With the Master in London and Paris

1. Gregory, *A Heavenly Vista*.
2. Tablet of 'Abdu'l-Bahá to Louise Mathew received c. 1910, USBNA, Translations of Tablets of 'Abdu'l-Bahá. Paraphrased by the author from the French.
3. Registration card completed by Louise Gregory in 1935 on her transfer to Eliot, Maine Bahá'í community, Spiritual Assembly of the Bahá'ís of Eliot, Maine Archives, Louise Gregory Papers.
4. Bahá'í World Centre, *Century of Light*, p. 20.
5. 'Abdu'l-Bahá, *'Abdu'l-Bahá in London*, pp. 19–20.
6. ibid. p. 21.
7. ibid. p. 27.
8. ibid. p. 85.
9. ibid. p. 91.
10. ibid.
11. ibid. p. 81.
12. ibid. p. 83.
13. Letter from the National Spiritual Assembly of the United Kingdom to the Bahá'ís of the United Kingdom, 5 November 2014.
14. 'Abdu'l-Bahá, *'Abdu'l-Bahá in London*, pp. 44–5.
15. ibid. p. 47, which gives the date 13 September when these words were spoken, but Redman in *'Abdu'l-Bahá in Their Midst*, p. 30 gives the dates 6 and 12 September for Mrs Thornburgh-Cropper's 'At Homes' and *Star of the West*, vol. II, no. 12 (16 October 1911), p. 4 also gives 12 September.
16. ibid. p. 49.
17. He visited again from 13 December 1912 to 21 January 1913 when He visited both England and Scotland.
18. See www.passmoreedwards.org.uk.
19. *'Abdu'l-Bahá in London*, p. 33 states that 460 people attended whereas *Star of the West*, vol. II, no. 13 (4 November 1911), p. 4 states that 200 attended.
20. 'Abdu'l-Bahá, *'Abdu'l-Bahá in London*, pp. 38–9.
21. *Star of the West*, vol. II, no. 14 (23 November 1911), p. 3.
22. Registration card completed by Louise Gregory in 1935 on her transfer to Eliot, Maine Bahá'í community, Spiritual Assembly of the Bahá'ís of Eliot, Maine Archives, Louise Gregory Papers.
23. *Star of the West*, vol. II, no. 14 (23 November 1911), p. 3.
24. ibid.
25. 'Abdu'l-Bahá, *Paris Talks*, no. 6, pp. 17–19.
26. ibid. no. 28, p. 81.
27. ibid. no. 39, pp. 124–5.
28. ibid. no. 40, p. 136.
29. *Star of the West*, vol. II, no. 18 (7 February 1912), pp. 6–7.
30. 'Abdu'l-Bahá, *Paris Talks*, no. 24, p. 69.
31. *Star of the West*, vol. II, no. 14 (23 November 1911), p. 15.
32. Behnam, *L'implantation de la foi baha'ie en France et impact de la venue de Abdu'l Baha à Paris au début du XXème siècle*.
33. 'Abdu'l-Bahá, *Paris Talks*, no. 37, pp. 115–16.
34. ibid. no. 53, pp. 157–8.

35 Letter from Marion Jack to Horace Holley, 11 March 1934, quoted in Jasion, *Never Be Afraid to Dare*, p. 134.
36 Letter from Louise Gregory to Agnes Parsons, 29 September 1920, USBNA, Agnes Parsons Papers.
37 Letter from Louise Gregory to Agnes Parsons, 18 January 1921, USBNA, Agnes Parsons Papers.

5. The seed is sown

1 *Star of the West*, vol. III, no. 2 (9 April 1912) p. 8. Other accounts give 27 March.
2 Zarqání, *Maḥmúd's Diary: The Diary of Mírzá Maḥmúd-i-Zarqání Chronicling 'Abdu'l-Bahá's Journey to America*.
3 ibid. p. 23.
4 Letter from Louise to Agnes Parsons, 18 January 1921, USBNA, Agnes Parsons Papers.
5 Letter from Louis to Pauline Hannen, 19 September 1912, USBNA, Hannen-Knobloch Papers, Pauline Hannen correspondence, quoted in Morrison, *To Move the World*, p. 64; Redman, *'Abdu'l-Bahá in Their Midst*, p. 99.
6 Zarqání, *Maḥmúd's Diary*, p. 24.
7 ibid. p. 27.
8 ibid. p. 30.
9 ibid. p. 33.
10 SS *Cedric* passenger manifest.
11 *Star of the West*, vol. III, no. 3 (28 April 1912), p. 4.
12 ibid. p. 3.
13 Thompson, *Diary*, pp. 232–4.
14 Zarqání, *Maḥmúd's Diary*, p. 38.
15 ibid. pp. 44–5.
16 ibid. p. 47.
17 ibid. p. 48.
18 ibid. p. 46.
19 *Star of the West*, vol. III, no. 3 (28 April 1912) p. 6.
20 Thompson, *Diary*, p. 273.
21 'Abdu'l-Bahá, *The Promulgation of Universal Peace*, p. 44.
22 Story related in the 'In Memoriam' article for Louis Gregory, *The Bahá'í World*, vol. XII (1950–1954), p. 668.
23 Excerpts from the *Cleveland News* and *Cleveland Plain Dealer*, May 1912, quoted in Ward, *239 Days*, pp. 60–62.
24 *The Bahá'í World*, vol. XX, p. 917.

6. The Seed Grows

1 Zarqání, *Maḥmúd's Diary*, p. 66.
2 Letter from Louise to Agnes Parsons, 18 January 1921, USBNA, Agnes Parsons Papers.
3 ibid.
4 *Chicago Daily News*, 29 April 1912, quoted in Whitmore, *The Dawning Place*, p. 57.
5 Zarqání, *Maḥmúd's Diary*, p. 67.
6 Petition drafted by 11 members of the Chicago 'House of Spirituality', quoted in Whitmore, *The Dawning Place*, pp. 4–5.

7   'Abdu'l-Bahá, *Tablets of 'Abdu'l-Bahá*, vol. 1, p. 19.
8   Letter from Carl Scheffler to Edna and Katherine True and Arna True Perron, 6 June 1961, in personal papers of Edna M. True, quoted in Whitmore, *The Dawning Place*, p. 36.
9   Letter from Mírzá Asadu'lláh to unidentified Bahá'ís, 4 June 1908, in personal papers of Edna M. True quoted in Whitmore, *The Dawning Place*, p. 46.
10 *Star of the West*, vol. III, no. 4 (17 May 1912), p. 32.
11 ibid. pp. 5–6.
12 Zarqání, *Maḥmúd's Diary*, p. 72.
13 *Star of the West*, vol. III, no. 4 (17 May 1912), p. 6; Whitmore, *The Dawning Place*, p. 263.
14 ibid. p. 7.
15 Mardíyyih Nabil Carpenter (later Marzieh Gail) in *The Bahá'í World*, Vol. VII (1936–1938), p. 219, quoted in Whitmore, *The Dawning Place*, p. 65.
16 Letter from Louise to Agnes Parsons, 18 January 1921, USBNA, Agnes Parsons Papers.
17 Registration card completed by Louise Gregory in 1935 on her transfer to Eliot, Maine Bahá'í community, Spiritual Assembly of the Bahá'ís of Eliot, Maine Archives, Louise Gregory Papers.
18 Letter from Louis to Louise, 8 July 1912, USBNA, Louise M. Gregory Papers.
19 Parsons, *Agnes Parsons' Diary*.
20 Zarqání, *Maḥmúd's Diary*, pp. 189–90. See also note 227, p. 481, clarifying the date.
21 Tablet of 'Abdu'l-Bahá to Louise Mathew from Dublin, New Hampshire, 1912, USBNA, Translations of Tablets of 'Abdu'l-Bahá.
22 Letter from Louise to Agnes Parsons, 18 January 1921, USBNA, Agnes Parsons Papers.
23 Letter from Alfred Lunt to Agnes Parsons, 4 April 1914, USBNA, Agnes Parsons Papers, quoted in Morrison, *To Move the World*, pp. 64–5.
24 Letter from Louis to Pauline Hannen, 30 September 1912, USBNA, Hannen-Knobloch Papers, Pauline Hannen correspondence, quoted in Morrison, *To Move the World*, p. 68.
25 ibid.
26 *Chicago Defender*, 28 September 1912, p. 4, col. 4, n.t. quoted in Egea, *Apostle of Peace*, vol. 2.
27 Letter from Louis to Pauline Hannen, 30 September 1912, USBNA, Hannen-Knobloch Papers, Pauline Hannen correspondence, quoted in Morrison, *To Move the World*, p. 68.

7. 'A fortress for well-being'

1   From a prayer revealed by Bahá'u'lláh, in *Bahá'í Prayers*, p. 118.
2   Letter from Louise to Pauline Hannen, 15 October 1912, USBNA, Hannen-Knobloch Papers, Pauline Hannen correspondence.
3   Letter from Louise to Agnes Parsons, 17 March 1914, USBNA, Agnes Parsons Papers.
4   Zarqání, *Maḥmúd's Diary*, p. 70.
5   Letter from Louise to Agnes Parsons, 11 March 1914, USBNA, Agnes Parsons Papers.

6   Letter from Louise to Agnes Parsons, 18 April 1914, USBNA, Agnes Parsons Papers.
7   Morrison, *To Move the World*, pp. 73-81.
8   Ward, *239 Days*, p. 181.
9   Letter from the Gregorys to the Washington Bahá'í community, 30 October 1912, USBNA, Hannen-Knobloch Papers, Joseph Hannen correspondence.
10 Letter from Louise to Agnes Parsons, 21 December 1914, USBNA, Agnes Parsons Papers.
11 Letter from Louise to 'Dear Sister in el Abha', 20 June 1916, quoted in Ruhe-Schoen, *Champions of Oneness*, p. 148.
12 Letter from Louise to Agnes Parsons, 21 December 1914, USBNA, Agnes Parsons Papers.
13 Tablet from 'Abdu'l-Bahá to Louis and Louise Gregory, 1914, quoted in *Bahá'í World*, vol. 12 (1950-1954), p. 669.
14 Letters from Louise to Agnes Parsons, 11 and 12 March 1914, USBNA, Agnes Parsons Papers.
15 Letters from Louise to Agnes Parsons, 12 and 17 March and 18 April 1914, USBNA, Agnes Parsons Papers.
16 Morrison, *To Move The World*, p. 103.
17 Roy Williams, from USBNA, taped personal recollections, Greensboro, NC, 1980; quoted in Ruhe-Schoen, *Champions of Oneness* p. 149.
18 Letters from Louise to Pauline Hannen, 15, 16 and 17 August 1913, quoted in Ruhe-Schoen, *Champions of Oneness*, p. 142.
19 Morrison, *To Move the World*, pp. 64-5.
20 Robert K. Merton, 'Intermarriage and the social structure: Fact and fiction', in *Psychiatry*, vol. 4 (August 1941), pp. 361-74, quoted in Sollors, *Interracialism*, p. 480.
21 W. D. Zabel, 'Interracial marriage and the law', in *Atlantic Monthly* (October 1965), pp. 75-9, quoted in Sollors, *Interracialism*, p. 60.
22 Letter from Louis to Edith Chapman, 27 September 1933, quoted in Morrison, *To Move the World*, p. 71; and in Ruhe-Schoen, *Champions of Oneness*, p. 211.
23 Letter from Louis to Edith M. Chapman, 17 June 1930, quoted in Morrison, *To Move the World*, p. 92.
24 Letter from Louis to Louise, 21 October 1917 from New York City, USBNA, Louise M. Gregory Papers.
25 Letter from Louis to Louise, 7 December 1917 from Chicago, USBNA, Louise M. Gregory Papers.
26 Letter from Louis to Louise, 5 November 1917 from Cleveland, Ohio, USBNA, Louise M. Gregory Papers.

8. 'Two birds in the nest of Thy love'

1   From a prayer revealed by 'Abdu'l-Bahá, in *Bahá'í Prayers*, p. 119.
2   Tablet from 'Abdu'l-Bahá to Louise Gregory, 16 October 1920, translated by 'Azízu'lláh S. Bahádur, USBNA, Louise M. Gregory Papers.
3   Letter from Louise to Agnes Parsons, 30 September 1920 from Portland, MA, USBNA, Agnes Parsons Papers.
4   Letter from Louise to Agnes Parsons, 18 January 1921, USBNA, Agnes Parsons Papers.

5   Letter from Louise to Agnes Parsons, 30 September 1920 from Portland, MA, USBNA, Agnes Parsons Papers.
6   Hutchison, Foreword to Parsons, *'Abdu'l-Bahá in America: Agnes Parsons' Diary*, p. xvi.
7   Letter from Louise to Agnes Parsons, 18 January 1921, USBNA, Agnes Parsons Papers.
8   Letter from Louis to Louise, 5 November 1917 from Cleveland, Ohio, USBNA, Louise M. Gregory Papers.
9   *Star of the West*, vol. VIII, no. 9 (20 August 1917), p. 120.
10 Letter from Louise to Joseph Hannen, 27 June 1919, USBNA, Hannen-Knobloch Papers, Joseph Hannen correspondence.
11 Letter from Louise to Agnes Parsons, 4 May 1916, USBNA, Agnes Parsons Papers.
12 Letter from Louise to Agnes Parsons, 18 January 1921, USBNA, Agnes Parsons Papers.
13 Letter from Louise to Agnes Parsons, 21 December 1914, USBNA, Agnes Parsons Papers.
14 Letter from Louise to Agnes Parsons, 4 May 1916, USBNA, Agnes Parsons Papers.
15 Will of Emma Mathew dated 11 November 1910, HM Probate Records.

9. 'Diffuse the divine fragrances'

1   'Abdu'l-Bahá, *Tablets of the Divine Plan*, p. 41.
2   Shoghi Effendi, *God Passes By*, pp. 303–5.
3   Message from the Universal House of Justice to the Conference of the Continental Boards of Counsellors, 29 December 2015, p. 16.
4   Shoghi Effendi, *God Passes By*, p. 305.
5   'Abdu'l-Bahá, *Tablets of the Divine Plan*, Foreword to the 1977 edition, p. xix.
6   *Star of the West*, vol. VII, no. 10 (8 September 1916), p. 86.
7   'Abdu'l-Bahá, *Tablets of the Divine Plan*, pp. 11–12.
8   Letter from Louise to Agnes Parsons, 4 May 1916, USBNA, Agnes Parsons Papers.
9   Letter from Louise to Agnes Parsons, 30 September 1920, USBNA, Agnes Parsons Papers.
10 'Abdu'l-Bahá, *Tablets of the Divine Plan*, pp. 70–71.
11 Letter from Louise to Agnes Parsons, 18 January 1921, USBNA, Agnes Parsons Papers.
12 Letter from Louis to Alfred Lunt, 23 September 1917, quoted in Morrison, *To Move the World*, p. 86.
13 Letter from Louise to Joseph Hannen, 10 June 1919, USBNA, Hannen-Knobloch Papers, Joseph Hannen correspondence.
14 Letter from Louise to Joseph Hannen, 11 June 1919, USBNA, Hannen-Knobloch Papers, Joseph Hannen correspondence.
15 'Abdu'l-Bahá, *Tablets of the Divine Plan*, pp. 53–4.
16 Morrison, *To Move the World*, p. 93.
17 Letter from Louise to Agnes Parsons, 29 September 1920, USBNA, Agnes Parsons Papers.
18 Letter from Louise to Agnes Parsons, 18 January 1921, USBNA, Agnes Parsons Papers.

19 Letter from Louise to Agnes Parsons, 29 September 1920, USBNA, Agnes Parsons Papers.
20 Letter from Louise to Agnes Parsons, 25 June 1920, USBNA, Agnes Parsons Papers.
21 Letter from Louise to Albert Vail, 19 May 1914, quoted in Ruhe-Schoen, *Champions of Oneness*, p. 143.
22 Letter from Louise to Joseph Hannen, 1 September 1917, quoted ibid. p. 163.
23 'Abdu'l-Bahá, *Tablets of the Divine Plan*, p. 41.
24 Letter from Louise to Joseph Hannen, 10 June 1919, USBNA, Hannen-Knobloch Papers, Joseph Hannen correspondence.
25 Letter from Louise to Joseph Hannen, 11 June 1919, USBNA, Hannen-Knobloch Papers, Joseph Hannen correspondence.
26 Tablet from 'Abdu'l-Bahá to Louise, 25 August 1919, USBNA, Translations of Tablets of 'Abdu'l-Bahá Collection.

10. The First Trip

1 Quoted in Shoghi Effendi, *God Passes By*, pp. 309–10.
2 ibid. p. 312.
3 ibid.
4 *Star of the West*, vol. XII, no. 15 (12 December 1921), p. 245.
5 ibid. no. 18 (7 February 1922), p. 273.
6 ibid. vol XIII, no. 1 (21 March 1922) pp. 17–18.
7 US National Teaching Committee, *Teaching Bulletin*, 31 March 1922, pp. 3–4, USBNA, Lunt Papers, quoted in Morrison, *To Move the World*, pp. 115–16.
8 *Star of the West*, vol. XIII, no. 4 (17 May 1922) p. 68; quoted in Rutstein, *Corinne True: Faithful Handmaid of 'Abdu'l-Bahá*, p. 155.
9 US National Teaching Committee, *Teaching Bulletin*, 31 March 1922, p. 11, USBNA, Lunt Papers, quoted in Morrison, *To Move the World*, p. 122.
10 US National Teaching Committee, *Teaching Bulletin*, 16 October 1922, p. 8, USBNA, Lunt Papers, quoted in Morrison, *To Move the World*, p. 122–3.
11 Thomas Cook, *The Traveller's Handbook for Belgium and the Ardennes with Maps and Plan* (1921), p. 210.
12 Letter from the Greatest Holy Leaf to nine-person body in Haifa, quoted in Rabbani, *The Priceless Pearl*, p. 57.
13 Rabbani, ibid.
14 Letter on behalf of Shoghi Effendi from 'Azízu'lláh Bahádur to Louise Gregory, 8 July 1923, USBNA, Original Shoghi Effendi Letters Collection.
15 Moojan Momen, *John Ebenezer Esslemont*.
16 The Hands of the Cause of God were appointed by Bahá'u'lláh, 'Abdu'l-Bahá and Shoghi Effendi with the duty of protecting and propagating the Bahá'í Faith. In some cases they were appointed posthumously in recognition of their services. For further information see note 183 in Bahá'u'lláh, *The Kitáb-i-Aqdas*.

11. 'Spiritual gladness'

1 Letter written on behalf of Shoghi Effendi by 'Azízu'lláh Bahádur to Louise, 5 January 1924, USBNA, Original Shoghi Effendi Letters Collection.
2 Morrison, *To Move the World*, p. 123.
3 Letter written on behalf of Shoghi Effendi by 'Azízu'lláh Bahádur to Louise, 5 January 1924, USBNA, Original Shoghi Effendi Letters Collection.

NOTES AND REFERENCES

4   Letter from Louise to Horace Holley, 24 June 1925, USBNA, Office of the Secretary of the NSA Files on Individuals 1925–1929.
5   Letter from Louise to Agnes Parsons, 5 February 1925, USBNA, Agnes Parsons Papers.
6   ibid.
7   Bahá'í Temple Unity, Proceedings of the Annual Meeting, 1922, p. 308, Bahá'í Temple Unity Records quoted in Morrison, *To Move the World*, p. 136.
8   Letter from Louise to Joseph Hannen, 23 July 1919, quoted in Ruhe-Schoen, *Champions of Oneness*, p. 181.
9   Letter from Louise to Agnes Parsons, 5 February 1925, USBNA, Agnes Parsons Papers.
10 Letter written on behalf of Shoghi Effendi by Dr J. Esslemont to Louise, 12 January 1925, USBNA, Original Shoghi Effendi Letters Collection.
11 Letter from Louise to Agnes Parsons, 5 February 1925, USBNA, Agnes Parsons Papers.
12 ibid.
13 ibid.
14 ibid.
15 Letter from Louise to Horace Holley, 24 June 1925, written on board *SS Zeeland*, USBNA, Office of the Secretary of the NSA Files on Individuals 1925–1929.
16 ibid.
17 ibid.
18 ibid.
19 ibid.
20 It seems likely that this is the same family that Renée Szanto describes in her autobiography *Rebirth: The Memoirs of Renée Szanto-Felbermann*.
21 Letter from Louise to Horace Holley, 24 June 1925, written on board *SS Zeeland*, USBNA, Office of the Secretary of the NSA Files on Individuals 1925–1929.
22 Harper, *Lights of Fortitude*, pp. 253 and 256.
23 *Bahá'í News Letter*, December 1925–January 1926, p. 7.
24 Letter written on behalf of Shoghi Effendi by his secretary to Louise, 10 June 1925, USBNA, Original Shoghi Effendi Letters Collection.
25 Letter written on behalf of Shoghi Effendi by Soheil Afnan to Louise, 28 September 1925, USBNA, Original Shoghi Effendi Letters Collection.

12. First Visit to the Balkans

1   Letter from Louise to Horace Holley, 1 January 1926, USBNA, Office of the Secretary of the NSA Files on Individuals 1925–1929.
2   *Bahá'í News Letter*, February 1926, p. 5.
3   Rabbani, *The Priceless Pearl*, p. 103.
4   Garis, *Martha Root: Lioness at the Threshold*, p. 88.
5   Letter from Louise to Horace Holley, 1 January 1926.
6   Letter to Louise from Martha Root, 21 August 1926, USBNA, Louise M. Gregory Papers.
7   Letter from Louise to Horace Holley, 1 October 1926, USBNA, Office of the Secretary of the NSA Files on Individuals 1925–1929.
8   Jasion, *Never Be Afraid to Dare*, p. 138.
9   Postcard from Dr Joi to Louise, 21 April 1927, USBNA, Louise M. Gregory Papers.

10 Talk given by 'Abdu'l-Bahá in Sacramento, 26 October 1912, quoted in 'Abdu'l-Bahá, *The Promulgation of Universal Peace*, p. 376; a slightly different translation is found in Esslemont, *Bahá'u'lláh and the New Era*. pp. 243–4.
11 Talk given by 'Abdu'l-Bahá in Washington DC at the Universalist Church, 6 November 1912, quoted in 'Abdu'l-Bahá, *The Promulgation of Universal Peace*, p. 396.
12 'Abdu'l-Bahá, Tablet dated January 1920, quoted in Esslemont, *Bahá'u'lláh and the New Era*, p. 247.
13 Letter from Louis to Horace Holley, February 1937, Inter-America Committee Files, US and Canada NSA records quoted in Morrison, *To Move the World*, p. 249.
14 Letter from Louis to Edith Chapman, quoted in Morrison, *To Move the World*, p. 71.
15 Letter written on behalf of Shoghi Effendi by his secretary to Louise, 21 April 1927, USBNA, Original Shoghi Effendi Letters Collection.
16 *Bahá'í News Letter*, August 1927, p. 3.

13. Czechoslovakia to Bulgaria and Back Again

1 Louis G. Gregory, 'Racial amity in America: An historical review', in *The Bahá'í World*, vol. VII (1936–1938), p. 658; quoted in Morrison, *To Move the World*, p. 181.
2 Letter from Annie McKinney to Horace Holley, USBNA, Office of the Secretary of the NSA Files on Individuals 1925–1929. From the researches of Pat Gorman.
3 Letter written on behalf of Shoghi Effendi to Louise, 3 February 1928, USBNA, Original Shoghi Effendi Letters Collection.
4 Letter written on behalf of Shoghi Effendi to Louise, 23 February 1928, ibid.
5 Letter written on behalf of Shoghi Effendi to Louise, 22 March 1928, ibid.
6 Letter from Louise to Horace Holley, undated, with copy of part of letter written on behalf of Shoghi Effendi, 22 March 1928, Office of the Secretary of the NSA Files on Individuals 1925–1929.
7 Letter from Louise to Horace Holley, 6 May 1928, Office of the Secretary of the NSA Files on Individuals 1925–1929.
8 Letter written on behalf of Shoghi Effendi by his secretary to Louise, 6 May 1928, USBNA, Original Shoghi Effendi Letters Collection.
9 Postcard from Louise to Horace Holley from Sofia, 10 May 1928, Office of the Secretary of the NSA Files on Individuals 1925–1929.
10 Undated note on copy in Louise's handwriting of Shoghi Effendi's letter of 6 May 1928. USBNA, Louis G. Gregory Papers.
11 *Summer in Czechoslovakia*, Thomas Cook brochure (1931), p. 195.
12 Postcard from Louise to Louis from Trenčianske Teplice, Czechoslovakia, 9 June 1928, USBNA, Louis G. Gregory Papers.
13 Letter written on behalf of Shoghi Effendi to Louise, 17 June 1928, USBNA, Original Shoghi Effendi Letters Collection.
14 Letter from Louise to Horace Holley. 21 November 1928, Office of the Secretary of the NSA Files on Individuals 1925–1929.

14. From Central Europe to the Holy Land

1 Postcard from Louise to Louis from Trenčianske Teplice, 19 August 1928, USBNA, Louis G. Gregory Papers.

NOTES AND REFERENCES

2 Letter written on behalf of Shoghi Effendi to Louise, 22 October 1928, USBNA, Original Shoghi Effendi Letters Collection.
3 Letter from Louise to Horace Holley, 21 November 1928, USBNA, Office of the Secretary of the NSA Files on Individuals 1925–1929.
4 Letter written on behalf of Shoghi Effendi to Louise, 19 December 1928, USBNA, Original Shoghi Effendi Letters Collection.
5 Letter from Louise to Horace Holley, 12 February 1929, USBNA, Office of the Secretary of the NSA Files on Individuals 1925–1929.
6 *Bahá'í News Letter*, April 1929, p. 4.
7 Postcard from Louise to Horace Holley, 17 February 1929, USBNA, Office of the Secretary of the NSA Files on Individuals 1925–1929.
8 *The Overland Desert Mail: The Direct Road to the East*, Nairn Transport Company brochure, 1925, from Thomas Cook Archives.
9 Letter from Louis to Louise from Brooklyn, New York, 18 March 1929, USBNA, Louise M. Gregory Papers.
10 *Star of the West*, vol. XX, no. 4, pp. 122–3, quoted in Redman, *Shoghi Effendi Through the Pilgrim's Eye*, vol. 1, p. 160.
11 *Star of the West*, vol. XX, no. 4, pp. 123.
12 *Star of the West*, vol. XX, no. 2 (May 1929), pp. 44–6, quoted in Redman, *Shoghi Effendi Through the Pilgrim's Eye*, vol. 1, pp. 161–2.
13 Ma'ani, *Leaves of the Twin Divine Trees*, p. 352.
14 Letter from Louis to Louise from Kansas City, 11 May 1929, USBNA, Louise M. Gregory Papers.
15 Letter from Louis to Edith Chapman, 21 June 1929, quoted in Morrison, *To Move The World*, p. 186; Ruhe-Schoen, *Champions of Oneness*, pp. 209–10.

15. 'Your Name Will Be Gratefully Remembered . . .'

1 Letter written on behalf of Shoghi Effendi to Louise, 29 January 1932, USBNA, Original Shoghi Effendi Letters Collection.
2 McKay, *Fires in Many Hearts*, pp. 96–7.
3 *Bahá'í News*, no. 58 (January 1932), p. 3, quoted in Morrison, *To Move the World*, p. 191.
4 Letter from Louise to Shoghi Effendi, 14 November 1930, written on board *SS Sinaia*, memorandum from the Bahá'í World Centre Research Department to the author, 23 August 2017.
5 Letter from Louise to Shoghi Effendi, 5 February 1931, ibid.
6 Letter from Marion Jack to an unidentified Bahá'í in New York, Christmas 1935(?), Bahá'í World Centre, Marion Jack Collection, quoted in Jasion, *Never Be Afraid to Dare*, p. 122.
7 Jasion, *Never Be Afraid to Dare*, p. 136.
8 Letter from Marion Jack to Louise, 1 March 1931, Bahá'í World Centre, Marion Jack Collection, quoted in Jasion, *Never Be Afraid to Dare*, p. 122.
9 Letter from Marion Jack to Emma and Louise Thompson (1931), Bahá'í World Centre, Marion Jack Collection, quoted in Jasion, *Never Be Afraid to Dare*, p. 121.
10 Shoghi Effendi, *God Passes By*, p. 288.
11 Letter from Louise to Marion Jack, 6 April 1931, Bahá'í World Centre, Marion Jack Collection, quoted in Jasion, *Never Be Afraid to Dare*, p. 136.
12 Letter from Louise to Shoghi Effendi, 2 April 1931, memorandum from the Bahá'í World Centre Research Department to the author, 23 August 2017.

13 ibid., and letter from Louise to Shoghi Effendi, 11 April 1931, memorandum from the Bahá'í World Centre Research Department to the author, 23 August 2017.
14 Marion Jack, 'Report of Bulgarian Progress' n. d. (1934?), Bahá'í World Centre, Marion Jack Collection, quoted in Jasion, *Never Be Afraid to Dare*, p. 143–4.
15 Letter from Louise to Shoghi Effendi, 13 April 1931, memorandum from the Bahá'í World Centre Research Department to the author, 23 August 2017.
16 Louise Gregory, 'Louise's Report', Bahá'í World Centre, Marion Jack Collection, quoted in Jasion, *Never Be Afraid to Dare*, p. 137.
17 Letter written on behalf of Shoghi Effendi to Louise, 29 January 1932, USBNA, Original Shoghi Effendi Letters Collection.
18 Postcard from Louise to Louis from Brno, 18 May 1932, USBNA, Louis G. Gregory Papers.
19 Postcard from Louise to Louis from Berchtesgaden, 12 August 1932, Louis G. Gregory Papers.
20 Letter from Louis to Louise from Richmond, Va., 3 February 1933, USBNA, Louise M. Gregory Papers.
21 Letter from Marion Jack to Shoghi Effendi, 22 May 1932, Bahá'í World Centre Archives, quoted in Jasion, *Never Be Afraid to Dare*, p. 141.
22 *The Bahá'í World*, vol. V (1932–1934), pp. 416–18.
23 Letter from Marion Jack to Horace Holley, 11 March 1934, Bahá'í World Centre Archives, quoted in Jasion, *Never Be Afraid to Dare*, p. 134.
24 Letter written on behalf of Shoghi Effendi to Louise, 30 April 1933, USBNA, Original Shoghi Effendi Letters Collection.
25 Letter from Shoghi Effendi to American & Canadian believers, 21 April 1933, in Shoghi Effendi, *The World Order of Bahá'u'lláh*, p. 93.
26 Letter written on behalf of Shoghi Effendi to Louise, 30 April 1933, USBNA, Original Shoghi Effendi Letters Collection.
27 Postcard from Louise to Louis from Stuttgart, 11 May 1933, USBNA, Louis G. Gregory Papers.
28 Letter from Louise to Louis, 14 May 1933, USBNA, Louis G. Gregory Papers.

16. A Change of Plan

1 Postcard from Louise to Roy Wilhelm from Portsmouth, New Hampshire, 5 September 1933, USBNA, Office of the Secretary of the NSA Files on Individuals 1930–1939.
2 Letter from Louise to Roy Wilhelm from Varna, 20 October 1933, USBNA, Office of the Secretary of the NSA Files on Individuals 1930–1939.
3 Letter written on behalf of Shoghi Effendi by his secretary to Louise, 4 November 1933, USBNA, Original Shoghi Effendi Letters Collection.
4 Postcard from Louise to Horace Holley from Varna, 25 November 1933, USBNA, Office of the Secretary of the NSA Files on Individuals 1930–1939.
5 Postcard from Louise to Horace Holley, 3 December 1933, USBNA, Office of the Secretary of the NSA Files on Individuals 1930–1939.
6 Letter from Louise to Louis, 24 January 1934, USBNA, Louis G. Gregory Papers.
7 Letter from Louise to Louis from Varna, 8 February 1934, Louis G. Gregory Papers.

8 Postcard from Louise to Louis at Fisk University, Nashville, sent from Varna, date unclear, Louis G. Gregory Papers.
9 Letter from Louise to Louis, 4 March 1934, Louis G. Gregory Papers.
10 Letter from Louise to Horace Holley, 6 April 1934, USBNA, Office of the Secretary of the NSA Files on Individuals 1930–1939.
11 ibid.
12 ibid.
13 *The Bahá'í World*, vol. VI (1934–1936), p. 133.
14 Letter from Louise to Horace Holley, 6 April 1934, USBNA, Office of the Secretary of the NSA Files on Individuals 1930–1939.
15 ibid.
16 Letter from Marion Jack to Louise, 19 April 1937, quoted in Jasion, *Never Be Afraid to Dare*, p. 138.
17 Letter from Marion Jack to Ella Robarts, 31 May 1949, quoted ibid.
18 Letter from Louise to Horace Holley, 6 April 1934, USBNA, Office of the Secretary of the NSA Files on Individuals 1930–1939.
19 Postcard from Louise to Louis, 18 April 1934, Louis G. Gregory Papers.
20 Postcard from Louise to Louis, 4 June 1934, Louis G. Gregory Papers.

17. A Summer in Salzburg
1 Letter from Louise to Louis from Salzburg, 17 July 1934, USBNA, Louis G. Gregory Papers.
2 Letter from Louise to Louis, 14 June 1934, USBNA, Louis G. Gregory Papers.
3 Undated letter from Louise to Louis from Hotel Elisabeth [1934], USBNA, Louis G. Gregory Papers.
4 Letter from Louise to Louis, 4 September 1934, USBNA, Louis G. Gregory Papers.
5 Letter from Louise to Louis from Frauenklub, Stuttgart, 17 August 1934, USBNA, Louis G. Gregory Papers.
6 Letter from Louise to Mr Abbott from Hotel Elisabeth, Salzburg. 19 July 1934, USBNA, Louis G. Gregory Papers.
7 Letter from Louise to Louis from Frauenklub, Stuttgart. 17 August 1934, USBNA, Louis G. Gregory Papers.
8 ibid.
9 Postcard from Louise to Louis from Stuttgart, 19 August 1934, USBNA, Louis G. Gregory Papers.
10 Letter from Louise to Louis from Salzburg, 4 September 1934, USBNA, Louis G. Gregory Papers.
11 Letter from Louise to Louis from Salzburg, 13 September 1934, USBNA, Louis G. Gregory Papers.
12 Postcard from Louise to Louis from Vienna, 17 September 1934, USBNA, Louis G. Gregory Papers.

18. Return to Belgrade
1 Letter from Louise to Louis from Hotel Royal, Belgrade, 28 January 1935, USBNA, Louis G. Gregory Papers.
2 ibid.
3 ibid.

4   ibid.
5   Letter from Louise to Louis from Hotel Royal, Belgrade, 1 April 1935, USBNA, Louis G. Gregory Papers.
6   ibid.
7   ibid.
8   ibid.
9   ibid.
10 Nakhjavani, *A Tribute to Amatu'l-Bahá Rúḥíyyih Khánum*.
11 ibid.
12 *Bahá'í News*, March 1935, p. 11.
13 *Bahá'í News*, September 1946, p. 10.
14 Letter from Louise to Louis from Hotel Royal, Belgrade 1 April 1935, USBNA, Louis G. Gregory Papers.
15 Letter from Louise to Louis, 13 April 1935, USBNA, Louis G. Gregory Papers.
16 Letter from Louise to Louis, 15 April 1935, USBNA, Louis G. Gregory Papers.
17 Letter from Louise to Louis, 13 April 1935, USBNA, Louis G. Gregory Papers.
18 ibid.
19 ibid.
20 ibid.
21 Letter from Louise to Louis, 15 April 1935, USBNA, Louis G. Gregory Papers.
22 Letter from Louise to Louis, 1 April 1935, USBNA, Louis G. Gregory Papers.
23 Note on back of envelope sent to Louis, 10 April 1935, USBNA, Louis G. Gregory Papers.
24 Letter from Louise to Louis, 13 April 1935, USBNA, Louis G. Gregory Papers.
25 Letter from Helen Bishop to Louise from Geneva, 12 June 1935, USBNA, Louis G. Gregory Papers.
26 Letter from Louise to Louis from Hotel Elisabeth, Salzburg, 17 July 1934, USBNA, Louis G. Gregory Papers.

19. The Last Trip to Europe
1   Registration card completed by Louis Gregory, Spiritual Assembly of the Bahá'ís of Eliot, Maine Archives, Louis G. Gregory Papers.
2   Registration card completed by Louise Gregory, ibid., Louise Gregory Papers.
3   Letter written on behalf of Shoghi Effendi by his secretary to Louise, 28 December 1935, USBNA, Original Shoghi Effendi Letters Collection.
4   See Smith, *The Bábí and Bahá'í Religions*.
5   Postcard from Louise to Louise Thompson, Eliot, 8 January 1936, Spiritual Assembly of the Bahá'ís of Eliot, Maine Archives, Louise Gregory Papers.
6   Letter written on behalf of Shoghi Effendi by his secretary to Louise, 4 April 1936, USBNA, Original Shoghi Effendi Letters Collection.
7   Letter written on behalf of Shoghi Effendi by his secretary to Louise, 29 May 1936, USBNA, Original Shoghi Effendi Letters Collection.

20. A Trip Together – Haiti
1   Shoghi Effendi, *Messages to America*, p. 6.
2   National Spiritual Assembly of the Bahá'ís of the United States, 'America's Spiritual Mission: National Spiritual Assembly Announces Teaching Policy for 1936–1937', in *Bahá'í News*, no. 101 (June 1936), p. 2.

3   Shoghi Effendi, *Messages to America*, p. 7; see also *Bahá'í News*, no. 103 (October 1936), p. 3.
4   'Abdu'l-Bahá, *Tablets of the Divine Plan*, p. 33.
5   ibid. p. 104.
6   Letter from Louis G. Gregory to the National Spiritual Assembly of the United States and Canada (secretary H. Holley), 31 December 1936, quoted in Morrison, *To Move the World*, p. 247.
7   Letter from Louis G. Gregory to the National Spiritual Assembly of the United States and Canada (secretary H. Holley), 21 February 1937, quoted ibid. p. 248.
8   ibid. pp. 248–9.
9   Louis G. Gregory, *A Teaching Campaign in Haiti*, USBNA, Louis G. Gregory Papers.
10 ibid.
11 Letter from Louise to Agnes Parsons, 18 January 1921, USBNA, Agnes Parsons Papers.
12 Annual Report of the Inter-America Committee, in *Bahá'í News*, no. 109 (July 1937) pp. 3–4, quoted in Morrison, *To Move the World*, p. 251.

21. 'Your Manifold and Truly Historic Services'

1   Letter written on behalf of Shoghi Effendi by his secretary to Louise, 27 February 1938, USBNA, Original Shoghi Effendi Letters Collection.
2   Zylpha Mapp, quoted in Atkinson et al., *Green Acre on the Piscataqua*, p. 77.
3   Undated note referred to in letter from NSA secretary, 17 September 1937, USBNA, Office of the Secretary of the NSA Files on Individuals, 1930–1939.
4   Letter written on behalf of Shoghi Effendi by his secretary to Louise, 27 February 1938, Original Shoghi Effendi Letters Collection.
5   Letter written on behalf of Shoghi Effendi by his secretary to Louise, 29 March 1939, USBNA, Original Shoghi Effendi Letters Collection.
6   Letter from Louise to Horace Holley, 24 July 1946, USBNA, Office of the Secretary of the NSA Files on Individuals, 1940–1949.
7   Cable from Shoghi Effendi to National Spiritual Assembly of the Bahá'ís of United States and Canada, 3 October 1939, in Shoghi Effendi, *Messages to America*, p. 30.
8   See Morrison, *To Move the World*, pp. 284–5.
9   Report of Holy Day observance, Eliot community, 23 May 1941, Minutes of the Spiritual Assembly of the Bahá'ís of Eliot, Maine Archives.
10 Letter from Horace Holley to Louise, 6 April 1943, USBNA, Office of the Secretary of the NSA Files on Individuals, 1940–1949.
11 *Bahá'í News* (November 1943), p. 4.
12 Message from Shoghi Effendi, January 1945, quoted in *Bahá'í News* (April–May 1945), p. 7.
13 Letter from Louise to Horace Holley, 26 May 1945, USBNA, Office of the Secretary of the NSA Files on Individuals, 1940–1949.
14 Ernest Reimer, memories of Louis Gregory, tape recorded 12 September 1979, USBNA, quoted in Morrison, *To Move the World*, p. 305.
15 Shoghi Effendi, *Messages to America*, p. 97.
16 Message from Shoghi Effendi, 25 April 1946, ibid. p. 88.
17 Letter from Louise to Horace Holley, 25 March 1946, USBNA, Office of the Secretary of the NSA Files on Individuals, 1940–1949.
18 ibid.

19 Copy of letter from secretary of Shoghi Effendi enclosed in letter from Louise to Horace Holley, 24 July 1946, USBNA, Office of the Secretary of the NSA Files on Individuals, 1940–1949.
20 Letter from Louise to Horace Holley, 24 July 1946, USBNA, Office of the Secretary of the NSA Files on Individuals, 1940–1949.
21 Postcard from Louise to Horace Holley, 27 August 1946, USBNA, Office of the Secretary of the NSA Files on Individuals, 1940–1949.

22. 'Your Hearts Are Young'
1 Letter written on behalf of Shoghi Effendi by his secretary to the Gregorys, 24 December 1949, USBNA, Original Shoghi Effendi Letters Collection.
2 Letter written on behalf of Shoghi Effendi by his secretary to Louise, 10 July 1947, USBNA, Original Shoghi Effendi Letters Collection.
3 *Bahá'í News* (September 1946), p. 10.
4 Winston Churchill, speech at Fulton, Missouri, 5 March 1946, reported in 'Britain and America In Peace', in *The Times* (London), 6 March 1946, p. 6.
5 Letter written on behalf of Shoghi Effendi by his secretary to Louise, 22 March 1948, USBNA, Original Shoghi Effendi Letters Collection.
6 Letter written on behalf of Shoghi Effendi by his secretary to Louise, 24 December 1949, USBNA, Original Shoghi Effendi Letters Collection.
7 Letter from Louis to Edith Chapman 20 October 1948, quoted in Morrison, *To Move the World*, p. 306.
8 Letter from Louise to Horace and Doris Holley, 23 December 1948, USBNA, Office of the Secretary of the NSA Files on Individuals 1940–1949.
9 Letter from Louise to Horace and Doris Holley, 25 December 1948, USBNA, Office of the Secretary of the NSA Files on Individuals 1940–1949.
10 Letter from Louis to Edith Chapman, 12 January 1949, quoted in Morrison, *To Move the World*, p. 306.
11 Letter written on behalf of Shoghi Effendi by his secretary to Louise, 22 March 1949, USBNA, Original Shoghi Effendi Letters Collection.
12 Letter written on behalf of Shoghi Effendi by his secretary to the Gregorys, 24 December 1949, USBNA, Original Shoghi Effendi Letters Collection.
13 Letter from Louis to Edith Chapman, 30 June 1949, quoted in Morrison, *To Move the World*, pp. 306–7.
14 Letter from Louis to Edith Chapman, 14 July 1949, quoted ibid. p. 307.
15 Emanuel Reimer, memories of Louis Gregory, quoted ibid. p. 308.
16 Letter from Louis to Edith Chapman, 27 Sept 1949, quoted ibid.
17 Letter from Louis to Edith Chapman, 9 May 1950, quoted ibid. p. 309.
18 Cable from Shoghi Effendi published in *Bahá'í News*, no. 247 (September 1951), p. 1; also in Shoghi Effendi, *Citadel of Faith*, p. 163.
19 Letter from Horace Holley on behalf of the National Spiritual Assembly to the Spiritual Assembly of the Bahá'ís of Eliot, Maine, 22 June 1954, Spiritual Assembly of the Bahá'ís of Eliot, Maine Archives, Louise Gregory Papers.
20 Letter from Horace Holley on behalf of the National Spiritual Assembly to the Spiritual Assembly of the Bahá'ís of Eliot, Maine, 29 May 1956, ibid.
21 Letter signed by Horace Holley on behalf of the National Spiritual Assembly to the Spiritual Assembly of the Bahá'ís of Eliot, Maine, 1 June 1956, ibid. Mr Holley transcribes the Guardian's cable. See also *The Bahá'í World*, vol. XIII (1954–1963), p. 876.

INDEX

Abbott, Robert S. 195
'Abdu'l-Bahá viii, 4, 6-7, 9, 12-14, 26, 31-5, 36-49, 50-69, 71-3, 77, 80, 88-9, 106-8, 239
  Ascension 110-14, 163
  during WWI 99-100, 125, 142-3
  in Britain 36-42
  in Budapest 123, 132, 237
  in France 36-7, 42-8, 160
  in Ramleh, Egypt 1-2, 4-7, 14, 34-5, 52
  in United States 48, 50-69, 71-3, 80, 91, 114
  Knighthood 111
  Tablets of the Divine Plan 99-102, 104, 108, 113, 118, 137, 145, 177, 213-14, 219
  teachings on
    interracial marriage 7, 60, 69, 71-2, 76, 78, 82, 84, 89-90, 170, 206-7
    racial harmony 6-7, 59-60, 74, 80-81, 84, 89, 91, 126
  Will and Testament 111, 118
  Young Turk Revolution 4
Advent of Divine Justice, The 223
Afnan, Soheil 135
Akka 3, 4, 8-12, 30, 52, 57, 65, 95, 99, 114, 124, 163-6, 170, 206, 233
Alabama 168, 219
Alexander, Agnes 108
Alexandria, Egypt 1, 3-4, 6-8, 34, 36, 48, 50-51
Algiers, Algeria 169
Allenby, Viscount 111
Alliance Spiritualiste 43
Am I My Brother's Keeper 227
Ansonia Hotel, New York 55-6
Antwerp, Belgium 133-5, 205, 240
Arras, Battle of 98
Asadu'lláh-i-Qumí, Siyyid 10-11, 50, 63, 65
Asia, SS 165, 241
Atlanta, Georgia 85, 122, 219
Atlantic City, New Jersey 75, 77
Ausonia, RMS 117, 240
Austin, Mr and Mrs 52
Austria 8, 28, 130-31, 135, 136-7, 139, 141, 175, 181, 191, 194-6, 201, 209, 226, 240-42
autobus service *see* Overland Desert Mail

Azores islands 165, 169
Avenue de Camoëns, Paris 42, 45

Báb, The 9, 11-12, 100, 110, 119, 163-4, 224
Bagdadi, Zia 78-9, 92, 146
Baghdad 4, 10, 52, 162
Bahádur, 'Azízu'lláh S. 119, 122
Bahá'í Temple Unity 64, 66, 84, 115, 207
Bahá'í Temple Unity Convention 63, 66-8
Bahá'í House of Worship, Chicago 63-8, 226
  ground breaking ceremony 66-8
Bahá'í House of Worship, Ashkhabad 63, 67
Bahá'í News/Bahá'í News Letter 134, 136, 145, 161, 168, 182-3, 189, 201, 213, 223-4, 231
Bahá'í summer school, Esslingen (1933) 179
Bahá'í summer school, Esslingen (1934) 191, 193-5, 242
Bahá'í World, The vii, 159, 188, 223
Bahá'u'lláh
  imprisonment and exile 4, 10-12, 52, 62, 64
  prophethood, message and teachings 4, 9-10, 13-14, 33, 37, 38-40, 48, 53-4, 56, 59, 71, 84, 86, 99-100, 117, 119, 125, 128, 132, 137, 157, 162, 164, 166, 194, 196, 200, 213, 216, 223, 225, 238
Bahíyyih Khánum 11, 34, 52, 111, 118, 165
Bahjí 4, 11, 164
Baker, Dorothy 223, 236
Baker, Effie 120, 163
Balkan League 142
Balkan Peninsula, States 142, 144, 147, 149, 152-3, 169, 173, 177, 184, 195, 201-2, 207-12, 217, 220, 227, 237-8
Balkan wars 98-9, 142-4
Balliol College, Oxford 112
Banchereau, Gabrielle Aliette *see* Mathew, Gabrielle Aliette
Barney, Laura *see* Dreyfus-Barney, Laura
Beauchamps, Jeanne 43
Beckenham, Kent ix, 15-16, 19-20, 22-3, 25, 30, 53, 96
Beede, Alice 45
Beirut, Lebanon 161-2

Belgrade, Yugoslavia 142, 185-90, 194, 196-7, 198-205, 208-12, 220-21, 226-7, 232, 237, 242
Bell, Alexander Graham 60
Benke, George Adam 173, 176-7
Benke, Lina 176
Berchtesgaden, Germany 175, 241
Bergen, Norway 212, 242
Berkeley Springs, West Virginia 107
Besant, Annie 38
Bethel Literary and Historical Society 61
Binder, Dr 150-52, 156-9, 237
Birch, Bishop 56
Bishop, Charles 188
Bishop, Helen 188, 195, 205
Blackwell, Ellsworth 218
Blackwell, Ruth 218
Bled, Yugoslavia 196
Blomfield, Lady 36-7, 42, 112
Bolles, May *see* Maxwell, May
Boris II of Bulgaria 141
Bosch, John 57
Boston, Massachusetts 84-5, 93, 116-17, 122-3, 140, 146, 172, 180, 203, 205, 207, 240-42
Botay, Marie L. 74
Boulogne-sur-Mer, France 145, 240
Bournemouth 120-21
  Local Assembly of 121
Bowditch, Nancy 234
Bowery Mission, New York 56
Boy Builder, The 95-6
Brackett, Nathan Cook Rev. 70
Brattleboro, Vermont 224
Bremen, Germany 152, 241
Brentwood, Maryland 101
Brindisi, Italy 171
Bristol 39-40
British Expeditionary Force 98
British Mandate, Palestine 110-11
Britannic, SS 172, 241
Brno, Czech Republic 175, 241
Bucharest, Romania 142, 169, 232
Budapest, Hungary 123, 128, 131-9, 141, 175, 232, 238, 240-41
Bulgaria vii, ix, 139-44, 146-52, 155-61, 169-77, 180-88, 195, 201-2, 207, 217, 220, 227, 237, 240-42
Burgas (Burges), Bulgaria 189, 202
Byfleet, Surrey 39

California viii, 30, 57, 73, 143
Cambridge, University of vii, ix, 27-8
Campbell, Rev. R. J. 37
Carpenter, Howard 177
Carpenter, Marzieh Gail 177
Carrido, Miss 198
Cator family 15
Cedric, SS 49, 50, 52, 54-5, 63, 113

Centenary of the Bahá'í Faith (1944) 213, 219, 226
Challis, Sister Grace 120-21
Chapman, Edith 166, 234-5
Chapman, Thomas C., Dr 233
Charleston, South Carolina 116
Chase, James B. Thornton 64-5
Chattanooga, Tennessee 122
Chicago 59, 61-71, 78, 84, 87, 125, 147, 178-9, 181, 206, 226, 236
Chicago Defender, The 74, 195
Chicago Temple *see* Bahá'í House of Worship, Chicago
Chicago 'House of Spirituality' 64-5
Chicago 'Women's Assembly of Teaching' 64-5
Churchill, Winston 111, 232
City Temple, London 37-8
Cleveland, Ohio 69, 93
Cleveland News 60
Cleveland Plain Dealer 60
Clifton Guest House, Bristol 40
Collins, Emma *see* Mathew, Emma
Collins, William 18
Collins, Betty 18
Columbia University 56
Commission on Interracial Cooperation 125
Committee for Europe 228
Committee on Assembly Development 223
Constanta, Romania 161, 169
Copenhagen, Denmark 210
Croydon canal 16
Crystal Palace 17
Cunard Steamship Company 117, 240
Czechoslovakia 153, 155, 175, 207, 241

Damascus, Syria 162
d'Ange d'Astre, Georgina Marie Baronne 47
Daniel, Everard W. Rev. 73-4
Danube River 155, 197
Daughters of the American Revolution 61
De Lagnel, Mrs J. C. 81
Denver, Colorado 52, 113
Detroit 223
Deux Sèvres, France 21, 117, 222, 240
Dobrudzha, Bulgaria 142
Dollfuss, Engelbert 194
Dresden, Germany 149, 241
Dreyfus, Hippolyte 30-31, 36, 47
Dreyfus-Barney, Laura 30, 36, 47, 81, 229
Dublin, New Hampshire 71-2, 125
Dyer, Andrew 91

Earl, Joy Hill 236
Edinburgh 27-8, 76, 77
Edinburgh Training College 27-8
Edinburgh, University of 27-8, 76, 77
Edirne (Adrianople) 4
Education Acts 26, 27

INDEX

Egg importing 18, 21-2
Eliot, Maine 114, 116, 146-7, 152-3, 166, 170, 206, 209, 211-12, 224-6, 230, 233, 238-9
Elisabeth Hotel, Salzburg 189
Equal Rights League 126
Esperanto 141, 149-50, 158-9, 161, 198, 238
Esslemont, Dr John 120, 156, 161
  in Bournemouth 120
  in Haifa 120, 127-8
  and *Bahá'u'lláh and the New Era* 120, 129, 131, 141, 150, 157, 180, 185, 198, 202, 203, 209, 210
Esslingen, Germany 133-4, 179, 191, 193-5, 208, 240, 242
Eurithra 61

Fabre Line 161, 165, 169
Fareed, Dr *see* Faríd, Amínu'lláh
Farid, Amínu'lláh 50-51, 53, 62, 68
Farmer, Sarah 114
Ferndown Lodge, West Moors 120, 240
Fontana, Adolf 136-7
Ford, Mary Hanford 42
Foyer de l'Ame, Paris 44
Frankfurt, Germany 133, 240
Freewill Baptist Home Mission Society 70
Fujita 163
Fulton, Missouri 232
Fürth, Steffi 181

Gastéa, Mademoiselle 47
Geneva, Switzerland 108, 150, 157, 171, 188, 205, 241
George, Florence 'Mother' 120
German Colony, Haifa 9, 163
German Templers 8
Getsinger, Edward 1, 57, 62
Getsinger, Lua 29, 68
Gibran, Khalil 56
Glenwood Springs, Colorado viii, 73
God Passes By 170
Goehring, Dr 205
Göppingen, Germany 195, 242
Grant, Percy, Rev. 56
Graz, Austria 130-31, 135, 136-8, 141, 240
Great Depression 169, 176, 181
Greatest Holy Leaf *see* Bahíyyih Khánum
Green Acre, Eliot, Maine 103, 114, 115, 122, 145, 146, 166, 169-70, 206, 211-12, 220, 223-4, 234-6
Gregory, Louis G.
  Bahá'í service 58-61, 68, 71, 82, 84-6, 93-4, 101-5, 107, 113-15, 117, 122, 124, 127, 139, 146-8, 166, 168, 176, 195, 196, 206-7, 208, 211, 214-18, 219, 222-4, 231, 235-6
  cable from the Guardian on his passing 236
  career as a lawyer 4, 58, 70, 77
  delegate at Wilmette ground breaking ceremony 68
  education 3-4
  family 3, 153
  marriage viii, 52, 62-3, 69-70, 71-5, 79, 83-4, 85, 87, 88-90, 92, 93, 126-8, 167-8, 170-71, 204-7, 238
  memorial services held at Green Acre and Wilmette 236
  passing 236
Gregory, Louise Mathew
  childhood 15, 19, 24-5
  collaboration with Martha Root 58-9, 134, 137-8, 140, 144, 149-51, 183-7, 199, 202, 207, 209, 223
  correspondence with Shoghi Effendi 113, 118, 119, 122-3, 127-8, 130, 134-5, 136-7, 144, 147-9, 151-4, 155-6, 159, 169, 171, 172-4, 177-8, 182, 185-6, 190, 192, 207-8, 209-11, 220-22, 227, 228, 231, 232-3, 235, 239
  declaration of faith 5, 30, 31-2
  delegate at Wilmette ground breaking ceremony 68
  education 20, 26-8, 76
  friendship with Marion Jack 12, 30, 41, 42, 49, 83, 169-70, 171-3, 176-7, 185, 189-90, 193, 195-6
  linguist 3, 24-5, 28, 108, 141, 149-50, 180, 214, 238
  passing 238
  passport application 116, 118
  personal qualities 76-7, 86, 93, 177, 197
  philanthropic projects 25-6, 32-4, 36, 76, 83
  pilgrimages 3, 5-14, 33-4, 35, 36, 76, 144, 148-9, 155-6, 159, 161-5
  singing talent 29, 224
  Tablets from, and talks and travels with, 'Abdu'l-Bahá 5, 31-4, 49, 51-2, 61, 62-3, 69, 72, 82, 88, 89, 92, 106-7, 108-9, 110, 225, 237
  teacher 3, 11, 26, 28-9, 53, 71, 92-4, 130, 190, 198-200, 203, 237
  training as a teacher 26-8
  marriage viii, 52, 62-3, 69-75, 76-7, 79, 83-4, 85, 87, 88-92, 126-8, 167-8, 170-71, 204-7, 238
  writing talent 95-6, 195, 221-2, 227
Grosse Point, Chicago 65
Grossmann, Dr Hermann 195
Guardian, Head of the Bahá'í Faith *see* Shoghi Effendi

Haber, Miss 234
Haifa 3-4, 7-12, 30, 34, 83, 99-100, 110, 112, 114-115, 118-20, 124, 127, 135, 136, 144, 148-9, 156, 159, 161-6, 170-71, 177, 188, 195, 201, 206, 220, 241

Haiti 214-18, 220
  first Local Spiritual Assembly 218
  National Spiritual Assembly established 218
Hamburg, Germany 178, 241
Hamburg, SS 178-9, 241
Hamburg-American Line 179, 241
Hannen, Joseph 5, 57, 80, 91, 92, 94, 103, 107, 108, 126
Hannen, Pauline 5, 13, 25, 52, 73, 77, 80, 84-5, 92, 146
Hawaii 108, 223
Hearst, Phoebe 30
Henderson, Professor George W. 85
Herald (Portsmouth NH) 224
Herbert, Bertha *see* Holley, Bertha
Herrick, Elizabeth 41
Herrigel, Wilhelm 119, 130-31
Hidden Words of Bahá'u'lláh 37, 71, 157, 187, 205, 208, 210
Hitler, Adolf 194, 208
Holley, Bertha 36-7
Holley, Doris 224, 233
Holley, Horace 36, 134, 136, 137, 139, 145, 150, 152, 154, 156, 159, 161, 182, 186, 188, 199, 201, 204, 220, 224, 225, 226, 228, 230, 233, 238-9
Holmes, Dr John Haynes 164
Holsapple, Leonora 145
Home Sanatorium, Southbourne 120
Homeopathic medicine 92, 205
Hopper, Marie 61
Hopper, Rene 61
House of 'Abbúd, Akka 11, 164
Howard University 4, 59
Hudd, Miss 83
Hull House, Chicago 67
Hungaria Hotel, Budapest 175
Hungary 123-4, 127-8, 132, 138-9, 141-2, 175, 207, 237, 240-41

Iceland 210
Ilić, Draga 186-8, 202-3, 205, 208-10, 220-22, 226-7, 208, 210, 232
Indian Army Reserve 98
Inter-America Committee 213
Interracial Bahá'í marriages, other (e.g. Mr Taite's and Mr Simpson's) 90
International Bahá'í Bureau, Geneva 171, 188, 205
Istanbul, Turkey 4, 8, 142, 169

Jack, Marion 12, 30-31, 41-2, 49, 83, 169-73, 176-7, 179, 182, 185, 189-90, 193, 195-6, 199, 201, 209, 237, 241
Jaffa 8, 34
Jamál Páshá 99
'Jim Crow' laws 86
Joi, Dr 141

Jounet, Albert 44
Jugoslavia *see* Yugoslavia
Jutland, Battle of 98

Kaiser Wilhelm II *see* Wilhelm II, Kaiser
Kalamazoo, Michigan 107
Kansas City, Kansas 166, 233
Kelsey, Curtis 163
Kent House Farm 15, 19
Khan, Ali-Kuli 59
Khan, Florence (Mme Ali-Kuli Khan) 59, 224
Khusraw, Áqá 50
King Alexander of Yugoslavia 194, 209
King Haakon of Norway 210
Kingston, Jamaica 218
Kinney, Carrie 54, 55, 56
Kinney, Edward 54, 55, 56
Kitáb-i-Íqán 205
Knobloch, Alma 13, 108, 176
Königsee Lake 175
Kossikowsky, Mrs 187
Ku Klux Klan 125

La Croix, France 53
Laconia, SS 205
Le Leu, Louis 43
Les Aubiers, France 21, 117, 145
Leeds, Yorkshire 117, 240
Le Havre, France 203, 242
Leipzig, Germany 176, 199
Leyland Line 123, 240
Library of Congress, Washington DC 59
Lisbon, Portugal 165
Liverpool 117, 123-4, 140, 172, 203, 205, 240-41
Local Spiritual Assemblies 115, 121, 172, 218, 219
Local Spiritual Assembly of Eliot, Maine 169-70
Locke, Alain 146
London 12, 13-14, 15-21, 24-6, 28, 30, 34, 36-42, 49, 55, 68, 77, 91, 111-12, 120, 142, 163, 184, 203, 206, 222, 237, 240
Lunt, Alfred 85, 103
Luxembourg 28-9, 77, 116, 118-20, 123, 124, 128-9, 134, 237, 240

MacNutt, Howard 74
McAlpin Hotel, New York 100
McClung, Lee 61
McKay, Doris 167
McKay, Willard 167-8
McKinney, Annie 146
McKinney, Edna 146
Macedonia 142
Madeira 165
Mahmúd-i-Zarqání 50, 51, 53, 78
Maida Vale College 26
Manassas, Virginia 71
Mansion, Bahjí 164
Marlowe, John 233-4

INDEX

Marlowe, Polly 233-4
Marseilles 35, 36
Mathew children, religious upbringing 20-21
Mathew, Edith 19, 22-3, 25, 96-7, 178, 184
Mathew, Emma 17-20, 24, 96-7, 98
Mathew, Ernest 17, 19, 21-3, 24-5, 31, 97, 117, 145, 222, 225, 228-9
Mathew, Ethel 19, 22, 25, 97, 203, 230
Mathew, Florence 18-20, 22, 96-7, 229
Mathew, Gabrielle Aliette 21, 24-5, 97, 117
Mathew, Harold 19, 22, 25, 98, 222
Mathew, Horace 19, 22, 25
Mathew, Leonard 19, 21, 25, 31
Mathew, Louise *see* Gregory, Louise Mathew
Mathew, Marie Claire 22
Mathew, Michael ix, 15, 17-19, 21-2, 24, 30-32, 96
Mathew, Percy 18-19, 21, 23, 31, 96, 98, 184, 229
Mathew, Ralph 19, 21-2, 25, 31, 184, 203
Mathew, Sydney 18-20, 96
Mathew, Vincent 19, 22, 25, 96, 178
Maxwell, Mary *see* Rúḥíyyih Khánum
Maxwell, May 29-30, 166, 201
Maxwell, Sutherland 30
Mazlúm, Mírzá 66
Meakin, Neville Gauntlett 2-14, 71
Metropolitan African Methodist Episcopal Church, Washington DC 61, 91
Mills, Mountfort 54, 114, 126, 145
Milutinović, Mrs 232
Mir newspaper 158, 160
Moody, Dr Susan 159
Moss, Marzieh 62
Most Great Prison 10
Mount Carmel 8-9, 11, 100, 110, 163, 170
Mount Pleasant cemetery, Eliot, Maine 239
Mühlschlegel, Dr Adelbert 195
Munavvar Khánum 11
Munich, Germany 195-6, 242
Munírih Khánum 12, 165
Munír-i-Zayn, Mírzá 50

NAACP *see* National Association for the Advancement of Colored People
Nachev, Mr 156, 159-60
Nairn Transport Company 162
Naples, Italy 48-9, 50-51, 113, 237
Nashville, Tennessee 4, 85, 122
Natchev, Mr *see* Nachev, Mr
National Association for the Advancement of Colored People 67, 126
National Socialism *see* Nazis
National Spiritual Assemblies 115, 226
National Spiritual Assembly of Germany and Austria 119, 226
National Spiritual Assembly of Haiti 218
National Spiritual Assembly of the British Isles 121

National Spiritual Assembly of the United States and Canada 115, 134, 140, 146, 207, 215, 238-9
Naw-Rúz festival 170
Nazis 194, 208, 222
New York 2, 5, 8, 50, 52, 54-8, 68, 73-4, 84, 90, 100, 103, 115, 117, 121, 126, 134, 137, 146, 164, 178-9, 212, 240-42
  City of the Covenant 55, 73, 100, 137
Norway 68, 210-12, 242
Nourse, Elizabeth 74

Ober, Grace 176
Ober, Harlan 176, 224, 236
Orient-Occident Unity Society 61, 82
Orient-Occident Unity Conference 59
Oslo, Norway 210, 212, 242
Ottoman Empire 4, 37, 99, 142
Overland Desert Mail 162

Paris 77, 91, 93, 257, 216, 224
  in the 'Belle Epoque' 29, 31
  Baháʼí Movement in 5, 12-13, 29-31, 34, 36-7, 42-9, 55, 70, 81, 157, 160, 169, 206, 228, 237
Parsons, Agnes 14, 49, 57-8, 61, 62, 69, 71, 78, 81-3, 85, 89-91, 94-5, 102, 104, 106, 124-6, 128, 129, 138, 146, 185, 206, 218
Passmore Edwards' Settlement 39, 41
Peary, Robert, Admiral 60
Penge, Kent 16-20
Persia 1-2, 4, 8-11, 31, 38, 42, 47, 52-3, 57, 59-60, 63, 66, 68, 74, 133, 159-60
Plaza Hotel, Chicago 66
Plovdiv, Bulgaria 151, 176, 185
Pöllinger, Franz 130-31, 135, 155, 175, 197
Ponsonaille, Monsieur and Madame 45-6
Popović, Mrs 198
Port Said, Egypt 8, 12, 34
Portland, Massachusetts 89
Portsmouth, New Hampshire 139, 146, 167-8, 171, 191, 192, 194, 204-5, 206, 210, 224, 225
Prague, Czech Republic 149, 151, 153, 175, 232, 241
Prince Paul of Yugoslavia 209
Prince Peter of Yugoslavia 209
Providence, Rhode Island 165-6, 169, 241

Queen Marie of Romania 186, 209

Race Amity Committee 124, 146, 207
Race Amity Conventions, Conferences 124, 126, 146, 207
  Chicago (1928) 147
  Washington DC (1921) 126, 131
  Washington DC (1927) 146
  Springfield, Massachusetts (1921) 126
  New York (1924) 126

New York state (1927) 126
Philadelphia (1924) 126
Portsmouth, New Hampshire (1927) 146
Race Unity Committee (1939) 223
Race Unity Conferences (1941 to 1946) 224
Ramleh, Egypt 1, 4-6, 12-14, 34-5, 52-3, 206
Randall, William H. 116
Regional Teaching Committees 213
Remey, Mason 134
Remick, Mr 225
Remington, Virginia 71
Revell, Mary 146
Revell sisters 146
Riḍván festival 10, 226
Riḍván Garden 11-12, 164-5
Rives, Isabel 163-4
Roger Williams University 85
Romania 139, 142, 161, 169, 209, 241
Roosevelt, Theodore, President 44, 61
Root, Martha 58-9, 120, 126, 134, 137-41, 145, 147-54, 157-9, 182-7, 189-90, 196, 198-9, 202, 207, 209-12, 223, 238, 241
Rosenberg, Ethel 34, 37, 40, 42, 140
Royal East Kent Regiment (the Buffs) 98
Royal Engineers 98
Royal Holloway College 26-7, 76
Royal Hotel, Belgrade 198-9, 209
Rabbani, Ruhangiz 112
Rúḥíyyih Khánum 201, 228, 231-3, 235
Ruse, Bulgaria 155

Sacramento, California 143
Sacy, Gabriel 46
Salonika, Greece 142
Salzburg, Austria 145, 178, 181-2, 189-91, 192-6, 205, 208, 241-2
Samuel, Sir Herbert 111
Sanderson, Edith 30, 32-4, 36, 157
Sanderson, Silas 30
Sanderson, Sybil 30
Schapira, Mr 157
Schopflocher, Lorol 145
Schubarth, Johanna 210
Schwarz, Mrs 195
Schweizer, Mrs (Frau) and Mr (Herr) 119
Scott, Edwin and Josephine 45-6
Second Seven Year Plan for North America (1946) 226
Serbia, Serbian language 142, 180, 187-8, 198, 202-3, 208-10
Seven Year Plan for North America (1937) 213, 219, 221, 226
Shanghai, China 198
Shaw, Dr 95-6
Shoghi Effendi 30. 99. 111-13, 118-19, 120, 122-3, 127-30, 133, 135, 136-8, 144, 147-54, 155, 158-60, 163, 165-6, 169, 170-77, 180, 182-3, 185-6, 190-91, 193-5, 201, 207-11,
213, 219-21, 223, 226-8, 231-3, 235-9
called 1922 meeting in Haifa 111, 114-15
in Egypt 7, 51, 206
meeting with pilgrims 114, 165, 170
rest and recuperation in Switzerland 118-19, 122
unable to accompany 'Abdu'l-Bahá to United States 50-51, 113
Shook, Glen A., Dr 224
Shrine of the Báb, Haifa 9, 100, 110, 163-4
Simplon Orient Express 161
Sinai and Palestine Campaign 99
Sinaia, SS 169
Slade, Isobel 120
Sofia, Bulgaria vii, 140-42, 147, 149-54, 155-8, 160-62, 169, 171-4, 176, 182-4, 189-90, 195, 209, 232, 237, 240-41
Sohrab, Ahmad 72
Some Answered Questions 188
Somerville, Massachusetts 122
Somme, Battle of 98
Southampton, England 121, 240
Spa, Belgium 29, 117, 128, 229, 240
Sprague, Mrs 228
Sprague, Philip 234
Springfield, Massachusetts 113-14, 126
Srebova, Olga 176
St George's Training College *see* Edinburgh Training College
St John the Divine Church, Westminster, London 38
Star of the West 13, 45, 47, 50, 100, 101, 111, 114, 163
Stara Zagora, Bulgaria 176
Stevenson, Margaret 120
Storer College, Harpers Ferry, West Virginia 70, 84
Storer, John 70
Stuttgart, Germany 13, 117, 133-4, 178, 195-6, 205, 240-42
Szántó, Mrs, and family 132-3, 138-9, 141
Szirmai, Mrs 132-3, 138-9, 141, 175

Tablets of the Divine Plan *see* 'Abdu'l-Bahá, Tablets of the Divine Plan
Tehran, Persia 52, 53
Theosophical Society 25, 38, 44
Thompson, Juliet 36, 54, 56, 58
Thompson, Louise 209
Thonon-les-Bains, France 36
Thornburgh-Cropper, Mary Virginia 40-41
Tobin, Esther (aka Nettie) 65-6, 68
Tokin, Mme Desanka Forgovice- 202, 221, 226-8, 231-3
Toulon, France 229
Treaty of London 142
Treaty of Versailles 117
Trenčianske Teplice, Slovakia 153-4, 241

INDEX

Trieste, Italy 138, 140, 232
Tripoli, Lebanon 161-2
True, Corinne 65-7, 166
True, Davis 66-7
Tudor Pole, Wellesley 6, 14, 37, 40
Turkey 47, 160, 162
Tuskagee, Alabama 219

Union Palace Hotel, Sofia 142, 150, 155, 189
Universal House of Justice 100, 115
Universalist Church, Washington DC 59, 143

Vail, Albert 107
Vanners, Byfleet, Surrey 39
Varna, Bulgaria 173, 176-8, 181-6, 188-9, 195, 202, 237, 241-2
Verdun, Battle of 98
Vienna, Austria 130-31, 134, 136-8, 141, 155, 175, 189-90, 197, 232, 240, 242
Von Wettstein, Mrs (Frau) 131-2, 141
Vrsac, Yugoslavia 202, 221

Wagner, Charles 44
Walker, Mary 27-8
Ward, Mary 41
Warsaw, Poland 150, 232
Washington DC 2, 4, 5, 13, 54, 55, 57-61, 68, 69, 70, 73-4, 77-87, 90-91, 94, 101, 104, 116, 124-6, 137, 143, 146, 163, 185, 204, 206, 216, 218, 220
Washington Public Library 59

Washington Working Committee 58
Western Pilgrim House, Haifa 163
Wiesbaden, Germany 117, 128, 133, 240
Wilberforce, Albert Basil Orme, Archdeacon of Westminster 38
Wilhelm II, Kaiser 117
Wilhelm, Roy 180-81, 183, 234
Williams, Roy 84
Wilmette, Illinois 66-7, 219, 226, 236
Wilmington, Delaware 220
Winifredian, SS 123, 140, 240
Wittmann, Mrs 197
Women's League for Peace and Freedom 131-4, 141
Woodcock, Percy and Mrs 52
World Economy of Bahá'u'lláh, The 199
World Order magazine 221, 223
World War I 95, 98-9, 117, 125, 141-2, 144
World War II 222-3, 230, 231, 237
Wragg, Charles 176

Young Turk Revolution 4, 142
Yugoslavia 185-6, 188, 193, 194, 196, 199, 201-2, 208-9, 220-21, 226-7, 231-3, 237, 242

Zagreb, Yugoslavia 196
Zamenhof, Ludvik Lejzer 149-50
Zamenhof, Lydia 150
Zeeland, SS 134, 240
Zlatarova, Mrs 150, 155, 158
Zuffenhausen, Germany 133, 240

ABOUT THE AUTHOR

Born in Surrey in the south of England, Janet was educated in Epsom and studied modern languages at the University of Edinburgh. She gained her diploma in librarianship at the Polytechnic of North London and subsequently worked in various roles, such as children's librarian, branch librarian, information officer at a children's charity, librarian in charge of a technical library for consulting engineers, librarian and factotum at a community centre on an island in the South Pacific and adviser to the head librarian at the National Library of the Maldives.

Some places where she has lived and worked include Scotland, Surrey, the London Borough of Sutton, Fiji in the South Pacific and the Republic of Maldives in the Indian Ocean. In addition, she had the bounty of serving for six years in Haifa as Acquisitions Librarian at the Bahá'í World Centre Library. She now lives in St Albans, Hertfordshire, with her husband Andrew, but they set off for far-flung destinations whenever possible.

If you enjoyed this book
you may also enjoy . . .

NEVER BE AFRAID TO DARE
THE STORY OF MARION JACK
by Jan Jasion

Among the graves in the Sofia War Cemetery is a simple granite headstone bearing a remarkable inscription:

> MARION JACK
> 1866-1954
> IMMORTAL HEROINE...

How did this lone Canadian painter come to be in Bulgaria? What brought her? Why did she choose to stay in this unfamiliar country all during the ravages and trials of the Second World War? Who was Marion Jack and why was she called an 'immortal heroine'? An adventurer who travelled by boat up the Yukon, an art student in Paris, a suffragette in London, a teacher in the Middle Eastern household of 'Abdu'l-Bahá, a 'pioneer' who took the message of Bahá'u'lláh to the heart of the Balkans – unstoppable, indomitable, she was 'General' Jack, who was never afraid to dare.

Although she spent nearly 30 years in Bulgaria, she never mastered the language. She had difficulties with money and with the authorities, was bombed and evacuated during the war, slept in a cold schoolroom and was often hungry and insufficiently clad. Yet Marion Jack's resting-place in Bulgaria is a shrine 'which the people of that country will increasingly honour and cherish'. She is for present-day Bahá'ís an 'inspiration and example'. *Never Be Afraid to Dare* is a fascinating and well-researched story of an artist who dedicated her life to the promotion of peace, brotherhood and the unity of humankind.

Jan Jasion was born in Canada of Polish parents. He studied in Canada, England and Poland and is author of several books and numerous articles.

ISBN: 978-0-85398-449-8
320 pages plus illustrations,
21.0 x 13.6 cm (8.25 x 5.5 in)

ETHEL JENNER ROSENBERG
ENGLAND'S OUTSTANDING BAHÁ'Í PIONEER
by Robert Weinberg

Who was Ethel Jenner Rosenberg?

A Victorian spinster . . .

A painter of miniatures and portraits . . .

The first Englishwoman in her native country to accept Bahá'u'lláh as the Manifestation of God for this day . . .

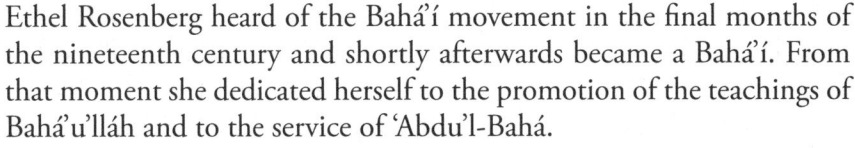

Ethel Rosenberg heard of the Bahá'í movement in the final months of the nineteenth century and shortly afterwards became a Bahá'í. From that moment she dedicated herself to the promotion of the teachings of Bahá'u'lláh and to the service of 'Abdu'l-Bahá.

Using Ethel Rosenberg's own diaries and letters, minutes and notes from the meetings of the first Bahá'í institutions in Britain, and other original documents, Robert Weinberg explores the life of this fascinating woman, described by Shoghi Effendi as 'England's outstanding Bahá'í pioneer worker'.

Includes the Tablet of 'Abdu'l-Bahá written to Ethel Rosenberg.

Robert Weinberg is a writer and researcher, a Web editor, journalist and radio producer, with many years experience working across a wide range of media, most particularly covering news and the arts. For four years he worked as the Director of the Office of Public Information for the Bahá'í International Community in Haifa, Israel.

ISBN: 978-0-85398-399-6
336 pages plus illustrations,
21.0 x 13.6 cm (8.25 x 5.5 in)

LADY BLOMFIELD
HER LIFE AND TIMES
by Robert Weinberg

The life of Sara Louisa, Lady Blomfield, spanned one of the most exciting periods in human history – the last half of the 19th and first half of the 20th centuries and the social and political developments that defined the era: the suffragist movement, the rise of eastern religious thought, Theosophy and spiritualism in Europe, the First World War, modernization. She experienced the poverty of rural Ireland and the ceremony of the royal court in London.

Beyond this, Lady Blomfield was one of the most socially distinguished adherents of the Bahá'í Faith, moving in social circles that included royalty, members of government and the celebrities of the day. She was the gracious and generous hostess to 'Abdu'l-Bahá on His historic visits to London in 1911 and 1912–13 and was a chronicler of Bahá'í history in her book *The Chosen Highway*.

Above all, she was a tireless advocate of the Bahá'í Faith's spiritual and social teachings; a defender of her persecuted co-religionists in Iran; a champion of the rights of women, children, prisoners and animals; and an ardent promoter of peace and interreligious understanding.

Robert Weinberg's detailed research has yielded a fascinating insight into the life of Lady Blomfield, her family and her circle, and into the life of 'Abdu'l-Bahá as it touched the lives of the British Bahá'ís. Punctuated by glimpses into London society and the rapidly developing Bahá'í community, Weinberg's book provides compelling grounds for Lady Blomfield's inclusion in the 'galaxy of unforgettable women' who 'became the principal exponents of the Bahá'í message on both sides of the Atlantic'.

ISBN: 978-0-85398-550-1
480 pages plus illustrations,
23.4 x 15.6 cm (9.75 x 6.25 in)

MAḤMÚD'S DIARY
THE DIARY OF MÍRZÁ MAḤMÚD-I-ZARQÁNÍ
translated by Mohi Sobhani

In the spring of 1912 'Abdu'l-Bahá set off from Alexandria on His historic journey to America. Among his small entourage was Mírzá Maḥmúd-i-Zarqání, who became, in the words of Shoghi Effendi, 'the chronicler of His travels'.

Mírzá Maḥmúd went everywhere with 'Abdu'l-Bahá, making extensive notes not only of the Master's many public talks and conversations with individuals but also of the new sights and experiences they found in America as well as the daily routines of eating, writing letters and travelling.

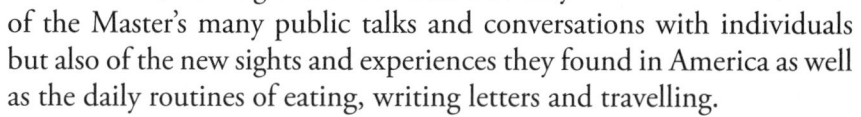

Maḥmúd remarks on the novelty of the New York skyscrapers, electric lights and American foods and customs for 'Abdu'l-Bahá's party as well as the picturesque spectacle provided to the Americans by His entourage in their *'abás* and Persian hats.

The result was a unique diary

> ... regarded as a reliable account of 'Abdu'l-Bahá's travels in the West and an authentic record of His utterances, whether in the form of formal talks, table talks or random oral statements. Mírzá Maḥmúd was a careful and faithful chronicler and engaged in assembling and publishing his work with the permission of the beloved Master ...
> *The Universal House of Justice*

The translations of the talks of 'Abdu'l-Bahá and His words found in the present volume were read and revised at the Bahá'í World Centre.

ISBN: 978-0-85398-418-4
530 pages plus illustrations,
21.0 x 13.6 cm (8.25 x 5.5 in)

'ABDU'L-BAHÁ IN THEIR MIDST
by Earl Redman

If the believers . . . establish, in a befitting manner, union and harmony with spirit, tongue, heart and body, suddenly they shall find 'Abdu'l-Bahá in their midst.

'Abdu'l-Bahá

'Abdu'l-Bahá in Their Midst is the story of the journeys of 'Abdu'l-Bahá to Europe and North America over the period 1911 to 1913. Rather than focusing on the public talks he gave, inspiring though these were, it narrates how 'Abdu'l-Bahá affected and transformed the lives of those he met, described in their own words. A revealing and heartwarming book.

Earl Redman is a geologist who worked for two decades studying mines and mineral deposits in more than 220 abandoned mine workings in the Juneau Gold Belt, Alaska. In 1999 he moved with his wife Sharon to Ireland, where although there are no mines in sight his experience has been put to good use in another field, exploring the gold mines of the stories included in this book.

ISBN: 978-0-85398-557-0
384 pages,
23.4 x 15.6 cm (9.75 x 6.25 in)